WORD AND WORLD: REFORMED THEOLOGY IN AMERICA

edited by
James W. Van Hoeven

The Historical Series of the Reformed Church
in America

No. 16

WORD AND WORLD: REFORMED THEOLOGY IN AMERICA

edited by
James W. Van Hoeven

Wm. B. Eerdmans Publishing Co.
Grand Rapids, Michigan

To M. Eugene Osterhaven

Copyright © 1986 by Wm. B. Eerdmans Publishing Co.
255 Jefferson S.E., Grand Rapids, Michigan 49503

Library of Congress Cataloging on Publication Data

Word and World: Reformed Theology in America

(The Historical series of the Reformed Church in
America; no. 16)
    Endnotes: p. 141
    Includes index.
    1. Reformed Church in America—Doctrines—History.
2. Christian Reformed Church—Doctrines—History.
3. Reformed Church—United States—Doctrines—History.
I. Van Hoeven, James W. II. Series.
BX9521.W67 1986   230'.5732   86-11627
ISBN 0-8028-0246-X

The Editor

James W. Van Hoeven received his undergraduate education at Hope College, Holland, Michigan. In addition, he earned the B.D. degree from Western Theological Seminary, Holland, Michigan, the S.T.M. degree from Oberlin College, and the Ph.D. degree from Vanderbilt University. He is a member of the American Society of Church History.

Mr. Van Hoeven, an ordained minister of the Reformed Church in America, was the organizing pastor of the Parma Park Reformed Church, Parma Heights, Ohio, where he served from 1960 to 1964. From 1964 to 1979 he was a member of the faculty at Central College, Pella, Iowa, where he held the rank of professor in the religion department. During that time he also studied and taught in Latin America and London, England. He has served as a member and moderator of the Reformed Church Historical Commission from 1970 to 1976, as a member of the Theological Commission from 1979 to 1985 and, since 1980, as a member of the Board of Trustees of Hope College.

He has written numerous articles and is the contributing editor of *Piety and Patriotism: Bicentennial Studies of The Reformed Church in America, 1776–1976.* In 1985 he was named the first editor of *Perspectives: A Journal of Reformed Thought.*

Since 1979, Mr. Van Hoeven has served as Senior Minister of The First Church in Albany, New York.

The Historical Series of the Reformed Church in America

This series has been inaugurated by the General Synod of the Reformed Church in America, acting through its Commission on History, for the purpose of encouraging historical research and providing a medium wherein this knowledge may be shared with the academic community and with the members of the denomination in order that a knowledge of the past may contribute to right action in the present.

General Editor

The Rev. Donald J. Bruggink, Ph.D., Western Theological Seminary

The Writers

The Rev. John W. Beardslee III, Ph.D., Professor Emeritus of Church History, New Brunswick Theological Seminary

The Rev. Elton M. Eenigenburg, Ph.D., Professor Emeritus of Christian Ethics and Philosophy of Religion, Western Theological Seminary

The Rev. Paul R. Fries, Ph.D., Dean and Associate Professor of Theology, New Brunswick Theological Seminary

The Rev. Eugene P. Heideman, Th.D., Secretary for Program, Reformed Church in America

The Rev. I. John Hesselink, D. Theol., Professor of Theology, Western Theological Seminary

The Rev. M. Eugene Osterhaven, Th.D., Albertus C. Van Raalte, Professor of Systematic Theology, Western Theological Seminary

The Rev. James W. Van Hoeven, Ph.D., Senior Minister, The First Church in Albany

The Rev. Dennis N. Voskuil, Ph.D., Associate Professor of Religion and Chair of the Department, Hope College

Contents

Preface

> What indeed has Athens to do with Jerusalem? . . . Away with all at-
> tempts to produce a mottled Christianity of Stoic, Platonic, and dialectic
> composition.
>
> Tertullian, ca. 200 A.D.

Christian theology exists in the context of history. This means that Christian theology is necessarily dynamic and developing, is shaped in each
new age by the interaction of the biblical Word with the contemporary
world and, in Sydney Ahlstrom's provocative image, "consists of a series
of footnotes to St. Paul." Thus no church, properly speaking, can claim
that its theology is original; in every period Christian theology is in
some sense "mottled." It is like a serious discussion being continued by
generations of people as they move into different worlds. This book
examines that discussion as it developed among generations of people
in the Reformed Church in America, from 1628 to the present.

I am grateful to my colleagues on the Theological Commission of the
Reformed Church, and especially to its moderator, James I. Cook, for
supporting the idea of this book. Moreover, I am profoundly indebted
to the writers in this volume for their contribution which in each case
was a labor of love in the service of the church. In addition, appreciation
is expressed to the consistory and members of the First Church in
Albany, and especially to Mary Elizabeth Williams and Robert Alexander, for their interest in this project and for their unfailing belief—
expressed in countless ways—that the work was significant and worth
doing; to Barbara Walvoord, Howard Hageman, and especially to John
Stapert, for reading the manuscript and offering valuable suggestions
along the way; to Grace Smith, Denise Lobdell, Margaret Schroder,
and most notably to Donna Kachadurian, for their assistance in typing
the chapters without remuneration; to the librarians at New Brunswick
Seminary, New Jersey, and Western Theological Seminary, Holland,
Michigan, for their patience in sending sensitively written notes and
not the police to retrieve overdue books; to Ellan Fladger, archivist at
Union College, Schenectady, New York, for her help in tracking down
material on Tayler Lewis; to Donald J. Bruggink for his counsel as the

general editor of the Historical Series of the Reformed Church in America; and to my wife Mary, who provided me with love, humor, and understanding during two summers of work on this enterprise, tolerated clutter without complaint, and helped by reading sections of the manuscript and making insightful comments.

Finally, I must say a word about M. Eugene Osterhaven, one of the writers in this volume, and to whom the book is dedicated. Through the years one has many teachers, but very few mentors. He was one such mentor for me. He was among the first to inspire in me a love for history and theology, to point out to me the strong social implications of Calvin's thought, and to model for me what it means to love God with your mind, body, and spirit. In the most profound sense of the word he was and is a mentor to me, and I gratefully dedicate this book to him.

James W. VanHoeven
Editor

Introduction

In June, 1984, the General Synod of the Reformed Church in America approved the recommendation of its president, the Rev. Dr. Leonard Kalkwarf, to "give high priority . . . to the study of [our] denominational identity."[1] Kalkwarf proposed that recommendation because he "repeatedly heard individuals raise the question"[2] during his travels throughout the church. Summarizing the issue, he asked, "What is the glue that holds us together?"[3]

It is an intriguing question, one that should interest not only members of the Reformed Church but also a wide variety of scholars working in American studies. Part of what makes the question intriguing is the anomalous character of the denomination itself. For example, the Reformed Church is Dutch in origin, confessional, and "American," and although it names these as primary elements in the "glue" that holds it together it has never felt altogether comfortable with any of them. Why is this? On the other hand, why has a Dutch-American network persisted in the Reformed Church when by all logic it should have "melted" into the American mainstream long ago? Or why has the Reformed Church felt somewhat uneasy in the American culture and with the American evangelical tradition when so much of its own life has embraced that culture and so much of its theology has shared in that tradition?[4]

This book studies the history of theology in the Reformed Church in America, and shows how theology has remained a crucial element in the "glue" that holds the church together. This does not mean that the denomination has always agreed on what is essential in its theology; as the volume will note, the church's history is filled with conflicts, disagreements, and even schisms on theological matters. What it does mean, however, is that from its beginning the Reformed Church gave a prominent place to intellectual discourse, and insisted that its theology inform and judge all of its actions. Examining this discourse and defining that theology is what this book is about.

The Reformed Church in America traces its theological roots to John Calvin (1509-1564), one of the great sixteenth century reformers. Calvin was converted to the evangelical faith around 1534, and became a dominant voice in the Reformation in 1536 with the publication of the first edition of his *Institutes of the Christian Religion*. In the same year he began the work of establishing the evangelical faith in Geneva, Switzerland. From that time on, except for a brief three year period when he was in Strassbourg, Geneva was his place of work; Calvin remade that city into a world-wide center of Reformed witness and influence.

Numerous leaders of the second Protestant generation were trained in Calvin's Geneva, and subsequently carried the message of the Reformed faith throughout Europe and beyond. John Knox (1513-1572), for example, studied there and returned to his native Scotland to lead its Reformation. English Protestantism also was influenced by Geneva's life and thought and its theology still bears the stamp of Calvin. In 1549 Zurich, where Ulrich Zwingli (1484-1531) had begun the Swiss Reformation, embraced most of Calvin's ideas. Shortly thereafter, much of Switzerland became Reformed. In addition, Geneva's influence reached into the Rhine-Palatinate, the dominion of the pious Elector Frederick III (1559-1576). Frederick's famous university in Heidelberg became an important evangelical center; the Heidelberg Catechism and the so-called Palatinate liturgy, both published in 1563, had their origin in that city. The Reformed faith also made significant advances in other German cities and territories and, in the 1550s, Calvinism replaced Lutheranism in Bohemia, Moravia, Poland, and Hungary. France, too, felt the influence of the Reformed Church. It threatened to capture that country but then was eclipsed after a long and bitter struggle.

After the 1550s, Calvinism also began its conquest of the Netherlands, a fact of great importance for understanding the theological history of the (Dutch) Reformed Church in America. The soil of the Reformation in the Netherlands had been prepared as early as the fourteenth century by a variety of religious groups and personalities, most notably the Brethren of the Common Life. Founded by Gerhard Groote (1340-1384), the Brethren formed a number of societies and taught the need for true repentance, the imitation of Christ, and the obedience of faith. The community's members shared their possessions, taught in the language of the people, and emphasized the importance of education; Groote instructed that "the root of your study . . . should be the Gospel; then the biographies and the sayings of the Fathers; then the epistles of Paul and the histories of the Apostles; and finally, the writings of Bernard, Anselm, Augustine and others."[5]

The Brethren restored old schools, some of them reaching back as far as the age of Charlemange, and young students flocked to them. The center of the movement was in Deventer, but it also formed communities and opened schools for learning and renewal at Zwolle, Groningen, Amersfrorort, Utrecht, Ghent, Leiden, Amsterdam, Haarlem, Antwerp, Brussels, and Delft. The Brethren's most famous student was Gerhard Geradsz, known later as Desiderius Erasmus (1467-1536), who began his training at Deventer when he was a young boy. Undoubtedly, the Brethren's simple piety, practical mysticism, and devotion to learning strongly influenced their many students toward a deeper spirituality, and provided a healthy antidote to the generally sad religious situation in the Netherlands in the century before the Reformation.

When news of Luther's reform reached the Netherlands in the early sixteenth century, the response was mixed, although most of the people rejected it; Lutheranism never significantly penetrated the Low Countries. Those who embraced this "new" evangelical gospel, however, began preaching it in an effort to reform the church from within. A few of these people were burned at the stake as a result: Henry Voes and Jan Esch in 1523, and Jan van Woerden (Pistorious) in 1525. Although these were isolated martyrdoms, they did have a sobering effect on the religious situation in the Netherlands.

Much more important, however, was the influence of the Anabaptist (rebaptizers) movement. The first Anabaptists appeared in Zurich, Switzerland, in 1522, and in a few short decades there were thousands of them in the Netherlands. Their principal ideas were the following: the sole authority of the New Testament; the restoration of the church to its original purity in faith and practice; the rejection of the state-church idea and of all governmental support or control of things religious; separation from the world; a heightened eschatology; and, as a sign of their discipleship, believers' baptism.

Some of these Anabaptist became extremely radical in their behavior and views which shocked the general public, but others, led by the Frieslander, Menno Simons (1496-1561), were more moderate and established a continuing community of faith. Simons was converted to the Anabaptist position in 1537, after which he became the movement's foremost leader in the Netherlands. Profoundly pious, Simons differed from other evangelical believers of his day in his refusal to take oaths or allow magistrates membership in his church, his pre-millenialism, pacifism, negative attitude toward culture and education, and rejection of infant baptism. His Christology also was peculiar in that he believed that Jesus had not really been born of Mary, but brought his flesh and blood with him from heaven. Simon reorganized the various Anabaptist elements in the Netherlands and made the movement respectable. Many Anabaptists, however, converted to the Reformed Church when it entered the country.

The history that brought about the founding of the Reformed Church in the Netherlands was inextricably interconnected with the people's revolt against Spanish domination. That began after 1555, when the Emperor Charles V abdicated and handed over the seventeen provinces of his Netherlands possessions to his son, Philip II of Spain. There were many reasons for the Dutch revolution against Philip; the struggle comprised a number of revolts by different classes and groups, often with conflicting motives. For example, in the early 1560s members of the Dutch nobility—bishops, abbots, lords, and the Prince, William of Orange, who was still Catholic at that time—resisted Philip's attempt to suppress their ancient rights and centralize the government. Moreover, the merchant class also entered the struggle in the 1560s, protesting Philip's decision to increase an already burdensome financial situation by demanding an additional excise tax, the notorious "tenth pence."

The catalyst for the revolt in the Netherlands, however, was the issue of religion. Philip was a militant Catholic who vowed to crush every vestige of Protestantism in the country, and in the 1560s that meant especially Calvinism. Two events triggered him to action in this regard. One was the report of wide-spread Calvinist worship in the open fields, which was prohibited, and the second was the destruction by fanatical mobs of church buildings; in Flanders alone, Philip learned that over four hundred churches had been desecrated, prompting him to say that "he would rather lose one hundred thousand lives than allow a change of religion in the Netherlands."[6] In 1567, Philip replaced his sister Margaret with the Duke of Alva as commander in the Netherlands, ordering him to extirpate the "heretics." Alva entered the country determined to do just that! He quickly established a council of disturbances, called by the people a "Council of Blood," which condemned almost the entire nation to death. During the next six years, Alva's council, supported by the Spanish army, unleashed its terror upon the hapless Dutch, killing over 18,000 people by "judicial" death, and tormenting and torturing countless others.[7] By such mad means Alva filled the nation with grief—but also determination.

One of those so determined was William, the Prince of Orange. The Prince had escaped the country during Alva's reign of terror, using that time to organize the Dutch provinces against Spain's domination. Moreover, in 1573 he converted to the Calvinist religion, which was a vital turning point in the nation's political and religious history. Six years later, in 1579, the Union of Utrecht was approved by seven northern provinces, and in 1581 Philip's domination over the Netherlands was renounced and independence declared: "We reject the King," wrote Marnix of St. Alegonde, "because he, the sworn enemy of the true

religion and of the Word of God, intends to retain dominion over the
land on no other condition than to be permitted to destroy the kingdom
of Jesus Christ."[8] This declaration assured the continuation of the struggle for independence, which the seven northern provinces achieved *de
facto* in 1609, and which became *de jure* in 1648 by the treaty of
Munster.

During this same period the Calvinists were making significant advances within the Dutch provinces, and profoundly altering the shape
of religion in the country. As we noted before, the Lutherans and Anabaptists had been the earliest Protestant groups in the nation, but by
the 1560s the Reformed witness was by far the most dominant. Calvin's
teachings had appeared first among the French-speaking southern
(Walloon) provinces of the Netherlands. Here several small congregations were formed which met secretly in private houses, held in 1563
the first Reformed synod in the nation, and began carrying the Reformed faith northward. Four ministers emerged as leaders among these
Reformed churches: Guido de Bres, who authored the Belgic Confession
and was martyred in 1656; Peter Dathenus, who translated the Heidelberg Catechism into Dutch, was court preacher in Heidelberg, wrote
the Palatinate liturgy, and presided at one of the first Dutch synods;
Henry Modet, who was a tireless and effective field preacher; and Fran-
ciscus Junius, who preached in Antwerp and later became professor of
theology at Leiden.

Encouraged by these leaders, the Walloon congregations continued
to hold worship services in secret, even though the penalty for such
action was imprisonment or worse. Equally important, these Reformed
Churches began to move toward some permanent form of organization,
which they succeeded in doing at the Synod of Antwerp in 1566. Held
in secret, those who attended this assembly were admitted by password
(La Vigne: The Vineyard) only. The delegates at Antwerp adopted, with
some minor revisions, the Belgic Confession as their basis of agreement.
This confession comprised thirty-seven articles, and had been written
and published in 1561 by Guido de Bres' to counter the charge that
Reformed churches were Anabaptist in character. The Antwerp assembly also provisionally adopted the Heidelberg Catechism. These two
creeds gave the fledgling Reformed Church in the Netherlands a much
needed "symbol of accord in the faith," which also became important
tools for Christian instruction.

Because the Spanish army continued its presence in the Netherlands,
it is not surprising that the Reformed Church chose to hold synod meetings in German towns near the Dutch border. These included Wesel
in 1568 and Emden in 1571. The delegates at the Wesel Synod, who

represented about twenty congregations, made important decisions regarding church order, approved Peter Dathenus' Dutch versification of the Psalms for use in worship, and gave further endorsement to the Heidelberg Catechism. The name which the syndics gave themselves reflects the pathos of their situation: "The Netherland churches which sit under the cross, and are scattered within and without the Netherlands."9 The synod of Emden confirmed the decisions made at the Wesel assembly.

Beginning in 1572 the military situation improved in the northern provinces, making it possible for the increasing number of Reformed congregations in that region to hold their meetings on Dutch soil. These included, among others, Alkmaar (1573), Dordrecht (1574), Middleburg (1581), The Hague (1586), and Groningen (1595). The first national synod to be held in the Netherlands was at Dordrecht in 1578. These synods debated and honed Calvinist positions on this doctrine and that, attempting by these discussions to articulate what it meant to be Reformed in the Netherlands in the sixteenth century. Predictably there was often disagreement on matters of dogma, order, and church government. Gradually, however, through this process agreement was reached on most fundamental issues, and an identifiable national Reformed Church began to emerge in the country.

One issue which often provoked heated discussion was the relation of the church to the state. Calvin's position on this issue was that the church should be independent of the state while at the same time being willing to cooperate with it. He argued for that position during much of his stay in Geneva, and did not win that struggle until 1554. The Dutch church generally was inclined toward Calvin's position on this issue, but some of its leaders, most notably the Leiden professor of theology, Casper Coolhaas (1536-1614), strongly favored state control over the church. This latter position gained wide popularity, moreover, when in 1575 the Prince of Orange ordered that consistories were to be appointed by local magistrates. This state-church controversy was hotly debated at most of the synod meetings, but especially at the synod of Middleburg in 1581.

Far more serious, however, was the so-called Arminian controversy, which surfaced early in the seventeenth century, nearly destroyed the Dutch Church, and precipitated the calling of the great Synod of Dordrecht (Dort) in 1618. The term Arminian refers to the teachings of Jacob Arminius (1560-1609), who was minister of "the great church" in Amsterdam before his appointment as professor of theology at Leiden in 1603. While at Leiden he began raising questions about Calvin's teachings on predestination (election), especially double predestination, and free will, which were immediately opposed by his colleague, Francis Gomarus. Arminius died in 1609, but his ideas were taken up by others who formed, in effect, an "Arminiam party" within the Dutch Reformed Church.

In 1610 this Arminian party issued a five-point "Remonstrance," which had the following points: (1) that God determined to save all who believe in Christ and rejected the teaching that election is unto faith; (2) that Christ died for all men, although "no one actually enjoys this forgiveness of sins except the believers"; (3) that while human nature has been impaired by sin, the will is still free "to prepare itself and to take the decisive steps" toward grace; (4) that grace is not irresistible; and (5) that faith may be lost—"[One] can only hope that he may persevere and be confident that divine grace will always be at hand and be sufficient."[10] In addition to challenging the doctrines of predestination, sin, grace, and the perseverance of the saints, the Arminian party (also called Remonstrants) declared that it was uncertain about other doctrines; original sin, justification by grace through faith, the atonement, and even the deity of Christ were called into question by the more extreme among the Remonstrants. This latter fact, which surfaced after the death of Arminius, contributed to the seriousness of the controversy in the Dutch Church, and also to its acrimony and divisiveness.

During the next several years, from 1610 until the Synod of Dort in 1618, the Dutch were embroiled in a heated party battle between the Remonstrants on the one hand, and the orthodox on the other, which nearly destroyed both the church and the nation. Arminian leaders succeeded for a time in getting civil authorities to order that no contested doctrines might be proclaimed from Reformed pulpits, and in a few instances they had pulpits closed to certain ministers. Orthodox churches retaliated, and where they could not secure support from magistrates they worshipped in houses or barns, even though they were fined for their civil disobedience. Governmental leaders were also deeply involved in the conflict, taking opposing sides. The situation became so stormy that in 1617 it appeared as though there might be a civil war in the country. Finally, on November 11, 1617, the States-General called for a national synod to resolve the controversy and bring peace both to the church and to the country. To insure the synod's success, the government invited to the assembly representatives from each of the provinces, as well as Reformed theologians from England, France, several towns in Germany, and a select number of cantons in Switzerland. King James I instructed the five English delegates to "mitigate the heat on both sides" and to advise the Dutch "not to deliver in the pulpit . . . those things . . . which are the highest points of schools . . . [and]

disputable on both sides," but are not relevant to the average person.[11]
When the synod opened on November 13, 1618, there were eighty-
four delegates present, twenty-six from foreign nations and fifty-eight
from the Netherlands. The Remonstrants wanted to be recognized as
equals at the synod and to move the delegates into a discussion of the
disputed questions. The majority at the assembly was orthodox, however, and summoned the Remonstrants to appear before it as defen-
dants. Thus, the outcome of Dort was certain from the start.

The Synod of Dort proved to be a watershed event for the Dutch
Reformed Church, marking the end of its formative period.[12] The delegates themselves sensed the historic nature of their meeting, and debated the varied and complex issues with careful seriousness. One such
issue was the nagging church-state problem. We have already noted
Prince William's decision in 1575 to have the civil magistrates select the
church's officers. This policy obtained throughout all of the Netherlands,
and in some places the state exercised even broader powers over the
church; in the province of Holland, for example, in 1612, the civil government called into force an earlier ordinance which mandated that the
civil authorities share both in the calling of ministers and the exercise
of church discipline. Most of the delegates at Dort favored rescinding
such ordinances, preferring the independence of the church in man-
aging its own affairs. They pressed their position twice at the synod, but
in both cases the government's officials refused their request. Thus, *per
force*, Dort accepted the continuation of the centuries-old practice of
state control over the church. There was, however, one saving note in
this for the church: as things turned out, the synod's success effected
a new spirit between the church and the civil government which resulted in the magistrates carrying out the synod's decisions in the life
of the nation. The church in the Netherlands did not gain its independence from the state until almost two centuries later.

A second problem with which Dort wrestled was the nature and role
of the church's confessions. Specifically, the delegates dealt with a pervasive anti-confessional humanist movement that had been present in
the Dutch Church for nearly a century. This movement's heroes were
Erasmus, whom we have already noted, Jacob Acontius (1492-1566?),
an Italian whose writings significantly influenced Dutch thought, and
Dirk Coornheert (1522-1590). Erasmus had been critical of the church
before 1517, the year Luther broke with it, but on the fundamental
issue of sin and grace he disagreed with the reformers as well, teaching
that the human will has the ability to choose to do either good or evil.
Acontius, who like Erasmus had immersed himself in the Greek and
Latin classics, was also like Erasmus in his inability to identify himself

with the creed of any church. His book, *stratagemata Satanae* (1565), which articulated his humanistic views, went through twelve editions and was widely read in the Netherlands. He argued for tolerance on issues of religion, strongly opposed executions for heresy, and believed that all Christian teachings could be reduced to a few essentials. Coornheert was equally opposed to Roman Catholics and Reformed Confessionalism and said that he did not prefer the one to the other. He delighted in criticizing the papacy, Roman superstition, and the Spanish occupation; he also rejected the teachings of Calvin, and wrote a pamphlet against the Heidelberg Catechism which he dedicated to "the States of Holland" and titled simply, "A Test." "Scripture," he declared, "knows nothing of original sin . . . or the teaching of predestination in the sense of Calvin because it makes God the author of sin."[13] In another place Coornheert's religious tolerance is revealed: "I hold as brethren all god-fearing people," he said, "who rest on the foundation of Christ, whether they be Papists, Monks, Baptists, Reformed, or Lutheran."[14] Erasmus, Acontius, and Coornheert were each brilliant controversialists, but their struggle for freedom of conscience in religious matters was too far advanced to be acceptable in the sixteenth or seventeenth centuries.

Their humanist influence, however, was profoundly felt at Dort. Indeed, the Arminian controversy cannot be understood without appreciating the enduring impact of their ideas. The Arminian party shared their anti-confessionalism and used their arguments to raise questions about the role of creeds at Dort; they argued for the time-boundness of creeds, and the need for confessions to be revised.

By far the most serious problem at Dort, however, involved discussion on the doctrine of predestination, especially that part of it known as reprobation. The Arminian party had already established its position on this doctrine in its five-point "Remonstrance," published in 1610. The issue, however, was far more serious than these few dogmatic statements. At stake was the method of religious inquiry itself; the Remonstrants had revived the rational side of the Christian faith—wrongly, the orthodox believed—and, for the first time in Protestant history, organized it into a significant power and gave it a definite place both in theology and the church. That was the deeper issue with which Dort wrestled in the predestination controversy. Indeed, it is the issue that has given this so-called Arminian controversy its continuing significance in the history of Reformed thought.

Dort responded to the five-points of the "Remonstrance" with its own five heads of doctrine. These so-called "Canons of Dort" were set forth in the following: (1) unconditional election and faith as a gift of God's grace; (2) that although Christ's death was "sufficient to expiate the sins

of the whole world," its "saving efficacy . . . extends [only] to the elect";
(3 and 4) that all are so corrupted by sin that they cannot effect their
own salvation. In sovereign grace God regenerates his elect to new life;
(5) those whom God elects and regenerates he preserves until the end.[15]

Dort's doctrinal decisions secured the Calvinist positions on sin and
grace against the Arminian "Remonstrance"; thus driven underground,
Arminianism later became an important influence on the theology of
John Wesley in "Old" England and on the successors of Jonathan Edwards in "New" England. Dort's decisions also secured the establishment of the Reformed Church in the Netherlands; its polity, liturgy,
and confessional statements were effectively adopted and enforced by
the state. In a little less than a century, therefore, roughly from 1560
to 1648, the ecclesiastical soil of the Netherlands was transformed, with
Calvinism replacing Catholicism as the religion of the nation. The Synod
of Dort, which concluded in May, 1619, stood at the mid-point of that
transformation, and determined its theological course.

During the period in which Dort was redefining the religious map of
the Netherlands, Dutch merchants, bankers, and seamen were expanding the nation's commercial influence, thus realigning its political map.
By 1609 that influence had reached the New World, and shortly thereafter the Dutch laid claim to all the land between the Delaware and
Connecticut Rivers. By 1613 they had a few trading houses on Man-
hatten (New Amsterdam, later New York), while a fort erected about
this time on Castle Island (Fort Nassau, later Orange) was transferred
in 1617 to the present site of Albany, New York. In 1623, the first party
of permanent Dutch settlers arrived in New Amsterdam and Fort Nassau, and five years later, in 1628, the Classis of Amsterdam commissioned the Reverend Jonas Michaelius to organize the first Dutch
Reformed Church in the New World. Subsequently, from 1628 until
the English conquest in 1664, the mother church in the Netherlands
sent seventeen ordained ministers to the new colony, who organized
thirteen congregations in scattered Dutch settlements here and there
along the Hudson River. By all odds these thirteen congregations should
not have survived the next several decades, given their adjustment to
a strange English-speaking culture, the imposition of English rule, and
the fact that there was virtually no new immigration from the Netherlands. Actually, however, quite the reverse happened. By 1700 there
were twenty-nine Dutch congregations in the New World, thus securing
the future of the Reformed Church in America.

The eight essays in this volume examine the history of theology in
the Reformed Church in America from its beginning in 1628 to the
present. The chapters are arranged chronologically, and for the most

part follow the outline of traditional texts in American Christianity. This is particularly the case with John Beardslee's essay on the colonial era (ch. 1) and my study of Reformed theology in the period from 1800 to 1850 (ch. 2). Two of the chapters are narrow in focus, and study the role of theology in specific events in Reformed Church history, namely, Elton Eeningenburg's essay on the Union of 1850 (ch. 3), and M. Eugene Osterhaven's chapter on the Schism of 1857 (ch. 4). On the other hand, both Eugene Heideman's chapter on Reformed missiology (ch. 7) and Dennis Voskuil's study of "Civil Religion" (ch. 8) are cast in broad strokes, and examine the unfolding history of single topics important in Reformed Church history. Finally, Paul Fries' chapter on modernity (ch. 5) and John Hesselink's essay on confessional renewal (ch. 6) critically study the response of Reformed theology to recent issues in American religion.

Although each writer worked independently, the story that unfolds in this volume is held together by a common issue in the American church, namely, the process by which an Old World denomination determines to hold to its faith and practice while at the same time refining that faith and practice in its developing history. This book carefully examines that process in the Reformed Church in America, and notes especially what remained constant and what was revised in the denomination's theology. Equally important, the book shows how through that process the Reformed Church carved out its own theological identity in America.

I

Orthodoxy and Piety:
Two Styles of Faith in The Colonial Period

John W. Beardslee III

The colonial period of the Reformed Church in America covers something over a century and a half, and at its mid-point, roughly 1720, lies the arrival of Theodorus Jacobus Frelinghuysen and the beginnings of an outburst of pietistic-revivalistic enthusiasm, which was a most significant turning point.[1]

The first half of the period, from the arrival of Dutch colonists in 1623 and the formation of the first consistory in 1628, to the arrival of Domine Frelinghuysen, can also be conveniently divided into Dutch and English periods, with the English conquest in 1664 marked as the decisive year of change. That event affected the life of the church very deeply, but its immediate effect upon theology was slight. The entire period was "colonial" in the full sense of the word—colonial rule, whether Dutch or English, and colonial dependence in commerce, education, and culture. Massachusetts acquired its own college in the first generation and was soon developing a creative, indigenous intellectial life. New Amsterdam, a much smaller community and one much more concentrated on satisfying old world commercial demands, did not. Dutch Church life, like that of the Anglicans, but again unlike that of New England was also colonial, lacking its own judicatory and remaining dependent upon Amsterdam even when the civil power was English.

The theology of the Dutch colonists was that of the homeland, but religion was not the primary motive of the colony, and most of the colonists lacked the educational background for significant contribution to theological development. The first ecclesiastical appointments were laymen—"comforters of the sick"—one of whom seems to have been illiterate until after his marriage.[2] The pastors, although usually meeting the educational requirements of the Amsterdam Classis, were rarely among the distinguished members of the colony, and in any event had few intellectuals with whom to interact. The quarrelsomeness and propensity to alcoholism that often characterized the Dutch colonial clergy

1

may be related to this loneliness of the ministers who found no social stimulation comparable to that in Europe.

The theology proclaimed by the pulpit was of course that of the Old Country and its schools. This was the "Calvinism" of the seventeenth century, the orthodoxy that was coming into being during the period. The Synod of Dort (1618-1619) completed its work less than a decade before the founding of the church in New Amsterdam. The controversies over orthodoxy—the limits within which the Belgic Confession was to be interpreted—had just been officially concluded, and the completion of systems of orthodox theology went on through the century. Colonists of the first generation brought with them, insofar as they participated in theological development, an earlier and less definitive form of orthodoxy than that which developed as time went on.

This ecclesiastical and theological life of the colony was to a large extent a pale reflection of the vigor and creativeness of the Dutch theological faculties of the century, the age of Voetius[3] and Cocceius,[4] which was also the golden age of the Netherlands in commerce, technology, and culture—painting, organ music, science—all of which was only vaguely felt in the colonies. The ministers who came from the Netherlands reflected the theological learning of their generation and no doubt tried to make it viable in the colonies, where new problems were often more troublesome than at home because of the lack of local tradition and social stability. That ecclesiastical disputes reflected both personal incompatabilities and differences between the theological traditions of different Dutch universities is probable (this latter issue demands further investigation), but the small number of theologically sophisticated people, and the low level of intellectual life generally, prevented the development of a consistent theological pattern. The general features of Dutch Reformed orthodoxy, as they developed, with emphasis on avoiding the "errors" of Roman Catholics, Anabaptists, and Arminians[5] were dutifully reflected, at least by common agreement of the pastors.

Orthodox pastors expected the support of the civil magistrates in the colony, following the practice of the Middle Ages and of the Reformation. Important teachings about the civil power commonly appeared in theological treatises as a secondary part of the doctrine of the church. This was the case with the fourth book of Calvin's *Institutes*, and with the *Medulla* and *Compendium* of Johannes a' Marck,[6] a writer of great influence in the eighteenth century, in which the question of civil power, like that of the family, is discussed in chapters entitled *De Regimine Ecclesae (On the Authority of the Church)*. The magistrate, like the minister, was expected to fulfill his functions under the rule of God and to enforce both "tables of the Law." On the assumption that truth is one, the responsibility of the magistrate was seen as including the maintenance of uniformity, and even as religious uniformity broke down, for example in the Netherlands, the magistrate, as a Christian functionary, was still seen as responsible for upholding Christian morality, for suppressing idolatry as well as theft and murder, and for being a "nursing father" to the church. Therefore, like the head of a seventeenth century family, the magistrate exercised authority in ecclesiastical affairs, always, in theory at least, subject to his religious responsibility. He protected the church, provided for the maintenance of public ministry, and saw to it that the "subject" had the opportunity for worship in peace. The good subject accepted the religious facilities provided by the ruler just as he accepted, with thanksgiving, the other facilities provided for him—markets, police, port works, and, occasionally, sanitation.

This system, that of the state church as a real part of the state's responsibility and effectiveness, was accepted in Europe for a couple of centuries after the Reformation and became, in effect, part of the common theology of a divided Christendom. Both Reformed and Roman Catholic theologians introduced important qualifications when the ruler refused to do his duty and enforced "heretical" practices, but both expected the individual's personal Christian life to be developed peacefully within a framework provided by the Christian magistrate. The good Christian, under "normal" conditions, was a passive receiver of a Christian environment.

Such was the framework within which theological development took place, and such was the framework that gave meaning to the developing forms of church life in the colonies. The debates of theological schools in the Netherlands require brief attention, but for all the excitement they may have caused, they became increasingly remote from the real interests of people even in that land, and much more in the New World.

With the defeat of the Arminians at the Synod of Dort, the limits of orthodoxy in the Dutch Church were definitively fixed. Arminianism, like Roman Catholicism and Anabaptism, had received an identifying definition that made it possible to exclude it. "Calvinism" presently acquired its "five points,"[7] expressed in the Canons of Dort and summing up the doctrine of the absolute, unconditioned, immutable decree by which God, from all eternity, had "elected" certain individual members of the sinful human race for eternal bliss with him, and had "passed by" the remainder. For purposes of human understanding, two decrees in particular were recognized, one to election for salvation, and, as its "necessary" opposite, abandonment to damnation ("reprobation"), but the quality of theology was determined by the description of God as absolute, who is sovereign over everything. A major concern of early orthodoxy was the concept of God's decrees as directed toward individuals, not to classes of people (believers or unbelievers) or other abstractions. God was seen as meeting people one by one, especially when he came in grace, and this, historically, is a vital point of contact between decreetal orthodoxy and the "pietism" which we will soon consider.

The development of theology in the Netherlands in the seventeenth century was, on its own terms, a significant and lively part of the intellectual excitement of that great period of Dutch history. The chief question which Reformed theology had set for itself was the doctrine of predestination. That every soul's destiny was purely in God's hands was the essential, or "fundamental" point. The argument between infralapsarians and supralapsarians—between those who thought of God as decreeing about fallen people or about unfallen, even uncreated ones— was active but seen as not touching the fundamentals.[8]

A more significant problem arose from the methodology of the discussion. In the sixteenth century, predestination, as God's infallible care of his chosen ones, had been indeed a comforting doctrine for "the church under the cross," that "lily among the thorns" which was the Reformed Church in Holland and France. In the seventeenth century, the Dutch Reformed Church ceased to experience persecution, and what had been a source of assurance more and more became an intellectual puzzle. The fathers of Dort, intent on upholding the great teaching that salvation is of God and that God's people cannot be overcome by the world, had undertaken a meticulous intellectual analysis of the doctrine and of the logical possibilities open to one who accepted it, but had urged ministers and teachers to use it for "the glory of God, holiness of life, and the consolation of dejected souls,"[9] and to "govern sentiments and speech by Scripture."[10] These were the Reformation's insights. They were brought into the world of the professional intellectual by the use of scholastic reasoning, a theological method criticized by the Reformers, but adopted by their heirs because it was the accepted university idiom. Answers to all questions were sought by logical reasoning from accepted first principles.

In this atmosphere, following the defeat of the Remonstrants, the debates between "Voetians" and "Cocceians" took place. Gisbertus Voetius and Johannes Cocceius were two of the most prominent academic theologians of this active period of Dutch cultural life. Voetius, a man of prodigious learning, approached theology with the idea of completeness, that is of doing as much as possible. Taking God's sovereignty with deadly seriousness, he proposed a doctrine of completeness and exactness—"precision" in his terminology—in obeying God, demanding this precision in doctrine, morals, polity, personal relations, social structures, and the inner life, all in accordance with the word of God. He claimed that such exactness was the Reformed, or original, Christian faith. Among the problems to be faced by Christians he listed: "whether the first reformers, and the first Reformed Churches . . . wanted, desired, and sought precision in the matter of reformation in doctrine, polity, discipline, ceremonies, and morals for every occasion, although they were not always able to achieve it? Reply: Affirmation. This is proved by the first ecclesiastical constitutions, the practice and decrees of synods, and the leading writers. . . ."[11] Not everyone agreed with, or tried to practice, Voetius' strenuous "Puritanical" morality, and few succeeded in reaching his standard of detail in dogmatic theology, but he set forth an ideal whose influence reached far. Absolute adherance to an orthodoxy based on the decrees and commandments of God and reaching into every phase of life, and supported by a community acknowledging God's lordship through Christian magistrates—such was the pattern Voetius proposed.

A variant of orthodoxy did appear with Cocceius, who distrusted the method of logical deduction from accepted principles, even if grounded on the Bible, and saw *sola scriptura* as meaning rather direct dependence on exegisis. The difference may be theoretical, for Voetius had found his abstract principles, and above all his conception of God as sovereign to be obeyed, in Scripture. Cocceius did, however, make a particular emphasis on the biblical idea of the covenant, seeing God first and foremost as one who made and kept agreements, not one who simply issued orders. Both men operated within the framework of a doctrine of predestination directed toward individuals, but Voetius presented God as legislator; Cocceius, somewhat more personally and concretely, as covenant-maker. He used Scripture with more emphasis on history and less on abstract logic, and distinguished between the covenants, old and new. It was consistent with this view to see more difference between Old and New Testaments than did the Voetians and to be less interested in enforcing the Old Testament law on members of the New Covenant. The practical difference between the parties in the Dutch community often expressed itself in terms of Voetian suspicion of Cocceian lax morality. Cocceian ladies in Dutch cities were seen doing their embroidery on Sunday, a piece of sabbath-breaking according to Voetians . The New Amsterdam women who in 1697 were seen shelling peas "at the door" on Sunday were doubtless unaware of the sophisticated theological argument, but they represented a Dutch Reformed ethos that avoided Voetius' precision.[12]

In the Netherlands, the two parties coexisted in an uneasy relationship in one ecclesiastical establishment, and in time the accepted theology came to include elements from both. With his emphasis on obedience as the primary Christian virtue and the importance of the decreeing, law-giving function of God, his acceptance of the Mosaic legislation, minus some ceremonies, as fully required by the gospel, and an emphasis on "ascetic theology," Voetius set the pattern for the future of Dutch Reformed theology. Cocceius, to some extent, softened and "humanized" the concept of God, and helped free exegesis from many presuppositions, pointed the Reformed world directly to the Bible, and popularized the concept of covenants. In common with the general trend of international Calvinism, however, the covenantal scheme came to be part of the accepted dogmatic framework. Popular theologians— Willem á Brakel,[13] and the teacher of John Henry Livingston, Gijstertus Bonnet[14]—are all designated "Voetians," in spite of the differences among them and their common tendency to lapse from much of Voetius' rigor and from his demanding academic ideals. Exegesis influenced by Cocceianism, covenant theology,[15] and a developed pietism are common elements in the new theological outlook.

The theological disputes were part of the activity of the elite who provided the ministry that the common people were expected to accept. Lay preaching was not encouraged; books of approved sermons were provided from which a layman could read if no ministers were available. In general, theological controversy took place in an atmosphere approaching paternalism, and the ordinary church member received his doctrine as he received his ministerial services, from those above. The Reformation's emphasis on correct doctrine as a bond of Christian unity degenerated into a debate over details of correct doctrine, and the doctrine of the priesthood of all believers tended to be forgotten; spiritual affairs became more and more the sphere of the established authorities. The controversial side of theological development, which in the Netherlands gave some excitement to church life, were less meaningful in the colony because of the lack of informed participation, the absence of regular ecclesiastical organization and channels for ecclesiastical action, the lack of a stable, traditional community life, and the resulting emergence of new forms of social relationship.

This new society sought stability, in part, through the traditional means of state-church establishment. The directors of New Amsterdam, although forced to make various concessions to religious pluralism, expected a state-church relationship of the European pattern, while the West India Company cooperated, formally, with the Classis of Amsterdam to fulfill the magistrates' expectation. The English conquest in 1664 was a shock to the system, and, although the Reformed Dutch Church originated in an extreme form of voluntarism, namely political-military revolt, the Dutch communities in the New World were ill prepared for the responsibility of volunteerism and self-support. By treaty, the English promised to respect the rights of the Dutch churches, but these rights were not defined, nor did the Dutch any longer enjoy the privilege of state support. They had, however, always borne the day to day costs of their churches, and the transition to a purely voluntary system, although an innovation both in practice and in theory, was furthered by a strong ethnic consciousness; the desire to speak and "be" Dutch provided an important social support for the Reformed Dutch Church after 1664, particularly where the local electorate was dominated by Dutch families. In those places, which were numerous, local governments went far toward replacing the central government as "nursing father" for the church. The church remained a necessary part of a cherished Old World way of life, even when the living, vital forms of culture in that homeland were no longer known. A few, for example the perceptive Domine Selyns[16] at the turn of the seventeenth century, sensed the possibilities of a new dynamic in the New World and of a Christian community that knew itslf as nonethnic.[17] Sometime later the Classis of Amsterdam sought at least a common college for the Dutch Reformed and Presbyterians. For the majority, however, the church was simply part of a traditional, ethnocentric way of life, ignoring, rather than opposing, "outsiders" when it could.

Social transformation resulting from English rule and the stopping of Dutch immigration brought the church face to face with a theological problem that the Reformers had regarded as solved. Was the church a separated community of those who have renounced the world, or did it embrace and have the obligation of including under its discipline all members of the civil community? The Anabaptists had held to the former teaching, and had paid the price of rejection. Zwingli and Calvin had taught the latter concept; the Reformed theologians from the beginning had at great pain separated themselves from the Anabaptists and integrated church and civil community. But circumstances in the New World, most dramatically the English conquest, led the Dutch to decide for the other side. Their church would not be integrated into the larger community. The price of that would be to "become English." Both in New Jersey and New York, the Dutch churches chose the path of the Anabaptists and became a separated minority. The kind of separated minority the Reformed church became during this period, however, was determined by a surprisingly different dynamic.

The movement known as "Reformed pietism" in church history had its roots in the original Reformation, represented an important emphasis to many of the Reformers, and was always present in the Reformed churches.[18] Its special characteristic was its emphasis on the fruits of the new life in the individual. Not only regeneration, but constant spiritual growth after regeneration was seen as essential. This led to an emphasis on the devotional and moral life, both important elements in Voetius' concept of completeness in obedience ("precision"). There was also room for the Cocceian effort to emphasize the Bible rather than philosophical ideas, but not for some of the liberal moral attitudes attributed to the Cocceians. Above all, however, the emphasis was on the work of the Holy Spirit in the individual and a desire to see public evidence of the fruits of that work. These concerns were prominent in Voetius as they were in Calvin, who also included the conviction that the civil community was responsible for keeping inviolate the glory of God and that the church must be so involved in the civil community that every person was subject to Christian discipline.

This last emphasis was not at first rejected by the pietists, nor did they criticize the existing structure or come forward with theological innovations. Their emphasis was on what could happen in and through the Christian, not on what the authorities, or the intellectuals, could do. The main task of the individual Christian was to develop his or her spiritual life. Prayer, Bible study, the practice of honesty, purity and charity, and similar matters that lay within the province of the individual, became equally important with doctrinal orthodoxy, which was never seen as an adequate end. Voetius had spoken of two "parts" of theology, dogmatic and practical, and had included under the heading of "practical" not only polity, homiletics, and liturgics, but ethics—personal and social—and the practice of prayer and aids to personal growth. The pietistic movement may be said to be the coming into its own of the second part, the "practical," and following the example of Voetius, much of it was based directly on the Heidelberg Catechism. Other catechisms, also stressing the practical and experiential side of faith, were also produced. In a world where the established institutions were falling short of the Reformation's ideals, this movement sought to fill in the gaps, beginning with its own members. In time, some of the social emphases of Calvin and Voetius were forgotten, and pietism acquired connotations of individualism. This gave it its special importance in the New World, where the social conditions were destroying some of the Old World sanctions of social stability and calling a new society into being.

The first crisis for the Dutch church following the English conquest emerged with the removal of official support. The determination of the Dutch people, however, kept the church alive, and ecclesiastical relations with Amsterdam continued. Slowly, however, it became obvious that many of those who voluntarily supported the Dutch churches did so from loyalty to the ethnic community rather than from theological motives. But pietism, almost unconsciously, provided the means whereby the long-term survival and Christian character of the church was secured. In this way it motivated a real theological revolution.

Pietist efforts to strengthen spiritual life within the church were followed by an increasing tendency to be critical of the "non-pietistic" brethren. The common charges of "formalism" and "dead orthodoxy" made against the official structures rested ultimately on the efforts of the church to be inclusive, and pietism, as time went on, came increasingly to mean emphasis on a small fellowship that pursued the Christian life and responsibility in earnest. Pietism, in short, was the natural fruit of one Reformation emphasis, namely, "the priesthood of all believers" and the call to make religion life-transforming, not merely a set of doctrines. Nearly all orthodox Reformed theologians had insisted that theology must not be allowed to become purely "theoretical" (academic), that devout prayer was necessary for Christian living, that the individual must not accept doctrine simply on the authority of the church but understand scripture itself, and, above all, that the work of the Spirit was necessary for Christian life. Thus orthodoxy, in theory at least, led toward the pietist ideal. The demands of social order and the emphasis on right doctrine—also genuine parts of the Reformation's ideal—had pushed these matters into the background. The pietists were determined to make them prominent, and if this could not be done through the official establishment, they would supplement or by-pass that establishment.

In the 1690s the Dutch Church in New Jersey sent Guilliam Bertholf, the Flemish immigrant and lay leader, to the Netherlands for ordination.[19] Rejected by the Classis of Amsterdam because he lacked proper academic credentials, the pietist Bertholf was ordained by the Classis of Walcheren. He returned to the Raritan Valley in 1694 to serve as the first Dutch pastor in New Jersey. Shortly thereafter the German pietist, Bernardus Freeman,[20] arrived in the New York colony to pastor the pioneer church in Schenectady, and then later a church on Long Island. Both Bertholf and Freeman served their churches with distinction and eventually won acceptance from the established clergy.

These details are significant for two reasons, one historical and the other theological. Historically the presence of these two clergy clearly indicates that pietism, which had gained influence in the Reformed church in the Netherlands, was present in the colonial Dutch Church before the arrival of Freylinghuysen. Theologically, it illustrates that when the pietist believed he had a clear vision of what the Lord called him to do, he pressed ahead with the task even if it meant by-passing the existing structures. On this level, their view of the church was quite different from the more orthodox clergy who insisted on working within established ecclesiastical mechanisms. Pietists revived the almost forgotten emphasis of Calvin and his colleagues, namely, that pure worship must be established with or without the consent of the religious or secular authorities. The arrival of the German Theodorus J. Frelinghuysen in 1720 may be taken, therefore, as the beginning of the second colonial period, when this principle began to grow into a dominant force in the Dutch churches of North America.

Frelinghuysen had been regularly ordained and commissioned by the church in the Netherlands, but his ministry (1720-1742) was marked by controversy which brought the special features of pietism to the fore.[21] His successors, notably his son Theodore Jr. (d. 1761),[22] J. H. Goetschius (d. 1774),[23] and Johannes Leydt (d. 1783),[24] formed a distinct party which precipitated a schism in the church, but which developed pietistic principles and practices into their characteristic American forms and, more importantly, determined a significant line of development for the future Reformed Church in America. At the end of the colonial period, the American-born John Henry Livingston and the Dutch-born Eliardus Westerlo[25] represented the combination of the older pietism and the moderating orthodoxy characteristic of eighteenth century Dutch universities, with an openness to the new revivalism which was more typically American.

One of the basic theological problems that surfaced shortly after Frelinghuysen's arrival, and which has troubled the Dutch Church from that day forward, concerned the nature of the Christian church. Because the formal definition of the church was not in dispute, this problem churned beneath the surface. It is best reflected in a popular eighteenth century textbook in dogmatics written by Johannes á Marck, and taught to future clergy of the Reformed church at New Brunswick Seminary. In his dogmatics, Marck lists the marks of the church, those visible signs by which the true church could be recognized in the world. He recognized at least five such marks: the classical three of Reformed theology (pure preaching, legitimate administration of the sacraments, and Christian discipline), plus holiness of life and fraternal love. Marck gives as his preference a two-fold structure: purity of doctrine as "a priori" and "antecedent," and holiness of life as "a posteriori and consequent."[26]

The shift in the Reformed doctrine of the church is obvious in this: The church of the word and sacrament was becoming the church of the word and personal holiness. The influence of pietism on mainstream Reformed orthodoxy was being felt. Moreover, it is very possible that the Anabaptist and Remonstrant elements in Dutch protestantism were also finding expression; the Anabaptists had criticized mainline practice for moral shortcomings, and the Remonstrants (Arminians) had argued that the doctrine of predestination was inimical to individual moral responsibility.

For his part, á Marck attempted to walk a tight-rope between orthodoxy and piety, stating that although holy living was surely a sign of the true church, it was possible only because of divine election. That caveat was becoming more formal than real in the practice of the Dutch church; the fact is that in the eighteenth century Reformed preaching put more emphasis on personal piety than orthodoxy, and for all practical purposes holiness, as defined by the pietists, became for many a new mark of the true church in Reformed theology. That shift from orthodoxy to personal piety had profound implications for the future history of the Dutch church.

That shift did not come without continuing conflict and controversy. In the first quarter of the eighteenth century that conflict focused on Frelinghuysen, who began his ministry in the Raritan Valley in New Jersey, a frontier community where traditional institutional support for religion was especially weak. Frelinghuysen was a zealous advocate of pietism who enforced holiness principles in his parish with the rigor of a man who was certain both of his own calling and of the unregenerate nature of many of his people. Determined to carve a kingdom out of the valley, he urged his parish toward an experience of Christ, demanded "precision in all holy living," and arbitrarily excluded the "impious" from communion and consistory appointment. He was intolerant of compromise on matters of spirituality, and not even well established orthodox clergy escaped the denunciations he delivered on a "lukewarm" Dutch church. Predictably this "noise from the Raritan" forced people to choose sides concerning Frelinghuysen's style of piety and, following the publication of a *Klagte*[27] (complaint) and a long series of appeals to the Classis of Amsterdam, there was a schism and not a kingdom in the valley. This schism in the Raritan anticipated the larger schism between *coetus* and *conferentie*[28] styles of faith that split the Dutch churches through the middle of the eighteenth century.

The formal debates surrounding the Frelinghuysen affair did not deal directly with doctrinal issues. Freeman made this point to Frelinghuysen's opponents, and their response fails to articulate any fundamental theological issue.[29] The new style of preaching, it is true, made heavier demands on the individual, inviting renewed discussion of the human will, and the charges of Arminianism made against Frelinghuysen and later his disciples are understandable. The real issue in the debates, however, was aimed at the nature of the church itself; the orthodox feared that the pietist emphasis on spiritual growth and separation from all worldliness would introduce Anabaptist heresy, or the more recent Labadist[30] and Quaker ideology, into the Reformed definition of the church. Significantly, the result of this debate, which continued throughout much of the eighteenth century, and especially into the *coetus-conferentie* dispute, and indeed has nagged the Reformed church to the present, was a new understanding of the church that made possible the Dutch becoming an independent, self-governing denomination in the New World.

Traditional orthodoxy viewed the church as an incarnational "given" which humanly speaking is a mixed society of "wheat and tares," but which is a divinely ordained institution, the "body of Christ," into which covenant people are born, are incorporated through baptism, and are nurtured and kept through hearing the Word and eating the Supper. Pietism, on the other hand, while also confessing that the church is incarnational, gave a significantly new emphasis to this confession. Pietism argued that the church is a divinely ordained community, not because it is grounded in established institutions—offices ordinances, confessions—but rather because it comprises a society of regenerate believers, freely associating together, who manifest their belief in Jesus Christ through worship and holy living. In traditional orthodoxy, the focus was on the established nature of the church, its "giveness" by God. In pietism, the emphasis was on the regenerate nature of the church, its "holy living" under God.

These two positions were hotly debated during the early stages of the *conferentie-coetus* schism, with Ritzema[31] of New York defending the orthodox (*conferentie*) side, and Leydt of New Brunswick, New Jersey, arguing the pietist (*coetus*) point of view. Both claimed the support of Voetius, although Leydt's position seems closer to Voetian piety than that of his opposition. Moreover, the *coetus* argument was helped by historical precedent. The initiative of the New Jersey colonists to arrange for the ordination of Domine Bertholf outside the accepted ecclesiastical structures clearly indicated the conviction that the church could manage its own institutional affairs. Indeed, the encouragement Calvin gave to the formation of "illegal" Reformed churches, as, for example, in France, was perhaps the only precedent needed. Calvin, of course, had also counselled a counter position, namely, the "avoidance of anarchy" and the search for "uniformity in truth" with the assistance of the state. That position had encouraged the idea that the role of the established church is essential in delivering Christian truth to the covenant community. In fact, however, that position had not worked well in Europe, and it was unworkable in the more individualistic and socially unstable situation of the colonies.

In any case, the pietists won the day among the Dutch churches, and both their practice and their theology made possible the organization of an independent Christian church in the New World. Ironically, in fixing this new church on solid theological grounds, the Dutch embraced a position that echoed the Anabaptist "heresy," namely, that only in the lives of Christian people can Christian truth be found, and that communities of Christian people cannot rely on the state for their establishment. These important theological lessons found expression in the "preface to the entire Constitution" (1792), which welcomes the separation of church and state and declares that the historic strictures against Anabaptists do not apply to any denominations of Christians now existing.[32] The influence of pietism in the colonial Dutch church made it possible to make such an expression of faith within a "Calvinist" or Reformed structure.

During the eighteenth century, pietism influenced the Dutch Church in one other way that needs to be noted here. Its insistence on a pure church focused attention on the virtues of people rather than on God's mercy to sinners as taught in classical Reformed theology. Consequently, Dutch pietism as practiced by Frelinghuysen and his successors during the colonial period tended to be censorious and self-righteous toward their opponents in matters of Christian faith and life.

There was, however, an antidote available to this self-absorbing attitude. James Tanis has shown the importance of Dutch pietism in developing a Protestant missionary theology.[33] He has also noted that Frelinghuysen showed no concern over evangelizing Indians. In fact, with the notable exception of the brief missionary career of Bernardus Freeman at Schenectady, Dutch pietists in general were not involved in any missionary activities during the colonial period. In this, however, Dutch pietists were not greatly different from Presbyterian protestants in the New York and New Jersey colonies.

As a consequence of the absence of a clear sense of mission beyond themselves, Dutch pietist groups failed to achieve the numerical growth they sought in the eighteenth century.[34] This inward-looking tendency fitted well the popular Cartesianism of the time,[35] one of the many cultural movements from which Reformed orthodoxy had distanced itself. A catechism by the younger Theodore Frelinghuysen in the 1750s assumed as fundamental truth, "that I am, and am a rational creature."[36] The Calvinist emphasis on knowing the self and God was, in some fundamental ways, subjectivized in pietism during much of the colonial period.

Near the end of the eighteenth century, however, the process of maturation made it possible for Dutch pietism to be delivered somewhat from its self-righteous inwardness, as well as its ethnic complacency, and to return to the classical Reformed emphasis on God's call to his people to work for his glory in the world. Dr. John H. Livingston, the towering figure in the Reformed Church at this time, was the person most responsible for effecting this transformation within Dutch pietism.

The heritage of colonial pietism persists in significant ways in the Reformed Church—ways which are congruous with the new American society. These include especially the emphasis on the voluntary, gathered nature of the church and on the work of the Holy Spirit in individuals, often without concern of the Spirit's work through the church. These emphases have led the Reformed Church to give less significance to the link between Word and sacrament; the church of the Word and sacrament in the minds of most Reformed Christians has become the church of the preacher. Thus it is that in the Reformed Church today the worshipping congregation, in spite of its liturgy and confessions, as well as its participation in mission, prayer, and other activities, has come to understand itself primarily as audience, listening to a person who brings the Word and claims the Spirit.

II

Dort and Albany:
Reformed Theology Engages a New Culture

James W. Van Hoeven

> We are strongly opposed to Hopkinsianism. We can never amalgamate
> with them. We can never go as a church into this Eastern Theology and
> Eastern policy. We are no half-way men![1]

So stated the Missionary Society of the Reformed Dutch Church in
1828. It was the society's response to those who wanted the denomination to cooperate with the Presbyterian and Congregational churches
in the missionary excitement of the period. As the statement suggests,
however, the issue went far beyond missionary strategy. It points to a
deep-seated theological controversy which exercised the Reformed
Church for more than a decade, finally resulting in a schism. It was one
of several such controversies within the Dutch denomination during the
first half of the nineteenth century, the consequence of an Old World
church finding its way theologically in a new cultural setting. How the
Reformed Church found its way theologically, and the path it found,
from 1800 to 1850, this chapter will attempt to make clear.

The Reformed Church entered the nineteenth century as a relatively
small denomination, recently organized as a self-governing body, its
nearly one hundred predominently Dutch speaking congregations scattered here and there in northern New Jersey and along stretches of the
Hudson River in New York State. The church bore battle scars, however, the most serious resulting from the long and difficult process by
which it finally freed itself from the church in The Netherlands and
formed an independent denomination. By 1800 that process was completed: the church approved its new constitution in 1792, which formally
organized "The Reformed Protestant Dutch Church in North America,"
and established the institutional mechanisms for it to move into the new
century on a fixed course.

The church's theological course, however, was less fixed as it entered
the nineteenth century. This was not for want of confessional clarity. In
its "Plan of Union," approved in 1772, and in its Constitution of 1792,

the church bound itself to classical Reformed theology by affirming the Belgic Confession (1562), The Heidelberg Catechism (1563), and the Canons of Dort (1619) as its "standards of unity," mandating that every minister in the Reformed Church adhere to those standards. By the turn of the century, however, this confessional clairty was already seriously challenged. Part of this challenge came from within the church's tradition itself: the persistent tension between those who favored the warm, personal tone and theological content of the Heidelberg Catechism on the one hand, and those who adhered to the formal orthodox statements of the Canons of Dort on the other.

The more insistent challenge, however, came from the outside, specifically from the evangelical crusades that dominated the religious life in North America during the nineteenth century. At the center of this movement were the revivals, the most pervasive force of religion in America from 1800 to 1860. "In fact," writes Perry Miller, "the dominant theme in America [during this period] is the invincible persistence of the revival technique."[2] Inevitably, all of this profoundly influenced the theological course of the Reformed Church. Indeed, the church's major theological task during the first half of the nineteenth century was to find a way to hold to its standards while at the same time adjusting itself to the new religious and intellectual realities in North America.

John H. Livingston (1746-1825) was the person most responsible for helping the Reformed Church find its way theologically during the first part of the nineteenth century. A precocious child of manorial parents, Livingston graduated in 1762 from Yale College, which was then a stronghold of New England "Awakening" theology. He intended a career in law, but a serious illness required that he return to New York City for rest. During that period "the finger of God intervened, arousing him to inquire if there might be hope" for his salvation.[3] The intensity of this religious experience caused Livingston to quit his intended study of law and to pursue a career in theology. Subsequently, he earned his doctor of divinity at the University of Utrecht in The Netherlands, which was then the center of Dutch experiential theology. Ordained in The Netherlands in 1770, Livingston returned to New York City the same year to begin his ministry at the Collegiate Reformed Church. In 1784, The General Synod appointed him professor of theology at New Brunswick Theological Seminary, and in 1810 he also became president of Queens College (now Rutgers University) in New Brunswick, New Jersey.

Livingston's contribution to the theology of the Reformed Church can be summarized in three general areas.[4] First, his emphasis on the experience of faith put the Dutch Church on the path of evangelical Christianity, which was the same path the majority of American protestants traveled during the first part of the nineteenth century. This did not mean, however, that the church embraced the methods of frontier revivalism. Nor did it mean a revolt against the intellect, or an abandonment of Reformed theology. Indeed, an examination of the course offerings and faculty lecture notes at New Brunswick Seminary, from 1800 to 1850, shows the school to be rich in scholarship and solidly orthodox. What it did mean was that the Reformed Church made the conversion of the individual primary in its preaching and teaching.

Under Livingston's influence the seminary became the catalyst for this emphasis. He turned the heart of the school eastward, toward New England, where the fires of "The Second Great Awakening" were then warming and filling the churches and where the experience of faith was emphasized over knowledge of faith. Moreover, a generation of students heard Livingston narrate the drama of his own conversion, beginning with "that awful work . . . where for several months I could do nothing but plead at the throne of grace, and weep over my wretched and lost estate," and concluding "joyously," with his affirmation "that Jesus Christ was able to save all who came unto God by him."[5] Students at New Brunswick formed prayer cells, Bible study groups, and a missionary society during the Livingston era, and learned from him that their primary calling was to challenge the unconverted, whether inside or outside the church, to repentance and salvation.

With few exceptions, these students began their ministries determined to fulfill that calling. Throughout the Reformed Church the clergy preached the evangelical gospel, stressing the necessity of the heartfelt religious experience and asking their listeners, "Do you believe that you have ever been dead in trespasses and sins . . . alienated from God, and under the awful sentence of condemnation? Has the grace of the Lord Jesus Christ recovered you? Are you converted? Are you renewed in mind by the power of the Holy Spirit?"[6] Moreover, these same clergy urged their members to adopt a life of piety, as "proof of faith," and in the early nineteenth century that included daily "seasons of prayer," Bible study, and strict Sabbath observance.

One consequence of this emphasis on the "experience of faith" was that the Reformed church began distancing itself from the orthodox formulations of Dort, especially the doctrines of election and limited atonement. We will note, however, that some in the church strongly objected to this. Unable to move the church from its experiential path, these left it to chart their own.

Livingston's second contribution to Reformed Church theology, one related to the first, was his emphasis on mission and millennialism. In a sermon preached before the New York Missionary Society in 1804, Livingston stated that the millennial period was drawing near, with the distinct possibility that the fall of "Great Babylon" would come immediately before the year 2000.[7] Before that event, this world would see "the signs and stirrings" of its approach, namely, the punishment of the nations who aided the anti-Christ in destroying the servants of God, the conversion of the Jews, the gathering of the gentiles into the church, and the "fall of Great Babylon . . . the Anti-Christ,"[8] that is, the pope in Rome. The cosmic scale of the event is compelling, as Livingston described it:

> In the physical order of things the event is possible; agreeably to the moral system it can be effected; and devoutly to be wished. When all nations receive the Gospel, and become real Christians; when men of every rank . . . shall know the Lord, and devote themselves to their redeemer, then all will be happy. Individuals will be happy, society will be happy, and peace, joy, and holiness will prevail throughout the whole earth.

The sermon concluded with the conviction that in clearly preaching the gospel the church participates in events that will inaugurate the millennial period. Livingston also believed that North America provided the most favorable conditions for vigorous missionary work as well as efforts of charity.

There are several reasons why Livingston's sermon was important to the developing theology of the Reformed Church. First, he preached it at an ecumenical gathering, thus nudging the Dutch Church further into the mainstream of American Protestantism. In addition, the sermon was widely circulated, and "was instrumental in kindling the foreign missionary spirit in this country."[10] Moreover, the sermon's unambiguous biblicism, as well as its strong affirmation of both the divinity of the Lord Jesus Christ and justification by grace, became characteristic of preaching and theological reflection in the Reformed Church during the nineteenth century. Finally, although Livingston's sermon reaffirmed the conviction that the conversion of the individual was the urgent and primary mission of the church, it also stressed that morality and social order in America depended on the church's preaching of the gospel. By this means Livingston connected evangelical Christianity with democratic goals in America, thus sowing the seed of "culture religion" on the path of Reformed Church theology.

It was Livingston's third great contribution to Reformed theology, however, that proved to be most decisive for the church. In 1791, the General Synod named Livingston chairman of a committee to revise the "standards . . . to fit local circumstances" in America. One such revision concerned the doctrine of the church. Both the Belgic Confession and the Canons of Dort had presupposed an established state-church arrangement, a position invalidated by the disestablishment amendment to the United States Constitution. In revising its standards in 1792, the Reformed Church accepted Livingston's adaptation of the American Puritan principle of voluntary church membership:

> In consequence of that liberty wherewith Christ has made his people free, it becomes their duty as well as privilege, openly to confess and worship him according to the dictates of their own consciences . . . wherever such explanation constitute a bond of union wholly voluntary. . . . The unerring Word of God remaining the only standard of the Faith and Worship of his people, they can never incur the charge of presumption, in openly declaring what to them appears to be the mind and will of their Divine Lord and Savior.

> The Church is a society, wholly distinct in its principles, laws and end, from any which men have ever instituted for civil purposes. It consists of all, in every age and place, who are chosen, effectually called, and united by faith to the Lord Jesus Christ.[12]

The Reformed Church approved Livingston's revised statement on the doctrine of the church apparently without debate. It became a fundamental principal of the church's faith and life, forming the context in which its theological decisions would be made in the nineteenth century. Inevitably, it introduced tensions into classical Reformed theology. Among the issues raised between 1800 and 1850 were the doctrines of election and limited atonement, the church and the sacraments, and the nature of ministry.

Thus led by Livingston, the Reformed Church began moving down the path of American evangelicalism as it entered the nineteenth century. Livingston's emphasis on the experience of faith, mission, and millennialism, and also his Puritan (and Anabaptist) adaptation into the doctrine of the church, profoundly influenced the shape and tone of Reformed preaching and teaching during this period, and initiated the process by which the church made the transition from classical Reformed orthodoxy to American style evangelicalism.

There were some, however, who were unhappy with this process and urged the church to return to Dort. These charged that the Reformed Church was moving beyond evangelicalism toward the more "liberal" New England Theology, specifically "Hopkinsian" theology. Samuel Hopkins (1721-1805), a Congregational theologian, had been a student and friend of Jonathan Edwards, the principal leader of the Great Awakening in the eighteenth century, and a creative and respected Calvinist. Although Hopkins himself remained within the Reformed tradition, he and his colleagues emphasized the freedom of the will more than Edwards, and thereby modified the doctrines of original sin, election, and limited atonement. Orthodox theologians opposed these modifications and identified them as "Hopkinsian."

The Hopkinsian issue first surfaced in the Reformed Church in 1814, when the General Synod raised the question of the "propriety of receiving licentiates for ordination from the Congregational Church . . . without examination."[13] The discussion at that meeting focused on two points: the difference between the Congregational and Reformed Churches regarding polity, and a suspicion of the theology of the Congregational Church "which maintains doctrines directly contrary to many of those which we believe to be the unadulterated doctrines of the Gospel."[14] On this latter point, those who raised the issue were thinking primarily of "Hopkinsian" modifications of the doctrines of election, limited atonement, and total depravity. In deciding this question, the General Synod reaffirmed its loyalty to the standards and ruled that ordinands trained in Congregational seminaries must be "examined in the particular doctrines and government of our church . . . and if they do not explicitly renounce every doctrine inconsistent with the Word of God and the Standards," they may not be ordained into the Reformed Church.[15]

The challenge from New England theology, however, did not go away with that decision. Indeed, the Reformed Church continued to debate this issue throughout much of the nineteenth century. The most celebrated of these debates occurred from 1818 to 1820, when the consistory of the church at Owasco, New York, charged that its minister, the Reverend Conrad Ten Eyck, had rejected the orthodox doctrine of limited atonement; it pressed the issue all the way to the General Synod. Specifically, the consistory charged Ten Eyck with preaching "Hopkinsianism," declaring that he "did not believe that Christ had atoned for any man . . . but for sin."[16]

The debate on this issue was long and acrimonious, and it finally reached the General Synod in October, 1820. At that meeting Mr. Ten Eyck answered six questions asked by the Synod. When the Synod declared three of his answers unsatisfactory, Ten Eyck made additional clarification, the key statement being the following:

> In answer to the second question, I did not mean to convey the idea that Christ died for sin in the abstract, but that the evil nature of sin rendered an atonement indispensably necessary, and that without such an atonement, it was impossible for God to extend mercy, even to the elect. By the words, he obeyed in the room and stead of his people, I meant and do mean to convey the idea of substitution; which doctrine I fully believe.[17]

The General Synod accepted this rather imprecise statement and then approved the orthodoxy of Ten Eyck while disapproving his "former opinions on the doctrine of atonement."[18] That Ten Eyck's "former opinions" may have been acceptable to others at the Synod is clear from the further resolution that

> Whereas, it has been repeatedly alleged on the floor of this Synod that some of its members have denied the infinite value and suffering of the death of Jesus Christ, to expiate the sins of the whole world. . . .[19]

The synod resolved that,

> The Word of God and the standards of this church teach us, that the Lord Jesus Christ died as an atoning sacrifice only for those whom the Father has given him; for whom in the divine love and wisdom, he became the substituted victim.[20]

The synod's decision on this issue carved a decisive path for the church in settling its theological controversies. On the one hand, by formally re-affirming the theology of Dort, The Reformed Church demonstrated its determination to maintain its bond with classical Calvinism. On the other hand, by approving Ten Eyck's imprecise answers to its questions the Reformed Church showed its willingness to tolerate more local and individual interpretations than some of the more orthodox members demanded. Indeed, in 1822, following the Ten Eyck decision, a small number of these orthodox members seceded from the denomination and formed "The True Dutch Reformed Church in the United States of America."[21] For most, however, the synod's compromise decision proved decisive for the long haul and became especially important during the next decade when the Reformed Church reopened its family quarrel on the orthodox-"Hopkinsian" question.

This quarrel began in 1822 and evolved into a major sectional conflict, pitting the northern, Albany Synod against the southern based New York (City) Synod, in New York State. Although the northern synod adhered to the Reformed standards, both its geographical proximity to the "liberal" New England theology to the east and its strong interest in winning converts on the neighboring frontier to the west, encouraged it toward evangelical Christianity, tempered its orthodoxy and ethnocentricity, and opened it to cooperative missionary ventures with the Presbyterian and Congregational churches. On the other hand, the southern based synod was situated in and around New York City, which at that time was egregiously provincial, anxious about the rumored excesses on the expanding frontier, and primarily concerned with purity in matters of doctrine and practice. Predictably, therefore, the southern based New York (City) Synod determined to hold its orthodox ground against the "liberal" north. Conflict became inevitable.

Consequently, during the decade beginning in 1822 the Reformed Church was involved in a major theological controversy, primarily along sectional lines. The meetings of the General Synod provided one of the forums for the protagonists to argue positions, make accusations, and scramble for support. A close examination of both the debates and resolutions on critical issues at these meetings shows the Reformed Church to be divided by sectional differences. Moreover, these differences seriously affected the denomination's missionary and benevolent programs, ecumenical affiliations, and issues involving both funding and professorships at New Brunswick Seminary.

The second forum providing opportunity for the protagonists to debate their differences were the Reformed Church's journals, *The Magazine of The Reformed Dutch Church* and the *Christian Intelligencer*. Each of these periodicals opened its pages to representatives from both sides of the controversy and wrote of it as the conflict between the "high ultras" in the south and the "extreme liberals" in the north.[22] The fundamental question in this debate remained theological: How can the Reformed Church innovate while at the same time hold firmly to its standards? Resting on this question, however, were the more practical issues of mission policy, ecumenicity, liturgy, and power.

This became especially obvious in 1828, when the Reformed Church revised its mission program and appointed John F. Schermerhorn, an Albany based clergyman, as its first missionary agent. Shortly after his appointment, the "liberal-conservative" conflict focused on him. "Has the march of error been checked since Schermerhorn's appointment?" a southern based cleric asked rhetorically.[24] He continued,

Have the changes in doctrine been limited to the extent of the atonement; or to the propriety of distinguishing man's inability into natural or moral? . . . Has [he] attempted, under the mark of religious zeal, to subvert the well established doctrine of original sin and of imputed righteousness?[25]

Responding to these questions, a northern ally defended Schermerhorn's orthodoxy, and called the attacks on him "Indian warfare—assaults in the dark . . . by the straightest sect in our church," and asked if the southern based Synod "resolved to go the whole length of South Carolinian nullification" on the issue, and secede.[26] Given all of this, it is little wonder that in his "State of Religion" address in 1831, the president of the General Synod referred to this north-south controversy as a "Civil War" and called for an end to the conflict.[27]

It is surprising that the Reformed Church made it through this decade of controversy without a major schism. Surely the passions on both sides were sufficiently heated for a division to occur. Moreover, both clergy and laity in the Dutch Church must have kept one eye on the Presbyterian Church, where brewed a similar controversy and which did result in a schism. One can only speculate on the reasons why the Reformed Church remained united during its conflict, while the Presbyterian Church split. Perhaps the most obvious reason is that some of the principal leaders on both sides of the conflict in the Reformed Church either died or became exhausted from the battle, and their mantles were not taken up by others, as they were in the Presbyterian Church. In addition, the Reformed Church was both smaller and more ethnocentric than the Presbyterian Church, making its "Civil War" more costly to sustain. Moreover, "Jacksonian Democracy" changed both Albany and New York City into major commercial centers during this period, thereby opening up money-making opportunities for Dutch entrepreneurs and making the desire for theological carping less compelling or interesting.

Eugene Heideman, in *Piety and Patriotism,* gives a theological reason for the Reformed Church staying together during its "liberal-conservative" controversies.[28] He notes that the (Presbyterian) Westminster tradition had placed the statement on election in the doctrine of the decrees, while the Reformed Church's Belgic Confession and the Heidelberg Catechism had related election more closely to God's work in Christ. In this the Dutch tradition remained closer to Calvin, who had located the discussion in Book III of his *Institutes* after the dicussion of the work of Christ, rather than in Book I where he writes on the doctrine of God. The effect of these differing approaches has been to allow the Dutch Church to give more weight to God's sovereign work in the process of history while the Westminster tradition emphasizes the sovereign decision of God before creation. Heideman rightly cautions that this distinction must not be overemphasized, for duing this period the leadership of the Reformed Church had great respect for the dogmatics of the Francis Turretin-Charles Hodge "Old School" tradition. It is significant, however, that Henry B. Smith, the great mediating historical theologian in the "Old School-New School" controversy of the Presbyterian Church, championed a position closer to Calvin and Dort than to Westminster on election, thus indicating that the difference is important in the attitude of the church toward historical events.

Whereas the New England evangelical-revivalist movement had tempted the Reformed Church toward "Americanizing" its theology, the appearance in the 1840s of another movement—the so-called Mercersburg theology—challenged the Reformed Church at the point of its Reformation heritage. The leaders of the Mercersburg movement, John W. Nevin and Philip Schaff, were professors in the German Reformed seminary at Mercersburg, Pennsylvania. Nevin emphasized the sacramental nature of the church, which he believed was present in the Reformation but which he found lacking in Reformed churches of his day. This emphasis was reflected in his two major works: *The Anxious Bench*, which was a trenchant critique of the sectarianism and nonsacramentalism of the revivals that he claimed were having too great an impact on Reformed congregations; and the *Mystical Presence*, which was an equally hard-hitting attack on Reformed orthodoxy for its failure to affirm the institutional (visible) church as the "body of Christ." An historical theologian, Nevin also wrote many other books and articles that emphasized an organic or developmental interpretation of Christian doctrine.

Philip Schaff, the most noteworthy church historian in North America in the nineteenth century, came to Mercersburg Seminary in 1844 following a brief career on the faculty at the University of Berlin. His controversial inaugural address at Mercersburg, "The Principle of Protestantism," clearly set forth his own developmental view of the church and Christian doctrine. Protestantism, he argued, emerged out of a long process of growth, and it was not the creation of any one man or country:

> No work so vast as the Reformation could be the product of a single man or single day. When Luther uttered the bold word which called [the Reformation] into being . . . he gave utterance to what was already . . . present to the general consciousness of his age, and brought out into full view that which thousands before him, and in his own time, had already been struggling in various ways to reach.[29]

Schaff established the "authority of the sacred Scriptures" as the formal principle of Protestantism, but also argued that scripture must be interpreted in the context of history and tradition. He eschewed static dogmatism whether in Roman Catholicism or orthodox Protestantism, and reserved his most stinging criticism for sectarians: "They seek to restore pure and primitive Christianity with entire disregard of the many centuries of Christian history."

In regard to the nature of the church, Schaff daringly called for a "Protestant Catholicism." Here he argued that the Roman Catholic and Protestant traditions each represented only half a truth, and he looked for a new synthesis which would incorporate the best of both traditions:

> We must look forward and not backward, if we wish [to be loyal to the Reformation] and finally achieve church unity. We must follow slowly

along the quiet historical way, for this is the way that we are led by the Spirit of the Lord. Not suddenly but [developmentally] . . . will the heavenly kingdom come to earth.[31]

The relationship between the Dutch and German Reformed Churches was close in the 1840s, with the synods exchanging delegates and proposing the idea of merger. But there could not have been a worse time in which to consider the idea of union. It was the beginning of a massive Roman Catholic immigration in America; the Dutch Church at that time stood in the vanguard of those who worked to maintain America as a Protestant fortress against "popery."[32]

Through its editor, Elbert S. Porter, the *Christian Intelligencer* led the assault against the Mercersburg men, stating that they held views of apostolic succession which would move the church toward Rome and away from historic Calvinism.[33] Porter also charged that they placed an emphasis on the church and its sacraments in preference to personal conversion and individual piety. Joining Porter and the *Intelligencer* in this battle were members of the faculty at New Brunswick Seminary, Charles Proudfit, a Dutch Church layman and professor at Rutgers College, and Joseph Berg, of whom we will have more to say later. Significantly, the leadership of the Dutch Church's attacks against Mercersburg resided in New York City and northern New Jersey, which was the "southern establishment" section of the church. Moreover, the most outspoken of the protagonists were Puritans in background, and several of them had come into the Dutch Church from other denominations.

Nevin wrote a stinging response to these attacks, referring to them as the "Dutch Crusade." He severely criticized the *Intelligencer*, arguing that it had

granted the free use of its columns to any disaffected minister, or layman, of the German Reformed Church who would be induced to make them the channel of his spleen or pride; besides encouraging every scribbler at home to write what trash he pleased in the same vein and for the same general purpose.[34]

Nevin further charged that the Dutch Church was losing its churchly and sacramental roots; liturgically, he said, "[your] church is becoming a sect, the product of private judgment and private will."[35] In any case, the heated battle between the two churches ended in 1852, when the Dutch General Synod formally condemned the Mercersburg theology, thus ending its relationship with the German Church.

The result of this episode proved decisive for the Dutch Church, at least in the short run. Shucking the Mercersburg men, it rekindled a love affair with the men from Princeton, namely Charles Hodge and the "Old School" theologians of the Presbyterian Church. These "Old School" men rejected the historical-developmental approach to theology of Mercersburg. They conceived of Christian doctrine as a fixed and unalterable system; orthodoxy was stable, a system of divinely revealed truth which could be mined from scripture. Thus, a theologian who was sufficiently trained could discern in the Bible God's perfect truth, complete and admitting of no development or improvement.

Joseph Berg was the person who championed this "Old School" theology in the Dutch Church during this period.[36] Berg had been a colleague of Schaff and Nevin at Mercersburg, but in 1852 he left the German Church for theological reasons and became a minister in the Dutch Church. Subsequently he served as a professor of theology at New Brunswick Seminary and became an outspoken critic of the Mercersburg theology. Berg interpreted the doctrines of Dort through the lenses of "Old School" theology and tried to influence the Dutch Church toward a narrow orthodoxy. Although he did not succeed in this, he was an eloquent spokesman for the orthodox position and gained a following in the southern region of the church. Philip Schaff had Berg and his followers in mind when he claimed that the Dutch Church was "almost more narrowly Calvinistic than the old school Presbyterians, and that in general it was the most rigid and unmovable of the churches in America that had their origin in the period of the Reformation."[37]

Schaff's characterization, however, did not accurately reflect the general theological situation in the Dutch Church. At the local level, the evidence suggests that Reformed theology was not "rigidly and unmovably" orthodox but diversely evangelical, even sectarian at places—here singing the gospel hymns of revival theology, and there egregiously Dutch and singing psalms; or here tilting toward "Hopkinsianism," and there holding solidly to Heidelberg; or here using the church's prescribed order in its worship, and there "doing what seemed right in their own eyes" with the liturgy. Indeed, the following description might be more representative of Dutch Church theology during the 1840s and 1850s than the rigid "Old School" orthodoxy:

> Though the Divinity of Christ was firmly held, the wide-reaching significance of the incarnation was little apprehended; and though the facts of His resurrection and Ascension were articles of faith, their bearing upon His priesthood and upon His future kingship were only dimly seen. . . . The great doctrinal topic of the pulpit was the way in which his death was related to forgiveness of sin. . . . The great channel of His operations was the preached word, not ordinances or sacraments. The sermon was therefore the center of interest, and the other parts of the service were regarded as introductory and subordinate. . . .

It was generally held that at the Lord's table that communicants ate and drank as a mere commemorate act—a vivid, way of bringing the Lord and His work to remembrance.[38]

The picture of Reformed Church theology at mid-century, therefore, was more mixed than generally is assumed. Formally, the Dutch Church subscribed to its standards and was solidly evangelical. In practice, however, the southern section of the church appeared more orthodox than its northern (Albany) counterpart; the church's southern region was more ethnocentric than the north and also felt more keenly the influence of the *Intelligencer* and the seminary. In the church's northern section the most immediate influence was the changing socio-cultural situation—a burgeoning frontier, the loss of Dutch political and religious hegemony to the Scots and Scots-Irish, inter-marriage between the Dutch and English, new transportation systems and the emergence of Albany as a major port city, and the attractiveness of New England theology to the new population. In an effort to adjust itself theologically to this new situation, the northern (Albany) region tempered its orthodoxy and for the most part moved toward American style evangelicalism. Such a transition is an often repeated story in American religious history, the consequence of an Old World church trying to remain faithful to its tradition while at the same time interacting with a new culture.

There is one other part to the story of this period that requires comment here, one that in the long run may have had the greatest influence on Reformed theology. Professor Theodore Appel, who became Nevin's successor at Mercersburg Seminary, hints at this in his study on the Dutch-German Church controversy of the 1840s and 1850s.[39] He lamented the "terrible disaster" that had befallen the two denominations and suggested the following as a cause: "Their leaders were not persons to represent the dignity and learning of the old Dutch Church . . . [nor] its orthodoxy and churchliness."[40] In this he was referring to Porter, and later Berg and the New Brunswick faculty, all of whom were "Old School" dogmatists. Appel then suggested that "Professor Tayler Lewis, one of the [Dutch Church's] brightest ornaments, or some one of the Van Dycks" would have been better qualified to lead the Dutch Church in that mid-century conflict.[41]

Given the obvious bias of Professor Appel, it might seem wise to discount his rather obscure reference to the influence of Lewis and the Van Dycks in the 1840s and 1850s. There is, however, evidence to suggest otherwise. Corwin lists five Van Dycks in his *Manual*. Of these, Cornelius V. served as a medical missionary to the Middle East, Leonard B. transferred to the Presbyterian Church prior to the Dutch-German controversy, and Hamilton served congregations in both the German and Dutch Churches before his untimely death in 1836. We can assume, therefore, that Appel was referring to Lawrence Van Dyck (1807-1893) and Cornelius L. Van Dyck (1804-1866). Both of these clergy spent the major parts of their ministries in the northern section of the Dutch Church, and the latter (Cornliues L.) "exercised more influence than any others in his classis."[42] Significantly, all of the Van Dycks listed by Corwin were related, and their ministries in various denominations suggests broad ecumenical commitments.

Tayler Lewis was undoubtedly one of the most influential and respected scholar-theologians in the Dutch Church during this period.[43] He was an active member of the First Church in Schenectady, New York, and from 1849 to 1877 he was professor of oriental languages at Union College in that city, teaching courses in Greek, Hebrew, Arabic, Syriac, Ancient Philosophy, Greek Poetry, and Biblical Studies. He was a prolific writer, publishing more than fifteen books and hundreds of articles, and he lectured widely in churches, seminaries, and colleges throughout the East coast. Lewis was a friend of both John Nevin, with whom he had studied at Union College, and Philip Schaff; Schaff wrote the preface to Lewis' edited translation of Langes' commentary on *Genesis*, stating that "[Lewis] was one of the ablest and most learned classical and biblical scholars of America."[44]

Lewis' most important work was *The Six Days of Creation*.[45] In it he suggests that the Genesis creation stories allow that God worked through natural evolutionary means to create humankind, thus presenting what must be the first instance of theistic evolutionary theology in Reformed Church history. Significantly, he wrote *The Six Days of Creation* in 1855, four years before the publication of Charles Darwin's *Origin of Species*! Lewis was vilified by both the evangelical and "Old School" press for this publication. Later, however, many of these critics, some of them within the Dutch Church, called Lewis a "prophet" and thanked him for providing a biblical response to the new science.[46]

Lewis also wrote books and articles on current social issues. Two of these, "Negrophobia,"[47] and "Slavery,"[48] which appeared in *The Christian Intelligencer*, were stinging critiques of the Dutch Church's attitudes toward the slavery issue. He opposed those who argued that "states rights" political theories were more important than the moral laws of God, and supported strong action, including military action, against the South's "evil institution."

Lewis was also an active participant in the theological issues of his age. He opposed revivalistic sectarianism, while at the same time championing the gospel preached by those same revivalists. He also challenged the liberal wing of New England theology which, Lewis claimed, substituted a refined morality for solid Reformation doctrine. Addressing this issue, Lewis declared:

> Our moralists are, in general, professed enemies of cant, but how often have we heard their canting whine: 'Ah, yes, men may talk about believing, but that is not the religion for me; give me James rather than Paul. Away with that hard dogma of justification by faith, . . . that gloomy Calvinism so subversive of pure morality.' . . . There is a strange blindness which leads men to credit to themselves as a virtue what they may thus admire in the abstract, or which they may some day think of doing. Salvation by faith demands the whole heart; it is the giving up by the bankrupt of all his poor assets; it is the entire surrender of the whole man into the hands of the Redeemer, with the earnest cry, 'be merciful to me, the sinner.' Salvation by works is too apt to content itself with 'good intentions.'[49]

Lewis was equally critical of "Old School" orthodoxy, particularly its Christology. Although not going as far as Nevin, he believed that Reformed orthodoxy did not do justice to the biblical and Reformation doctrine of the mystical union of Christ. Against Berg, Hodge, and other "old School" theologians, Lewis wrote:

> It is, however, a matter of great surprise that those who rigidly . . . hold to a real union with the first man, a real imputation of his guilt and on real psychological grounds . . . should break the Apostle's analogy, should make a mere figure or, at most, a moral influence of that regeneration by which the believer is really transferred to a new life, and engrafted into the humanity of the Second Adam—the Lord from heaven.[50]

In short, while Berg, Hodge, and other orthodox theologians had argued that union with Christ was the result of God's justification, Lewis stated that it was the ground. Correspondingly, Lewis criticized orthodoxy's doctrine of the church, and for the same reason; he claimed that orthodox theologians failed to take seriously the mystical presence of Christ in the sacraments, liturgy, and the nature of the church itself, which he believed was present in Reformation theology.[51]

It would be inaccurate to argue from all of this that Lewis and the Van Dycks represented a major influence on Reformed theology during the 1850s. We do know, however, that Reformed theology was in flux during this period. Moreover, the evidence suggests that Lewis and the Van Dycks may have been leaders of a significant "underground movement" in the church, which rejected both revivalist sectarianism and "Old School" Presbyterianism and which also was displeased that the proposed merger between the German and Dutch Churches had failed. This "movement" was solidly Reformed and evangelical, but preferred

the warmer accents of the Heidelberg Catechism to the narrower orthodox formulations, accepted the historical-developmental approach to
theology, raised its voice here and there against social wrongs, promoted
mission and ecumenicity at home and abroad, and embraced the new
American culture while at the same time pressing the church toward
more Reformed positions in both faith and worship. If this suggestion
be accurate, it can be argued that in the long run the theological perspectives of this "underground movement" prevailed in the Reformed
Church.

Various developments in the church beginning in the 1850s support
this view. For example, in 1857, and again in 1873, the denomination
approved revisions in its liturgy, following almost precisely the pattern
of the German Reformed Church. Moreover, in 1867 it voted to drop
the word Dutch from its official title.[53] It also reopened merger discussions with the German Church in 1886, and in 1893 it started work with
the Presbyterian Church to organize a "Federal Council" of Reformed
Churches.[54] There were similar developments in the twentieth century,
as succeeding chapters in this book make clear, so that by 1950 nearly
all of the emphases of Lewis, the Van Dycks, and the "underground
movement" of the 1840s and 1850s had become accepted in one form
or another as standard Reformed theology.

But 1950 was still a long century from the period considered in this
chapter. During the years 1800 to 1850 the various segments of the
Dutch Church struggled to find a common theological path down which
to walk. Indeed, for the most part, the theological history of the period
was marked by pique, conflict, suspicion, grudging compromise, and one
minor schism. Perhaps that was inevitable in the early nineteenth century. The church then was finding its way theologically and was determined to remain loyal to its confessions while at the same time trying
to become a truly American denomination. In the mix of that tension
the polar edges of Reformed thought began to be defined, and the
process by which a Reformed Church goes about finding a path "truly
Reformed, truly evangelical, and truly catholic," became more apparent. When the period ended, however, that work remained unfinished.
Perhaps the history of the era suggests that Reformed theology in some
fundamental sense must always be unfinished and in tension with itself,
its culture, and the Word of God. Understanding that may be the period's most important legacy—and challenge—to our own age.

III

New York and Holland:
Reformed Theology and The Second
Dutch Immigration

Elton M. Eenigenburg

The union in 1850 between the Dutch immigrant churches of Holland, Michigan, and the eastern-based Reformed Protestant Dutch Church was not hastily contrived. In a real sense it built upon a courtship of several years, during which firm bonds of confidence, trust, and mutual respect were established. The Reformed Dutch Church had welcomed these "Holland immigrants" in the New York harbor in December, 1846, had assisted them on their journey westward, and periodically had provided information on them in its journal, *The Christian Intelligencer*.[1] Moreover, in 1847 and 1848 the General Synod had passed favorable resolutions about them, expressing genuine concern that they not be neglected, and adding "they are of the same origin, springing from the same branch of the Reformation, and adopting the same standards" as our own.[2]

In June, 1849, and then again in the following spring, the Board of Domestic Missions commissioned The Rev. Dr. Isaac N. Wyckoff, minister of the Second Reformed Church of Albany, New York, formally to open conversation with this new Dutch colony in Michigan. In his report to the board, Wyckoff wrote of the immigrants' piety and theology: "Their religious habits are very strict and devout. They do all things with prayer and praise . . . The appearance and tone of piety is pure, and higher than anything I have ever seen, and seemed like the primitive Christians, and most beautiful." He remarked favorably about their attention to schools and to Christian education, with reference particularly to the catechising of the children and to their training in the singing of the psalms. On theological issues Wyckoff commented briefly: "On comparison of doctrine, a perfect agreement with our standards, was found."[3]

Wyckoff also commented on an issue he considered potentially troublesome, namely the immigrants' preference for a congregational rather than a presbyterial polity: "In the order of their churches, they believe each church and consistory should direct and manage its own concerns, and incline to the idea that an appellate jurisidiction of superior judicatories is not so scriptural as a . . . fraternal conference and advice."[4] Wyckoff urged patience with the "Hollanders" on this issue, however, and reminded the board of the immigrants' generation-long harrassment at the hands of the Netherlands government: "They have so felt to the quick the galling chains of ecclesiastical domination, and have seen with sorrow how exact organization, according to human rules, leads to formality on the one hand, and to oppression of tender consciences on the other, that they hardly knew what to say."[5] Wyckoff reported that he had assured the immigrants that the Reformed Dutch Church had no intention of exercising ecclesiastical tyranny over them; they would be "most perfectly free, at any time they found an ecclesiastical connection opposed to their religious prosperity and enjoyment, to bid us a fraternal adieu, and be by themselves again."[6]

In April of 1850, the Classis of Holland appointed Albertus Van Raalte its representative to the meeting of the Particular Synod of Albany, with full powers to give and secure the information needed to facilitate the desired union. That synod, which met on May 1, approved the organization of the Holland Classis and reported the same to the General Synod at its June meeting. The proposed recommendation to the General Synod urged the reception of the Classis of Holland as a member classis of the Particular Synod of Albany. The recommendation was adopted without debate.[7] That, briefly, is the sketchy outline of the story that brought about the Union between the four immigrant churches of the Classis of Holland and the Reformed Protestant Dutch Church in North America in 1850.

That brief history introduces the principle concern of this essay, which is to determine, if possible, the theology represented by both the existing eastern church and the immigrant mid-Western church at the time of the Union. Wyckoff had reported a happy agreement on this issue, but something more than merely noting similarities and dissimilarities and weighing them in the balance is necessary. The quest is for evidences of deep agreement which, despite very different historical and cultural milieus, made possible an almost instant recognition of one another as being in "perfect agreement" theologically. Wyckoff had a sharp sense of it, and so did the colonists.

There were no doubt many differences between the two groups, but what moved them toward union with each other was the intuition that they were, before God, very much alike, and therefore meant for one another. Neither their common ethnic identities nor their shared Calvinist roots are sufficient to explain that intuition; there were other Hollanders and other professed Calvinists in the Netherlands at that very time who, had they come to settle here, would not have evoked the same sparks of amity and acceptance. The search for the roots of that sense of compatibility requires looking back some decades—a good many in the case of the immigrants—to see what and why they believed as they did in the year 1850. We shall first inquire into the theology of the Reformed Protestant Dutch Church at that time and then examine the immigrants' background.

If by a denomination's theology we mean its belief in and adherence to its creeds and confessions, there was a remarkable agreement between the Reformed Dutch Church and the newly arrived immigrants. Both professed loyalty to the three principal doctrinal standards of the Reformed churches—the Belgic Confession (1562), the Heidelberg Catechism (1563), and the Canons of the Synod of Dort (1619). Van Raalte seemed to sense the depth of that agreement when he visited New Brunswick Seminary as early as 1847 or 1848. Years later he recounted his impressions:

> I listened to the teachings and conversations of the Professors, saw the workings of their heart, and understood their love to God and their devotion to His truth. I blessed my God that I there found the faith of my fathers—the historical church of the Netherlands—and because I found it, and I loved it, I determined to bring the immigrants into intimate connection with the Dutch Reformed Church of America.[8]

The Reformed Church's standards represent the principal beliefs and convictions of Reformed Christians throughout the world, and most particularly of the Netherlands Reformed Church and the Reformed Church in America. To be orthodox, in the opinion of the Reformed community, requires adherence to the standards, and serious deviation might well raise questions about one's soundness in the faith.

Such questions were raised by the General Synod in 1834, concerning the orthodoxy of Professor Alexander McClelland of New Brunswick Seminary. The issue first surfaced in the Classis of New Brunswick, following McClelland's publication of his "Sermon on Spiritual Renovation, connected with the use of Means," based on the text, Luke 11:9.[9] Apparently the Classis of New Brunswick sensed some doctrinal faults in the article and referred it to the General Synod for examination. The committee appointed to study the matter concluded that there were serious differences between McClelland's sermons and the standards, particularly on the issues of depravity, good works, and grace. Unfor-

tunately, we are not given the reasons for that judgment. McClelland's
sermon, however, is printed in the *Minutes* of the General Synod, and
he appears to give a more favorable view of the gifts and attainments
of the "natural man" than the standards allow. He insisted, for example,
that when unbelievers are confronted with the gospel invitation, they
need simply exercise their faith to believe it. That is, the gospel's invitation is a genuine offer.[10] The standards, on the other hand, state
that the natural man, of himself, cannot exercise the faith to believe;
faith is given only to the elect by the Holy Spirit.

When the synod called upon McClelland to explain the apparent
discrepancies, he made clear that he believed the doctrine of election
to be clearly revealed in the Scriptures. He insisted, however, that it
is not a doctrine to be preached to the general public; it has its proper
place in the church, for which it is "peculiarly designed," as the Canons
of Dort declare (I.14). It must be dealt with there reverently for God's
glory and the benefit of his people, "without vainly attempting to investigate the secret ways of the Most High."[11] The gospel preached in
the world must not permit the unbeliever to plead an inability to believe
because he does not know himself to be elected to salvation. The onus
of rejecting the gospel's invitation rested squarely upon the unrepentant
sinner. Whatever the "secret counsels" of God may be with respect to
such matters was the business of neither the preacher nor the hearer
of the gospel. McClelland was convinced, however, that salvation is
God's gift; in no way was the unbeliever able to appropriate it on his
own, however great his gifts and abilities.[12]

McClelland's defense of his sermon is a remarkably brilliant one if
not precise, theologically. The General Synod declared itself completely
satisfied with him and with his "unequivocal approbation of the standards of the church." It pronounced its "continued confidence in the
correctness of his theological views."[13]

The deep concern for faithfulness to the Reformed standards evi-
denced in the McClelland case finds affirmation again and again in
synodical minutes, sermons, essays, and other writings of the Dutch
church from colonial times through the period now under examination.
Prior to the independence of the American church from the church in
the Netherlands in 1792, the former was a reflection of the latter in the
New World. Theologically, that meant adherence to the Reformed creeds
and confessions. Following 1792, however, there were many challenges
to Reformed orthodoxy, a fact reported on at the General Synod of 1817:
"We cherish, we love, we preach, and we profess our steadfast adherence
to that form of sound words, contained in the excellent standards of our
church." But, "Whilst purity of doctrine is still our happy and honorable

distinction—whilst we have hitherto not swerved from the good old way; yet let not him that buckleth on the harness boast as he that putteth it off. It is an evil day . . . Deceivers have gone forth to deceive."[14] The worst of the "deceivers" are named: Socinians (Unitarians) and Arminians, who "are not Calvinists."[15] In 1824, the General Synod also condemned "Hopkinsianism" as being contrary to the Word of God and the standards.[16] In short, the documents of the Dutch church, from the colonial period to 1850, suggest that it was formally committed to the classical doctrines of Reformed orthodoxy.

The attempt to identify the theology of the "Holland immigrants" who settled in Michigan in the mid-nineteenth century is something like trying to find the proverbial "needle in a haystack." You know it is there, but it will take quite a while to find. More than that, the search for the needle has a distinct advantage: you probably know what the needle looks like; in the case of the immigrants' theology, you do not. If the clergy who led the migration had had the time and the library resources for it, they might have written learned treatises on a wide range of theological tenets. They were not equipped for that. Among them only Albertus Van Raalte and Hendrick Scholte[17] had the advantage of a university education. More importantly, they were primarily pastors and preachers who lived and worked in primitive settings on the advancing American frontier. Henry Dosker wrote concerning Van Raalte that he found it necessary to be occupied all day long and frequently into the night with pastoral responsibilities and that he found no time to give adequate attention to the studies necessary to his heavy preaching schedule.[18] That kind of life style, which was typical of the imigrant clergy, is not conducive to creative theological thinking and writing.

The pastors and most of their people were, however, very religious, and religious people do have a theology. It is the theology formed in their earliest years—the special beliefs and attitudes now set deeply in minds and hearts. It is acquired through years of hearing the Scriptures explained in home, church, and school—and often enough, in earnest conversation and debate in the marketplace. It is not a textbook theology but a kind of "practical theology" in which the understanding of what the Bible says is so thoroughly merged with the details of everyday life that the word of Scripture has "become flesh." It may or may not be good theology, but it is definitely theology—a way of comprehending how the eternal God is related to, and engaged in, the human situation.

All of this is not to say that the immigrants' theology was little more than a love affair between their religious instincts and the Bible. We noted above that their theology was acquired through years of hearing the scriptures explained. That is what we have to get at if we are to find

the needle we are concerned about in the haystack of a maddening
jumble of several centuries of Dutch cultural and ecclesiastical history.
Sometimes the search has been made to seem too easy. For example,
it is common to read that the immigrants were stern, orthodox Calvinists. The impression is left that all one need do is to find out what Calvin
taught on this or that doctrine, and then impute the same to the immigrants. By this means one would know what was "explained" to them
when they were growing up in the Netherlands in the first half of the
nineteenth century. For us, that will not do.

By the seventeenth and eighteenth centuries, Calvin's theology had
in many respects become hardened into Calvinism in the Netherlands
and other places where it had taken root. Indeed, there was much of
seventeenth and eighteenth century Reformed theology from which
Calvin himself would have wanted to be disassociated. Large blocks of
it, for example, fell under the heading of what came to be called "Protestant scholasticism."[19] The name suggests complex doctrinal systems,
developed with more concern for rational and logical distinctions than
for the meaning of biblical truth. Such heavy rationalism in the interpretation of the church's theology profoundly determined both the shape
of dogmatism and its sometimes violent debates with opposing schools
of interpretation. That was eminently true in Holland for more than a
hundred years following the Synod of Dort. In some cases dogmatic
views were formed with the aid of philosophical tools and materials
borrowed from the Greek philosopher Aristotle and the French sceptic,
René Descartes.

It is not strange, therefore, that theological conceptions appeared
from time to time that were quite distant from Calvin's original thought.
A case in point concerns the meaning of the "covenant," a term that for
centuries has had great significance for Reformed Christians.[20] Covenants are God's primary method of relating to his redeemed people,
together with the program he desires to accomplish on earth in and
through his people. Calvin frequently refers to the covenant in his
writings; it is the focus of much of his theology. Calvin never employs
it as an all-embracing structural principle, a device that enables one to
go into considerable detail with respect to such matters as to how God
must, in the nature of the case, organize his work on earth and go about
his business.

An extraordinary example of covenantal thinking is that furnished by
Johannes Cocceius, one of the foremost Dutch theologians in the post-
Dort era. The full range of his discourse on covenant theology need not
be detailed here. Indeed, much of his writing did not enjoy widespread
acceptance. One part of his thought, however, namely his "federal the-

ology," which was favorably received by Reformed and Presbyterian churches requires brief comment.[21] Cocceius taught that the Bible sets forth a "covenant of works" prior to the Fall, in which Adam and Eve are held responsible for obeying God. After the Fall, however, God established a "covenant of grace." This new covenant comprises three stages—before the law, after the law, and under the gospel—and each stage is an advance on the one that precedes it. Each covenant carries with it the promise of rewards or punishment, depending on the faith and obedience of the individual. Moreover, God, and not man, established both covenants and sets their terms.

Cocceius' unrelenting foe in the theological strife of the seventeenth century was Gisbertus Voetius, professor of theology at Utrecht.[22] If Cocceius is viewed as a scholastic or rationalistic Calvinist, he is far surpassed in this by Voetius. The latter went to extraordinary lengths to expound Calvinist dogma in logical and philosophical thought forms that made neat distinctions at critical points, thus resolving difficulties. Voetius' goal in this was exactness—"precision" in his terminology—in everything that had to do with Christian faith and morals. The continuing strife between Cocceius and Voetius and their followers nearly brought about the spiritual demise of the Reformed Church in the Netherlands. Ironically, with all his reliance on the vaunted powers of the intellect to solve the puzzles of theology, Voetius possessed what seemed to be a deeply practical and pious side—an insistence that true religion for any Christian is to be found in the warm, evangelical center of an intensely personal and heart-felt piety.

While Voetius remained a principal spokesman of Dutch pietism for more than a century, he was by no means the only significant one. Many of the Dutch who emigrated to the midwest in the mid-nineteenth century were nurtured in pietist writers such as Voetius, Abraham Hellenbroeck,[23] Willem à Brakel,[24] Joducus van Lodensteyn,[25] and Hermannus Witsius.[26] Indeed, the strain of pietism is so pervasive in the feeling and thinking of the Dutch immigrants that it is necessary to set out its main accents here.[27]

It is important, first of all, to understand the way the pietist viewed the relationship between the church's standards and "religion of the heart." The standards were always affirmed by the pietist, but he did not consider intellectual assent to the standards, or, for that matter, proper conduct of one's life according to the ordinances of the church, as primary in the Christian faith. That place belonged to a person's piety, construed as a godly life. For the pietist the Christian faith was much more a matter of the heart than the head. His focus was on the inner life of feeling, a condition that is effected through one's union with

Christ. In this union, Christ joins himself with the true believer and conveys to him his power and Spirit.

Pietism drew a sharp distinction between the converted and the unconverted person, between being "born again" and continuing as the "natural man." Only the former walks in the light of God, because only the Spirit can enlighten the heart. In addition, the "born-again" Christian understands the meaning of the revealed Word, while the "natural man" has only an external grasp of it. This implied, of course, that true theologians and teachers must be "born-again" Christians; the theologian who is not "born-again" knows the letter but not the spirit of the gospel.

Moreover, the pietist gave faith an active character; it is more than a matter of believing certain truths. Faith has its beginning in justification, understood as union with Christ, which is at the same time the beginning of one's sanctification. Faith, if authentic, will become fruitful in good works. Thus, faith requires effort and spiritual diligence. One grows in grace through the discipline of a faith that issues in an increasing sanctification. In that context the "imitation of Christ" was paramount for the pietist.[28] The goal of the Christian is to become more Christlike, especially in the experience of suffering. Every "cross" of this life, whether it be a temptation, spiritual conflict, illness, poverty, or persecution, needs to be borne in obedience to God in accord with the pattern of Jesus' genuine submissiveness.

This theology of "cross bearing" was particularly comforting to the Dutch pietists who emigrated to the New World in the 1840's. The story of that emigration is packed with peril, adventure, and stubborn determination. It begins with more than a decade of religious persecution under King William I, during which many of them were fined and imprisoned.

Moreover, when the secessionists finally decided to leave Holland for North America in 1846, they were ridiculed, vilified, and threatened by townspeople and friends. The Atlantic crossing provided no relief from their difficulties: heartless crews ignored their miseries, and many of the emigrants died at sea. The journey from the New York harbor westward was also a perilous one of frightful journeying conditions and attacks by thieving Americans. When the emigrants finally arrived at the primitive forests of Michigan, they quickly began the arduous task of cutting trees and piecing together logs for houses, barns, churches, and roads, and all of this during a punishing winter and under desperate economic conditions.[29]

The ground that held those Dutch emigrants through those years of peril and adventure was the rich soil of Calvinist doctrine which had nurtured their emotions as well as their minds. Van Raalte related how their much-loved Heidelberg Catechism often spoke to their need and sustained them on their way. We can picture them discussing truths about their creator God who made all things and who upholds and governs them by "his eternal counsel and providence"; that that God is for the sake of Christ "my God and my Father"; and that I rely so entirely on him "that I have no doubt, but he will provide me with all things necessary for soul and body; and further, that he will make whatever evils he sends upon me, in this valley of tears, turn out to my advantage, for he is able to do it, being almighty God, willing, and a faithful Father."[30]

Further, God's government of this world is so complete that all things "come not by chance, but by his fatherly hand." They include "herbs and grass, rain and drought, fruitful and barren years, meat and drink, health and sickness, riches and poverty." The faith corollary of this knowledge of a God who so creates and sustains all things is clear: "That we may be patient in adversity; thankful in prosperity; and that in all things, which may hereafter befall us, we place our firm trust in our faithful God and Father, that nothing shall separate us from his love: since all creatures are so in his hand, that without his will they cannot so much as move."[31] It may be noted that the second part of Article 13 of the Belgic Confession ("Of Divine Providence") expresses sentiments very similar to those above.

It is impossible, of course, to determine whether pietism or the nineteenth century Calvinism of the standards exercised the greater influence on the faith of the seceders during this period. More than likely, one individual was affected by one of them, someone else by the other. The fact that there had to be an admixture of the two at all is highly significant. If the original teachings of John Calvin himself had been retained in the generations following his demise, there may not have been need for a "religion of the heart," forcing a "religion of the head" into second place. But we cannot be certain. Perhaps powerful emotional needs would have insisted that heart religion be given a significant place notwithstanding. While there is a strong subjective note in many of Calvin's writings—an accent on the true inwardness of genuine religious experience—it is a different kind of inwardness from that demanded by Voetius and other pietists. For Calvin, subjective religion was an inwardness always in the control of correct scriptural understanding. It is descriptive or objective in character—because this or that is true theologically, the Christian may properly have an inward conviction and personal experience that corresponds to it.[32]

The inwardness component in the standards is also of the same general character in the relatively few places where it makes an appearance.

It is always the implication or corollary of a doctrinal truth, as for example, of God as creator or provider. It is possible for the Christian to believe with all his or her heart whatever is declared to be true doctrine and how that is related to good Christian practice—with the latter remaining in the area of an intellectual grasp of what should be the case. Then both doctrine and practice are held sincerely as true propositions. That does not issue, *per force*, in Christian living that is vibrant with fervor, aflame with love for Christ and his gospel, alive with compassionate feelings for the "lost," and continually vigorous in doing the work of the kingdom. That comes about only when one gives oneself unreservedly to it. It is the characteristic life style of the pietist.

The Dutch seceders did not become thoroughgoing pietists on the above model. From the relatively scanty descriptions we have of their day-to-day Christian behavior in those difficult decades prior to their coming to North America, they appear to exhibit a determined Calvinist character. This was not that original Calvinism which was noted above; such was not to be found anywhere. Rather, it was a Calvinism modified by scholastic, rationalistic formulations of doctrine, having as its proper addendum a structure of stern morality as befitting Christian conduct under the imperious demands of a sovereign God. As Voetius himself seemed unable to tolerate such unrelieved rigor and thus developed a religion of the heart, so the seceders could rejoice in their inheritance of a well-developed tradition of a stern, scholastic Calvinism that was softened by an inwardness that seemed to bring forth a new form of Calvinism—a veritable merging of two powerful traditions.

That modified Calvinism furnished the Dutch Protestants who were to become the seceders of 1834 and the generation following with the religious and theological dynamic that formed them into a special kind of people of God. In the early stages of becoming that people, they found the strength of purpose to distinguish themselves from the Netherlands Reformed Church which, because of its rationalism and liberalism, appeared to be spiritually lifeless. By the 1840's the seceder's identity in the Netherlands was clearly established, even though they did not become a separate denomination. They remained a group of scattered congregations, often troubled by disagreements and contentions, but unified, nevertheless, by a singular vision of God's purpose and direction for their lives.

In the New World it was Albertus C. Van Raalte who, more than any other, gave vivid expression to the Calvinism of the immigrants. This emerged most clearly in his sermons, although the general conduct of his life in the colony as well as his leadership in both the church and the community, also gave evidence of his Reformed spirit. Dr. Gordon J. Spykman provides a helpful analysis of Van Raalte's sermons in his book, *Pioneer Preacher: Albertus Christiaan Van Raalte.*[33] Spykman's study reveals the composite character of Van Raalte's theology. The specifically Calvinist component was solidly there in a blending of some elements of original Calvinism with those characterizing the scholastic elaboration of Calvinist dogma. Joined to these, as if having an unquestioned right to be there, were some of the familiar notes of the pietism described above.

Calvin's thought was frequently present in Van Raalte's preaching. He quoted especially from Calvin's *Institutes of the Christian Religion.* While Calvin occasionally used the logical argumentation of earlier Roman Catholic scholasticism to support doctrinal positions, his work for the most part attempts to interpret Scripture in a straightforward manner. Van Raalte apparently sought to follow his "spiritual father" in this. Doubtless he found two of the standards, the Heidelberg Catechism and the Belgic confession, close to the *Institutes* in mood and simplicity of expression. He frequently quoted the Heidelberg Catechism in his sermons, probably because of its deeply experiential accents. In addition, the Catechism's simple, straightforward questions and answers were useful tools for the instruction of the immigrants, few of whom were educated.

The Canons of Dort, with their detailed description of God's method of saving the lost, appear less frequently in Van Raalte's sermons, although he surely affirmed their strong predestinarian position. The Canons, coming out of the Synod of Dort in Holland, provide a bridge between the simplicity of statement in the earlier Heidelberg Catechism and Belgic Confession and the later dogmatic complexities of the developing scholasticism. It contains elements of both. Having been trained in scholasticism in the University of Leiden, it would have been striking, indeed, if Van Raalte had not expressed himself approvingly with respect to at least some of Dort's content and style.

Some scholastic emphases are, in fact, easily detectable in Van Raalte's preaching. Spykman correctly observes a clear tension between a highly intellectualistic view of God, as developed by the scholastics, and the historical picture of God characteristic of the Bible. Van Raalte made much of the attributes of God, which are described quite abstractly and apart from his concrete redemptive activity. "There is a kind of scholastic logic at work which leads the preacher to explain all kinds of things which God must necessarily be and do as logical deductions drawn from the established concept of God."[35] In Van Raalte's explanation of the efficacy of prayer, he employed the principle of causality in nature as a useful analogy. Just as God authored the principle of causality as the necessary means of securing his desired results in the natural order, so he ordained that prayer should be the appointed means for securing desired ends in the spiritual and moral realms. God's decree ordains it so; prayer in itself does not achieve those ends. Nor can prayer alter the decrees in any way. Van Raalte expounded a variety of other themes with equal logical rigor. In doing so he was not at all an original thinker; he was simply repeating patterns learned at the university.

There was however, another, less rationalistic side to Van Raalte's theology, which was also found in his preaching. Here the focus was not on how or why God acts as he does, but on the personal Christian faith and life of each believer. Its fountainhead was not the rationalistic structures taught in the schools but the deeply subjective piety derived from two quite different sources. The first was the personal implications of doctrinal truths for the Christian life, as emphasized by Calvin, the Heidelberg Catechism, and the Belgic Confession. The second was the pietist accent of the "religion of the heart," of which Voetius, perhaps, was the most noteworthy model. Van Raalte's sermons seem often to be dominated by the spirit and content of this "inwardness." Indeed, the believer's relation to Christ was regularly treated on the level of inner piety, calling upon the people to cultivate their personal spirituality as their chief goal. In the process certain important emphases of historic Calvinism seem excluded, such as Christ's rulership of the world or the securing of his sovereignty over all areas of human experience, including the primary institutions of human society. These matters are not so much disbelieved; they simply were not part of that people's vision at that time.

The "practical theology" of the Dutch immigrants (that needle in the haystack for which we have been looking) is substantially that of Van Raalte himself. The immigrants did not learn it from him in any original sense; he was expert in reinforcing what they had long been taught. Only Hendrick Scholte, founder of the immigrant colony at Pella, Iowa, could have given their theology a somewhat different direction, because he was a premillenialist. Scholte, however, never became a minister of the Reformed Church, and his peculiar theological accents had no lasting influence on the people in the Pella area.

The Calvinism of the seceders is still present within many of the Reformed congregations in the Midwest. There are few traces of scholasticism in their theology today. What persists are certain Calvinistic accents about the way God pursues his goals in history and the church and particularly in the lives of faithful believers. The old pietistic emphases are also very much alive among many of these Reformed congregations, refurbished now, however, through the influence of American fundamentalism.

The Reformed Dutch Church in the East found the immigrants' theology quite to their liking. Wyckoff made that clear following his visit to the Michigan colony. It was not identical with the theology of the eastern church, but how could it be? The historical and cultural forces that shaped their respective theologies were different. Significantly, both traditions were influenced by Voetian "Old World" piety. Perhaps that was the familiar note that Wyckoff found "pleasant to his ears" on his visit to the "Holland immigrants." The warm evangelical piety of the immigrants was more than likely similar to that espoused by the already existing Protestant Dutch Church in North America.

IV

Saints and Sinners:
Secession and The Christian Reformed Church

M. Eugene Osterhaven

The secession from the Reformed Church in America in 1857, and later in 1880-82, understood theologically, concerned the doctrine of the church. Called into question was whether that denomination was a true church or a false church, a liberal church or the old pure Reformed Church. That was the issue and those expressions, or their equivalents, were often heard in the new world to which the Dutch had come. Examined more closely, the issue was whether the church in essence is one and catholic, and whether the Reformed Church in America was a member of it; whether the Reformed Church was lax in doctrine, discipline, and worship; whether its goverment was in accord with cherished Reformed principles; whether its conditions for church membership were based on Scripture; whether it was proper to cooperate with other evangelical churches and to sit at the Lord's Table with their members; and whether the Reformed Church in America had to be a pure church for the immigrant congregations in the West to remain in fellowship with it. In addition, there were one or two minor theological concerns which divided people, and, no less important, there were non-theological factors, sometimes disguised or given theological justification, which swayed the hearts of believers and predisposed their decisions. We shall look at each of these presently, but first it is necessary to consider the major theological issue which agitated and then set Dutch-Americans at odds with each other and with the American branch of the old Dutch Reformed Church.

Shortly after their arrival in the New World in 1846 the Dutch immigrants who had left Europe primarily for religious reasons united with the Reformed Protestant Dutch Church, and their leaders said that they did so for theological reasons. Their *Confession of Faith,* following Calvin, maintained that there is only "one catholic or universal church," that it consists of those who are saved, and that believers should unite with it.

. . . no person, of whatever state or condition he may be, ought to withdraw himself, to live in a separate state from it . . . all men are in duty
bound to join and unite themselves with it; maintaining the unity of the
church . . . those who . . . do not join themselves to it, act contrary to
the ordinance of God.[1]

The immigrants were highly conscious of their confessional statements
and particularly aware of the teaching of the unity of the church. They
were heirs of the Calvinistic tradition which in the Netherlands had
brought to maturity Old Testament ideas of covenant and theocracy and
the *volkskerk*, the vision of the whole community living together as the
people of God.[2]

It was with anguish therefore that Albertus C. Van Raalte, the leader
of the emigration to Michigan, and others separated themselves from
the church in the Netherlands. Rather than leaving the old church, they
considered themselves as its heirs. Correspondingly, they believed that
the state church in the Netherlands had gone astray and put them out.
Their lamentable experience with that leadership did not embitter these
persons but served to intensify their confidence in the old religious
tradition and to quicken their love for the ancient faith. That is why the
leaders of the *Kolonie* in Michigan responded as they did to the questions put them on the occasion of the visit of the Rev. Isaac N. Wyckoff
of the Reformed Protestant Dutch Church. Traveling from Albany and
representing the Board of Domestic Missions of his denomination, Dr.
Wyckoff met with "quite a large company," including the pastors and
elders[3] of the colony on June 4, 1849, after visting each of the congregations. His questions were 1) about their doctrinal standards and form
of church goverment; 2) whether they wished to unite with the Dutch
Reformed Church in America; and 3) whether the congregations needed
help.

Dr. Wyckoff was no stranger to the colonists. He and Dr. Thomas
DeWitt, of the Reformed Church in New York City, had done much
for the immigrants before their arrival, each having organized a society
to lend assistance to them. Wyckoff's organization, called *The Protestant
Evangelical Holland Emigrant Society*, was founded on October 8, 1846,
a month before the arrival of Van Raalte and his party. The groups of
immigrants arriving in New York were assisted there and in Albany on
their way west, Dr. Wyckoff especially giving them great assistance. At
the meeting of the Holland Classis on September 27, 1848, an invitation
from the Reformed Church to attend its synodical assemblies was read,
but the colonists felt unable to accept "because of the pressure of local
business and the difficulties connected with a new settlement." When
Wyckoff appeared in the colony the next spring, he was received with

great joy, but the cautious settlers waited a full month before they framed a reply on July 10 presumably in order to give the matter an adequate hearing. It is the answer to the second question that interests us. It reads:

We feel a very great need for the communion of saints. We hate sectarianism. By God's Word and by complete persuasion we affirm: 'the eye cannot say to the hand, nor the head to the foot, I have no need of you.' And we consider it an abomination to say: 'I am holier than you.' Therefore we are looking for the greatest possible union with God's people wherever they appear on earth if they know and follow the way of salvation. So how much more we feel ourselves [to be] *one* with the churches which have the same expression of faith, the same liturgy, and form of government, and [which] publicly defend the truth of God against falsehood. We have never considered ourselves to be other than a part of the Dutch Reformed Church and therefore desire to live in fellowship with those churches and wish to send our representatives to their ecclesiastical assemblies.[4]

The document is signed by the four ministers of the colony, A. C. Van Raalte, of Holland; M. A. Ypma, of Vriesland; C. Van der Meulen, of Zeeland; and S. Bolks, of Overisel; Graafschap and Drenthe being without ministers at the time, and twenty elders. The plan was then evidently submitted to the congregations, as the minutes of Vriesland July 30, 1849, and other testimony of the period show.[5]

At a meeting of the Holland Classis the next April, Van Raalte was delegated to attend the meeting of the Particular Synod of Albany in order to "facilitate the desired union." The letter of authorization given him by the classis and directed to the synod is further witness to belief in the unity and catholicity of the church. It reads in part:

In consideration of the precious and blessed unity of the church of God, and the clearly declared will of our Saviour that they should all be one; as well as the need which particular parts of the whole have of one another—especially we, who feel our weakness and insignificance—our hearts thirst for fellowship with the beloved Zion of God. Since the day that we stepped ashore in this new world, our hearts have been strengthened and encouraged by meetings with people of God. The children of God are all dear to us, living in their respective denominations, but in guiding and caring for the interests of our congregations we find ourselves best at home where we are privileged to find our own confessional standards and the fundamental principles of our church government. Thus it was gratifying to us to experience from the other side no narrow exclusiveness, but open, hearty, brotherly love. This awakens in us a definite desire to make manifest our fellowship and to ask for the hand of brotherly fellowship in return.[6]

The Particular Synod met in Albany in May and recommended the reception of the Holland Classis to the General Synod which met in June. The union was consummated and at the next meeting of classis, October 30, 1850, Van Raalte related the "affection and sympathy" with which he had been received at the meeting of the particular synod and the debate about the legality of receiving an already organized classis into the synod rather than individual churches.[7]

The strong protestations of the leaders of the *Kolonie* for the unity of the church at the time of union with the Reformed Church in America were no passing phenomenon. They represented a profound, enduring conviction whose roots lay deep in the Reformed/Calvinist tradition in which they had been nourished. That conviction was intensified through experiences which those leaders had had as a part of the secession from the state church in the Netherlands and through the sectarian spirit and secessions with which they had to struggle within the *Kolonie* in the New World.

In Europe the colonists had been thrust outside the established church because of their religious convictions. Van Raalte, admittedly a man of conviction but no extremist, was refused ordination even though he was eminently qualified. Once outside the established church, he was subjected to persecution, repeated fines, imprisonments, the quartering of four soldiers in his home, threats, and other harassment. What happened to him happened to hundreds of others. Dissenters were fined many thousands of gulden when one gulden was a day's wage for a worker; when financial resources were exhausted, the accused's property was sold. In a town in Friesland eight soldiers were quartered in a home of one room in which a man lived with his sick wife and five children. In November, 1836, a small, seceding congregation at Hattem was ordered to provide lodging for sixty-five soldiers. Ten of them stayed with Van Raalte's brother-in-law, the Rev. A. Brummelkamp, and his wife, six of them with a deacon named Geerlings, and six with the couple in whose home worship was held. Our purpose is not to narrate this history, however, but to note it in relation to the strengthening of conviction. The fact that it was the established church which, at the meeting of its synod in 1835, petitioned the government to enforce certain articles of the Napoleonic penal code, thus setting in motion the persecution, galvanized the beliefs of multitudes of people and forced them to consider themselves in relation to the *Hervormde Kerk* out of which they had come.[8]

In spite of all that he had experienced, Van Raalte and many others with him retained the ideal of the unity and catholicity of the church and eschewed the idea of separation. The beginning of the *Afscheiding,* or Secession, in 1834, under H. de Cock at Ulrum, troubled him and he felt an aversion toward much that had happened within that movement since then.[9] Spreading rapidly, the Secession soon had thousands of adherents throughout the country and these, although united in their loyalty to the Reformed faith, separated into a number of factions each with its own notions about church government, the Christian life, worship, or the education of ministers.[10] These internal divisions saddened and disheartened leaders of the Secession as well as other leaders of the revival which had begun in the *Hervormde Kerk* leaving some of them with a deep desire for unity. Recalling those days, Van Raalte wrote:

> The alienation among the faithful in the Netherlands was for me a continuous tearful and heart-rending sorrow. This made me more fearful than all the persecution. I was profoundly impressed by the spiritual devastation wrought by unbelief and the enhancement given carnality by this estrangement and hopeless conflict. It often consumed all my zest for living and made me afraid of life.[11]

It is little wonder that with this situation in the seceding churches and Van Raalte's attitude toward it, the Synod of 1840 was the last that he attended.

Over against the quarrelsome, disputatious, and sometimes petulant element among those with whom they worked, Van Raalte, his brothers-in-law, Brummelkamp and Van Velzen, and other heads of the *Afscheiding*, were in constant touch with leaders of culture in the Netherlands of a different stripe. These people, while orthodox in their faith, were broad-minded, confident, and impatient with both the dominant liberal-rationalism of the age and the petty strife that they observed in some advocates of Secession. Two of these men. Dr. Abraham Capadose and Isaac Da Costa, were converted Jews. Two others, the poet Willem Bilderdijk and G. Groen Van Prinsterer, were intellectual leaders of rare insight, the latter the official historian of the House of Orange. All were guiding lights of the religious awakening and sympathetic toward the leaders of the Secession. Their breadth of interest and catholic spirit quickened the pulse of the future leaders of the immigration and helped prepare them for the difficult days ahead. Groen Van Prinsterer, who remained in the state church, spoke the mind of all on the oneness of the church:

> No believers, no company of believers, may consider themselves isolated from this divine whole, of which Christ is the head. Many do not consider that the root is often disowned by seceding from one of the branches, the foundation denied in the denial of part of the living stones of the building and the Head rejected in the rejection of the members. The

church must be tested by the Scriptures, but we must be careful not to reject divine truth, in whatever form it appears, lest we reject the unity of the Church, and deny what God works in the Church.[12]

Before the emigrants left the Netherlands their leaders were well aware of the threat that a *strijdlustig,* or contentious spirit, is to the unity and peace of the church. Their fears were soon realized. Within a few years of their arrival there was a repetition of the wrangling that had plagued the Secession in Europe. One of the chief figures in these disputations was Gijsbert Haan who had emigrated in 1847 and had stayed in New York and New Jersey before moving west. Received into the Vriesland church on August 10, 1849, Haan soon began agitation within the classis against the union which had been consummated with the Dutch church in the East, a subject to which we shall return, and concerning various other matters. Although he was not a delegate from his church, he brought complaints to classis on October 14, 1851, about the retirement of elders and the non-observance of festival days: Christmas, Good Friday, Easter, and Pentecost. Haan charged that the failure to retire elders in some instances showed that the adoption of the church order of Dort was "nothing more than make-believe." Classis replied that retirement was in order with the understanding that those retired are "inactive overseers" who "in important cases can be called upon to serve the consistory," and that when there was a lack of qualified persons, if the congregation so desired, elders need not be retired. The observance or non-observance of festival days was also declared an optional matter, particularly since workers in Grand Haven, Grand Rapids, and Holland could not be excused from their labor on certain week days and were free only in the evenings. Moreover, in both instances, it was declared these matters had been dealt with previously in classis, "often in extended discussion." In its judgment, classis affirmed that "Christian love makes us very yielding and tolerant in such non-essentials" and that "no one should be burdened herein, since the Lord in his Word has left us free. . . . in the churches unity and peace are constantly to be sought." The classis warned against "accusations, as if we favor looseness, arbitrariness, and an anti-Reformed system of church government" which is "not only unfair [but] it is also very dangerous and destructive" leading to "schisms" and "the nefarious system of the Independents" in which "each congregation will keep itself to itself."[13]

The desired "unity and peace" in the churches was not to be achieved. Haan, who had not been elected an elder in Vriesland, moved to Grand Rapids where he was soon elected to that office and served as a delegate to the classis meeting of April 27, 1853. His elevation to office gave him greater opportunity to condemn the union of 1850. He did so on the grounds of laxness in doctrine, worship, and practice in the Dutch church of the East, and his "influence must have penetrated to every church in the colony."[14] The agitation reached its peak at the meetings of classis on September 5, 1855 and April 2, 1856. At the latter meeting, Haan was severely rebuked, and on October 9 of that year he left the denomination with a few friends in Grand Rapids.

Haan's departure from the classis was not the first, however. There had been a schism at Graafschap as early as 1851 over a marital problem and a demand on the part of some there that an elder, J. J. Schepers, be ordained by the classis as a minister.[15] Drenthe, which had experienced difficulty since 1849,[16] lost two-thirds of its congregation in 1853. The seceding minister, R. Smit, had had a history of difficulty in the Netherlands,[17] and Hessel O. Yntema, an elder from Vriesland who lived between Drenthe and Vriesland, testified that Smit began slandering Van Raalte within "a fortnight" of his arrival in Michigan.[18] Deposed by Classis Holland, Smit led his group into the Scotch Associate Reformed Church and continued to sow dissension within the *Kolonie*.

That dissension was felt acutely in the neighboring congregation at Vriesland where two elders, Hendrik Dam and T. Ulberg, shared the view of Haan about the Reformed Church in the East. At a meeting in a schoolhouse in 1851 Ulberg had reported an experience in Albany similar to that of Haan. He had heard no catechetical preaching in Wyckoff's church and had noted that church festival days were not observed. Moreover, baptism was sometimes administered apart from public worship.[19] Haan, Dam, and Ulberg won other families to their position, and here, according to Dosker, "the separatistic spirit first strongly revealed itself."[20] There were other leaders in the church there of a different spirit, however, who believed that Christians are called to unity and peace as well as the pursuit of truth. Their thinking prevailed so that the early secession in Vriesland was limited to a dozen families. Dam had left the Reformed Church in March of 1856, but the seceding group was not organized as a congregation until April 17, 1857 with H. Dam and T. Ulberg as elders and G. Haan, Jr., as deacon. Although that fellowship was to triple during 1881 and 1882 as a result of a controversy over Freemasonry, internal dissension so weakened the congregation that it was dissolved on April 4, 1893.

The congregations in Holland, Zeeland, and Overisel escaped the secessions experienced in Graafschap, Drenthe, Grand Rapids, and Vriesland during the 1850s. That does not mean that all was at peace, for in each settlement within the *Kolonie* the church dominated the life of the people, many of whom continued to weigh the reports that they had heard about "the East" and to wonder if it might not be better "to

be by ourselves again." The church in Holland in particular had a problem with a member, A. Krabshuis, who first appears in the minutes of
consistory on December 5, 1853, because of his complaint by letter of
the circulation of a Dutch translation of Richard Baxter's *Call to the
Unconverted*, which is said to contain Arminian heresy.[21] On February 12, 1855, he was elected an elder but because of misgivings about
his fitness for office he was not installed until May. In the meantime,
the blood pressure of both congregation and classis seems to have risen
alarmingly. On March 5 the consistory entertained Krabshuis' renewed
complaint against Baxter and his dissatisfaction with the minister, Van
Raalte. On March 16 the consistory discussed Krabshuis at length, with
Van Raalte speaking in Krabshuis' defense. On April 11, the question
of his installation came before classis by petition from members of the
congregation who declared him to be "unfit for that office on account
of his public attacks upon ministers in [the newspaper] *De Hollander*."
After lengthy discussion, the matter was resolved with the Rev. Cornelius Van der Meulen pointing out "the good and bad sides of the
elected brother, and that, if he should employ his gifts in humility and
love, he would be an excellent blessing for the church of Holland, but
that if he should fall into the love of contention, he would be a fearful
scourge." When the vote was taken, a majority saw "no sufficient reasons
not to proceed with the installation." The installation took place and, in
Dosker's words, "the misery began already in October of the same year,
1855. At the consistory meeting of October 22 Krabshuis came with a
long list of objections. He was at war over the last meeting of classis."[22]

The classis had met on September 5 in Vriesland. Among the issues
that came before it were 1) reports by Van der Meulen and Elder J. Van
de Luister of Zeeland on the last meeting of the General Synod in which
they gave a favorable report of the church in the East; 2) a discussion
initiated by Haan's question about the celebration of the Lord's Supper
at Synod to which non-delegates, including professors and students from
New Brunswick Seminary, were invited; 3) the interpretation of Article 28 of the *Belgic Confession*, which was read, and "whether we must
still in this age, acknowledge only the Reformed as the true churches,
and whether the Lord's Supper may be administered only to members
of the Reformed church, so excluding other converted people"; 4) a
letter from four consistorymen from Grand Rapids, including Haan,
protesting the circulation of Baxter's book; and 5) a letter from the Reverend H. G. Klijn of Grand Rapids urging fidelity to the Reformed
confession as "the standard of faith and the only way of salvation."

Krabshuis' complaints at the October consistory meeting were directed against Van Raalte who was charged with 1) being too free in the

use of the Lord's Supper; 2) defending Baxter's errors; 3) dominating the consistory; 4) rejecting the Secession in the Netherlands; and 5) holding that points of difference should not be taught children. During the prolonged discussion it became clear that Krabshuis had no support.

At a consistory meeting on November 3 he acknowledged that he should have discussed the issues raised with the minister before bringing them before the consistory. He absented himself from the meeting of December and sent notice of his separation from the church to the consistory meeting of January 18, 1856, with the request that he and his family not be troubled by a visitation from consistory. A week later the consistory unanimously accepted his resignation from office "after long patience with the ranting weaknesses [*schreeuwende zwakheden*] of the brother." Then it was said: "However, the impropriety [*verkeerde*: wrongness] of his schism must be called to his attention, although his right of conscience to separate himself is not challenged. To his own Lord he stands or falls."[23]

The withdrawal of Krabshuis from the consistory and congregation in Holland preceded Dam's sucession from the Vriesland congregation by two months and that of Haan from the church in Grand Rapids by nine months. These events were but prelude, however disturbing they were in themselves, to what was soon to come. The seeds of discontent sown in every corner of the colony were to come to fruition at the meeting of classis a year later. At its spring session, on April 8, 1857, four communications lay before the assembly, two of them from ministers and two from congregations. The first was over the name of the Rev. Koene Vanden Bosch who had left the Netherlands the previous year and had been received into the classis on August 20, 1856.[24] It reads as follows:

Noordeloss, March 14, 1857.

To the Consistory of Zeeland:

By this I notify you that I can hold no ecclesiastical communion with you, for the reason that I cannot hold all of you who have joined the Dutch Reformed Church to be the true church of Jesus Christ, and consequently I renounce all fellowship with you and declare myself no longer to belong to you. I am the more constrained to do this by the fear of God, on account of the abominable and church-destroying heresy and sins which are rampant among you, which, if the Lord will and we live, I shall present to the next meeting of Classis.

I hope that your eyes may yet be opened to see your extreme wickedness, to take it to heart, and to be converted therefrom.

(Signed)   K. Vanden Bosch
                                          Minister at Noordeloos

The second document was from the Rev. H. G. Klijn [or Kleijn] of Grand Rapids:

> To the Classical Assembly of the Dutch Reformed Church, to be held at Zeeland, April 8th, 1857.
> Reverend brethren:
> The God of love cause you to be one in Christ, by the power of the Holy Ghost.
> In connection with the report of my withdrawal from the American denomination, the Reformed Protestant Dutch Church, presented to your assembly by the delegates, I hereby give expression to my cordial thanks for the love and honor enjoyed among you, together with this sincere desire, that you could join with us in our standpoint.
> Brethren, ministers of the gospel, we are together ministers of the secession, in so far as your overseers in the midst of you walked in that same path with us in the Netherlands. Yea, we were separated from all Protestant denominations. Brethren, I exhort you in love not to lose this your character. The Church, the Bride of Christ, is a garden enclosed, a well shut up, and a fountain sealed. The Lord open your eyes, that you may follow your calling, whereby the Church of Christ may walk in one way, to the glorification of his holy name.
> I commend myself to a continuance of your fraternal friendship, that no spirit of bitterness may reign in us and among us, for we are brethren, beloved of the Lord, bought by Christ, in order that we should serve him without fear, in holiness and righteousness all the days of our life. The King of Glory dwell in your assembly, that you may do his will. Now the Lord of Peace himself give you peace at all times and in every way. The Lord be with you all.
>
> Your affectionate brother in Christ,
> (Signed)   H. G. Kleijn
>
> Grand Rapids, Michigan
> April 6, 1857.

The third letter was from the congregation at Graafschap:

> Graafschap, April 7, 1857.
> To the Classical Assembly, Reformed Protestant Dutch
>   Church, to be held at Zeeland, April 8th, 1857.
> Reverend Brethren:
> We are obliged to give you notice of our present ecclesiastical standpoint, namely, separating ourselves from your denomination, together with all Protestant denominations, with which we thoughtlessly became connected upon our arrival in America. We are uniting ourselves with the Afgescheidene Gereformeerde Kerk in the Netherlands, and exhort you herewith affectionately to walk in the same way with us. The reasons for this our secession, namely, 113 members, or communicants, are as follows:

(1) The collection of 800 hymns, introduced contrary to the church order.

(2) Inviting (men of) all religious views to the Lord's Supper, excepting Roman Catholics.

(3) Neglecting to preach the Catechism regularly, (to hold) catechetical classes, and (to do) house visitation.

(4) That no religious books are circulated without the consent of other denominations, directing your attention to the Sabbath booklet, with the practice by J. Van Der Meulen, in 1855.

(5) And what grieves our hearts most in all of this is that there are members among you who regard our secession in the Netherlands as not strictly necessary, or (think that) it was untimely.

(6) In the report of Rev. Wyckoff he gives us liberty to walk in this ecclesiastical path.

Brethren, we are glad that almost the entire congregation, the number of members given above, with us, the consistory, and our dear little children, again stand upon the same standpoint on which our fathers enjoyed so great blessedness, and oh, we should rejoice still more if the King of the Church should bring you to this conviction. This is the duty of us all. The God of love be your counsellor and guide to walk in the way of truth.

Your affectionate brethren in Christ,
   In the name of the Consistory,
                     (Signed)   J. F. Van Anrooij, Pres.
                                        Henry Strabbing, Clerk

The fourth was from a congregation in Polkton:

                                        Polkton, April 1, 1857.
To the Classical Assembly of the Dutch Reformed Church.
Reverend Brethren:

Hereby we notify you that we declare ourselves, as members of consistory of the above mentioned church, with the congregation, no longer to belong to your denomination, and have betaken ourselves to the standpoint we had when we left the Netherlands, in order thus again to be in connection with the church of the Netherlands; and the reason is this, that your denomination fraternizes with those who are in opposition to the doctrine of our fathers, and (this) is very well known to you, if you are honest, not to touch upon all points. Since there are others who have told you the points item by item, it is not necessary for us (to do so). In the hope that God, who alone is able to make a roaring sea calm and smooth, may also make your hearts so calm and smooth that you will walk with us in the way of our fathers, is our heartfelt desire and prayer.

   (Signed)   J. H. Van Der Werp, Elder
                                      Lukas Elbers, Elder
                                      Henry Vinkemulder, Deacon[25]

The first meeting of the seceding group was held in April, 1857, with Klijn, president, and Vanden Bosch, clerk, but the minutes of that meeting are lost.[26] The first classical meeting was held on October 7, 1857, in Vriesland with five churches represented, Grand Rapids, Vriesland, Graafschap, Noordeloos, and Grand Haven.[27] The Polkton group, represented at a meeting of the new classis on February 3, 1858, then disappears from the scene for a decade, its members returning to the older fellowship. Klijn, who at the meeting of the Holland Classis on April 2, 1856, had admitted his having been influenced by Haan and had left the old Dutch Reformed Church on January 25, 1857, having served as the president of the new group at its first meeting in April, was back in the Reformed Church by September 9 of that same year. Confessing his "error and guilt" for having "offended against fraternal fellowship" and for the "pain he caused the brethren," he professed renewed confidence in the integrity of the old denomination and was received warmly by the classis.[28] Haan too had a change of heart. Perhaps having mellowed with age, or through chastening received during the maturation of his nine children, perhaps for other reasons, he was back in the Reformed Church in Grand Rapids by June 10, 1868.[29]

That, in brief, is the story of the beginning of the division within the *Kolonie* in the first decade of its existence. Among the reasons given for secession in the four documents presented the Classis of Holland few are theological. Vanden Bosch mentions "abominable and church-destroying heresy and sins which are rampant," and which he will present (*sic!*) at the next meeting of classis. He was not at the next meeting of classis, so we do not know what he had in mind. What we do know is that he was as entangled in the web of controversy after 1857 as he was before.[30] Klijn wants separation "from all Protestant denominations." That *is* a theological issue to which we shall return. Graafschap does not mention a single theological issue in its list of grievances. Polkton objects to fraternization "with those who are in opposition to the doctrine of our fathers" without specifying who these are. We know from the early history of the colony, however, that fraternization with Methodists was objectionable to some. The theological question, then, in the history that we have been reviewing is the doctrine of the church in its unity and catholicity. It involves association with other Christians, even other Reformed Christians, and the desire of some to forego such associations and "to be by ourselves again." Behind that expressed desire lay varying measures of fear, distrust, and carry-over from the Netherlands of old prejudices and quarrels, as well as commitments, into a vast, strange, new world.

Was it theologically proper; was it ecclesiastically legitimate; was it prudent for the Classis of Holland to unite with the old Reformed Church in the East? Indeed it was. They were both members of the same family; they shared the same faith, polity, and forms of worship. Granted there were some differences, for the process of Americanization had been proceeding for centuries in New York and New Jersey, and this is bound to alter forms and practices at least superficially, as is evident in both the Reformed and the Christian Reformed denominations in "the West" today.[31] But that the Reformed Protestant Dutch Church of 1850 was a fundamentally sound church, orthodox in its teaching and conservative in practice, the record shows, Haan and Ulberg notwithstanding.[32] This is seen in the *Digest of the Minutes of the Reformed Church in America* in the reports on Sabbath observance, dancing, intemperance, catechetical instruction, devotional exercises for students at Rutgers College, candidates for baptism, the call for days of humiliation and prayer, and other matters.[33] It is seen more impressively in the issues of the *Christian Intelligencer*, the denominational paper, which, as Van Eyck testified, in "those days was a terror to evildoers, and it kept to the front its tremendous opposition to liberalism."[34] It was declared in the Netherlands by Van Prinsterer, Da Costa, and Capadose[35] and by Philip Schaff in a lecture on America on his tour of Europe at the time of the union. Schaff, who was in a position to know, said that the Reformed Church in America was bound to the Heidelberg Catechism and the Articles of the Synod of Dort, that it was "almost more strictly Calvinistic than the Old School Presbyterians," and that in general it was "the most rigid and unmovable of all the churches in America that had their origin in the period of the Reformation."[36] Schaff was able to make that statement because he knew the denomination in the East in a general way and its seminary at New Brunswick in particular.

Founded by John Henry Livingston, the most influential man in the history of the denomination and a model of Reformed theological integrity and piety, New Brunswick had been served by a number of distinguished men known for their adherence to the old orthodoxy. In his visit to the seminary, Van Raalte came to know these men, some of whom, like Samuel A. Van Vranken, could converse with him in English or in Dutch.[37] The other ministers from the *Kolonie* met the New Brunswick professors at meetings of synod, and from the late 1850s on, young men from the West, like Roelof Pieters and the Vander Meulens, traveled east to study theology. There is nothing in the record to indicate dissatisfaction with the theological integrity of the seminary from any of these. Rather, they agreed with Van Raalte who repeatedly expressed his confidence in the church in the East and its seminary.[38]

At the centennial of the seminary in 1884, President Charles Scott of Hope College recalled Van Raalte's sentiment:

> Once I heard the venerable Dr. Van Raalte, in an evening conversation, relate the tearful history of the Holland immigration to this land in which they now dwell. He told how they left the loved homes of their fathers, and the fair surroundings of the Netherlands, and suffered in the forests of Michigan. I can almost repeat his very words, 'Our deepest anxiety was for ecclesiastical connections and the educational needs of these immigrants. Oh, it was upon my heart as a leaden weight, for so I felt my responsibility before God. One of my first missions was to the Theological Seminary at New Brunswick. I listened to the teachings and conversations of the professors, saw the workings of their hearts, and understood their love to God and their devotion to His truth. I blessed my God that I there found the faith, the faith of my father—the historical church of the Netherlands—and because I found it and loved it, I determined to bring the immigrants into intimate connection with the Dutch Reformed Church of America.' Well did Van Raalte fulfill that promise. When he went home he gave his attention and efforts to bring about such a connection of the churches; he succeeded, and among the last prayers of that good man's life was this that, in the Providence of God the Holland congregations might ever dwell in love and peace with our American Reformed Church.[39]

A word needs to be said about the secession from the Reformed Church at Hackensack in 1822, inasmuch as that has been cited as evidence of laxness in doctrine and discipline in the old denomination. Solomon Froeligh, who made that charge, had had a short stint at teaching theology but did not receive a permanent position. Reportedly a talented, aggressive person with extreme theological views, he fell into difficulty with a neighboring congregation, was censured by classis, and seceded, taking four other ministers and parts of their congregations with him. The new group then drafted and passed a series of resolutions excommunicating all officers of the Reformed Church and members who remained in fellowship with them, giving them over to Satan until their conversion. Picking up a few more small congregations, the new group, calling itself "The True Reformed Dutch Church in the United States of America," refrained from all association with other believers until its union with Dutch dissidents in the West late in the century. The secession of 1822 does not evidence weakness in the old denomination; it is rather a sad lesson in what one-sidedness in doctrine, irascibility, and ambition can do to destroy Christian fellowship and enfeeble the witness of the church.

In the account thus far there is no theological justification for the secession from the Reformed Church in the 1850s. Admitting the imperfections of the denomination and all who were a part of it, it was orthodox in confession and conservative in denominational life. Within some congregations there were weaknesses, as immigrants en route to the West had observed. Some of these immigrants had spent months in Albany and later reported that they had witnessed a lack of discipline and cathechetical instruction, irregularities in the use of the sacraments, ignorance of doctrine, and poor church attendance. While not excusing such shortcomings, it must be remembered that those observing them had just come out of an intense religious revival in the Netherlands and that Haan, Ulberg, Dam, Vanden Bosch, and few others who made the charges, were among the most conservative persons in the colony. Moreover, the imperfection of every denomination and differences among congregations must be kept in mind. The vast majority of the immigrants did not share the feelings of the critics, or, if they did share them, they did not feel that they were sufficient reason for secession. Why then the difference of opinion toward the old Dutch Church among the immigrants in the West? If anything, their theology of the church should have bound the newcomers to their Reformed brethren in the East, as Van Raalte and the classis said time and again. Why the split?

The real reasons were non-theological. They were attitudinal and emotional, often misunderstood and lying deep in the hearts of the people. They had to do with the party spirit that had developed in the Netherlands; with pride in one's own position and the inability or unwillingness to admit that an opponent might be right; with ignorance and narrowness and accompanying prejudices; with jealousies and pride and the irritation that comes when one feels that he is not receiving his due; with the isolationist mentality driven by fear and/or resentment, fear of the strange, new environment and resentment over the multitudinous difficulties encountered in making the transition to the new world. The real reasons were geography, distance, the speed of Americanization, and the realization of the eventual loss of one's own language. Some of these require consideration.

A prime reason for the secession was the quarrelsome, contentious nature of many of the immigrants. This was no new quirk which they acquired when they arrived in Michigan; they brought it with them from Europe. Outsiders, without an intense religious life, may fail to understand this. Or, even if they are zealous believers but are not biblically informed and theologically oriented, they may not comprehend the mentality of the Dutch Calvinists who settled in the virgin forest of Michigan in the mid-1800s. There have been periods in the history of the church when whole populations seem to have enjoyed discussing—and arguing—theology. That was true in the fourth and fifth centuries of the church, and it was true in parts of Europe in the sixteenth and seventeenth centuries. That was also true of many Dutch immigrants who came to North America in the nineteenth century. They loved theology, and they loved to debate it.[40] In the Netherlands they had become Van Velsianen, Brummelkampianen, Scholtianen, of the Club of Scholte, Congregations of the Cross, Van Dijkeanen, Bakkerianen, the Gelderschen, or adherents of some other group.[41] Unfortunately, factionalism and a party spirit[42] were highly visible characteristics of the religious life of many orthodox Calvinists at this time. In America this meant that the immigrants were headed for difficulty. Thus, John H. Kromminga writes that their "disputes make manifest the smallness of spirit of the immigrants, and demonstrate the fact that trouble would have arisen even without the union [of 1850 with the Reformed Church].[43] N. H. Dosker, who was a part of the secession in the Netherlands before emigrating in 1873 to minister to a church in Grand Rapids, develops as a thesis of his history of the secession in America that the reason for that schism was the quarrelsomeness of the immigrants, and that the alleged poor condition of the Reformed Church as the reason for the split was "simply a later fabrication that was picked up."[44] The result of the contentiousness of the immigrants was not only a secession of some of them from the Reformed Church but, in the words of Dosker, "the rending of congregations, the sowing of discord and division among brethren, and the extinguishing of spiritual life by factionalism."[45]

A second reason for the secession was the personalities of certain leaders. This has been observed in the previous discussion. Haan, Krabshuis, Smit, and Vanden Bosch, and undoubtedly some on the other side, were difficult contentious persons. Skeptics need to read only the minutes of the Classis of Holland to be convinced. A good place to begin is the meeting of April 2, 1856, where Haan is seen in action.[46] Or, they may read the *Minutes of the Highest Assembly of the Christian Reformed Church, 1857-1880*, which tell the same story.[47] Little wonder that after years of having to work with a few such people, Van Raalte exploded at a meeting of the Classis of Holland as follows, in part:

> Rev. Van Raalte says that although there is nothing else for the Classis to do than to receive these letters of secession as notification, as it is the fruit of a lust for schism already for a long time manifested by a few leaders, against which there is no weapon, which will do us less damage outside of the church than inside of it; and although the speaker has no desire to abridge the liberty of those who are separating themselves, also is even earnestly desirous that we may not be involved in quarrels, and (thus) arouse (mutual) bitterness among the Holland people, but may

avoid everything that may give occasion thereto, and may, as far as possible, promote (mutual) love—yea he could also wish that those who fancy that they can create a holier and purer church than the Dutch Reformed Church of this country may serve to put us to shame and to be a blessing to us by spiritual prosperity and an active fruit-bearing Christianity—nevertheless he is constrained with his whole soul to testify against this conduct that tears asunder the church of God, and warns each and every one against such a reckless course of conduct, which will bring ruin upon our posterity; (and to point out) that the whole affair (excepting a few leaders who fan the fire of distrust and suspicion), is a mixture of ignorance, sectarianism, and a trampling under foot of the brethren, of which the ministers of the Classis of Holland have been constantly for years the prey, which trampling under foot now extends itself to the entire old Dutch Reformed Church and the orthodox denominations—(a spirit) which has never been characteristic of the Reformed Church (and) which shall bear the judgment of God.[48]

Considering all that Van Raalte had done for the *Kolonie*—serving as minister, physician, judge, counselor, clerk of classis, correspondent, businessman, advocate, comforter, financier, colonizer—and the gruding response that he often received for his effort, his reaction to the secession was mild. Few people of his gifts and training, having to endure so much from those who should have been so grateful, would have continued. What sustained him was his faith in God and sense of calling. Those who knew him and wrote about him[49] agree concerning his greatness. Equally at ease in addressing a day-laborer or state governor, Van Raalte was determined to carry out the vision he had for his people. By the end of the first summer they numbered 1700, two hundred more than there were in the city of Grand Rapids, and two years later, when he wrote a long letter to both the United States Senate and House of Representative about improving harbor facilities, there were 3000. He was able to sell state leaders on his plans and to get them to serve on his committees. Former Governor, and later Senator, Lewis Cass and Judge John R. Kellogg were his friends. It was said that he was the dictator, pope, ruler, and owner of the whole *Kolonie*.

Dr. Van Raalte's remarkable leadership was not accepted with appreciation by everyone, unfortunately. There were those who resented his firm hand, strong will, and versatility. Though he had control of his emotions, his patience was sorely tried by some, and he was not always able to hide his feelings. He knew what had to be done and had the will to do it, and others lacked his clear vision, boundless energy, and determination. Or, if they had certain gifts, they did not have them in the variety and degree that he had them. Hence, there was bound to be friction. Thus it could be said by one who had been on the scene and, after Van Raalte's passing, had reflected long and hard:

> The town meeting in Holland was Van Raalte; the consistory in Holland was Van Raalte; the Holland Classis was Van Raalte, The state of affairs was such [in the early period of the colony] that it could not be otherwise; and, when all is said and done, it was well that it was that way. However, the unavoidable result was that, insofar as the adjustment of mutual coexistence was concerned, in all of this there was, to all intents and purposes, no appeal, and for the dissatisfied, rightly or wrongly, there was little else left but secession."[50]

A study of the secession of the 1850s in the *Kolonie* therefore leads to the conclusion that certain people are a part of the explanation for it. Among them was the great pioneer and leader at whose funeral the vice-president of the United States, pro tem, was present and concerning whom there is written on his memorial tablet the words ascribed to Jesus in Luke 24:19: *Mighty in Works and Words.*[51]

A third reason for the secession was the language question and the speed of Americanization. Seldom admitted, sometimes unconsciously affecting the attitudes and moods of people, they were nevertheless powerful factors in creating dissension and then schism within the Dutch communities. There is nothing more sensitive than language, which, for good reason, has been called "the soul of a people." Touch it and you touch that which lies deepest within. That was true in western Michigan. The *Kolonie* was not yet five years old when the language question first surfaced officially. At the spring meeting of classis in 1852 there was a complaint that "the pure use [of the Dutch language] is being lamentably lost, although all are convinced that the interests of religion make it absolutely necessary that this language, which cannot be dispensed with for many years, shall be kept up, in order that the preaching may not become ridiculous by reason of the mixing of languages." The same appears in the minutes of the seceded group where "the brethren consider it the highest necessity to preserve the Dutch language for generations, and the congregations are strongly urged to provide for instruction in the Dutch language . . . in school and preaching."[52]

It was a hopeless struggle, and the story has been repeated in hundreds of communities across the land. First in school, then here and there, and finally in church the new language takes over. Some accept the inevitable; others resist it, these latter conservatives determined to preserve this dear symbol of the old way of life, the liberal progressives willing, perhaps reluctantly, to make the necessary adjustments. The minutes of the various consistories record the grim struggle and the repeated voting until, at long last, there is acceptance. In the process people are pitted against each other and some have another reason for secession.[53]

The change of language, however, was but a symbol of a more subtle, more profound variation. It represented the giving up of much more than the mother tongue; it meant Americanization with its manifold implication. As the gradual displacement of the old language cast a gloom over some persons, the many other signs of cultural change brought feelings of impotence, frustration, anger, and grief. The story has been told often in the history of ethnic communities; here, where Calvinist religious fervor could burn white hot, the cultural clash could be severe. Zwaanstra records the struggle in the Christian Reformed Church.[54] The same occurred, in greater or lesser measure, in the various Dutch communities and contributed to their divisions.

Of great importance in this connection was Van Raalte's promotion of Americanization. A man of vision and cosmopolitan interests, he believed that the Dutch settlers should become good Americans. He worked hard to learn English from the day he boarded a ship for America, used it brokenly but unashamedly, felt genuine warmth toward many American friends, and encouraged his people to do the same. His patriotism was real and his enthusiasm for the new land was contagious, as is seen in the response within the *Kolonie* during the Civil War. Van Raalte's progressive attitude is reflected in the minutes of the Holland Classis just two years after the complaint lodged there about the loss of Dutch noted earlier. In the spring of 1854, the growing "American population of the village of Holland, and the influence of the same upon the young people, as also that a gradual passing over from Dutch to American (religious) services is necessary and natural" are noted. Classis requests the Reformed Church for an American preacher who can help in a variety of ways including "the religious education of the youth, work among the American population, and the gradual transition of our children to the American (religious) services." At the fall meeting of classis synodical approval of the request was recorded.

Not all were happy over the transition to English and the growing Americanization. This is seen in the attitude of many toward those of other denominations. Van Raalte's open attitude toward Presbyterians and Congregationalists irritated them even though these others too professed the Reformed faith. Worse, his friendship with Methodists, including Judge Kellogg of Allegan, and later toleration of a Methodist evangelist in *"De Stad,"* the city of Holland, bewildered some and incensed others. The different preaching style of the evangelist appealed to many, and Van Raalte, who could have prevented the intrusion but did not do so, was thought to have compromised the truth. Had he not declared earlier at classis, when the Reformed Church was accused directly and he by implication of laxity, that letters of dismissal from Methodists "are not accepted by the Dutch Church?"[55] Yet, he welcomed them and thus condoned their error, it was rumored.

Moreover, Van Raalte defended the practice of cooperation with other denominations in the production of Sunday school materials and occasional joint worship. Concerning the latter, he said that a Reformed church does not advocate or practice an "exaltation of itself" or "a hard and arrogant rejection of the other churches, but on the contrary, fraternal fellowship."[56] Van Raalte's six years of study at the University of Leiden and his wide circle of friends had given him breadth and a tolerance that others could not understand. His approval of "the East" was convincing proof that he was not to be trusted, and as early as August 22, 1853, it was reported at consistory in Holland that Van Raalte had been accused of bringing "the congregation into an impure church for the sake of money." The slander spread when it was recalled that the Reformed Church in the East had given the *Kolonie* repeated and substantial help over the years, much of it at the request of the colony, a fact which seems to have been forgotten. Rather than expressions of gratitude, what came from the lips of some was that they had been "sold out to the East for the sake of gold." Had the rank and file known the financial risks that Van Raalte took personally in borrowing large sums to buy land and to keep the colony afloat, and the energy he had expended in securing gifts from the church and laymen in the East for the new settlement and its college, the voices of the dissidents might have been quieted, but not altogether. From the time that some of the settlers stepped off the flatboat at the eastern end of Lake Macatawa it was evident that they would have difficulty adjusting to the new environment. As the colony developed these people increasingly resisted the pressures toward Americanization and contributed to the break with the Reformed Protestant Dutch Church in the East, a church which they felt had become thoroughly Americanized and hence tainted with corruption.

A fourth, and related, reason for secession was the desire of some for isolation and their consequent antipathy toward fraternization with outsiders. All, even Van Raalte, wanted a degree of isolation; that is why they had gone into the wilderness, to found a Christian settlement where, while close enough to railroads, seaports, markets, and some contact with the culture of the East, they would yet live in relative isolation so that they could develop their own religious and civil life in accord with what they conceived to be the will of God. To some, however, this meant no significant contacts with others, even with other

Christians. Klijn had stated this in his letter of secession; he wanted the Reformed immigrants to be "separated from all Protestant denominations . . . not to lose this [their] character." Others objected to cooperation in the production of Sunday school materials. The Polkton letter of secession gives as the reason therefor fraternization. Groen Van Prinsterer's famous saying, "In our isolation lies our strength," had been wrenched out of context and had become a slogan. The social ethic of Calvinism, which fosters a penetration of society in Christ's name, was being perverted; believers so devoted to missions that they originally wanted to go to Java "to work as missionaries with the whole of this colony," and then, after emigration to America, began building a missionary ship even before their fields were cleared, to preach the gospel overseas, were in danger of introversion; Calvinists, who should have known the cultural mandate, were losing their character by turning in on themselves.[57]

Not all, however. Nor was isolationism to be the continuing posture or ideal of the church that succeeded the original seceders. Evidence to the contrary is the present witness of the Christian Reformed Church in society and the labor of the president of its seminary.[58] Within the first decade of their life in America, however, and for some time afterwards, isolation and an antipathy towards fraternization with other Christians was a contributing factor to secession.

A fifth reason for secession was the singing of hymns and choral music. Although the latter had no place in the *Kolonie*,[59] American churches did have choirs, and there was concern that the practice might spread. Moreover, hymns were being sung in some Dutch churches and there was controversy over that practice.[60] The imposition of hymn-singing in the Netherlands in the new church order of 1816 had led many to associate hymns with everything else they disliked about the new arrangement. A hymn book, prepared by the authorities, was placed in the churches with the requirement that one or more hymns be sung at each service. The reaction was as might be expected and, when the Dutch migrated here, sentiment against hymn-singing was strong in some quarters. Klijn, in Grand Rapids, opposed them, as did the church at Graafschap and others in the colony. The matter sounds strange today, but it was a live issue at the time of settlement and for many years later.[61]

A sixth factor which contributed to the secession, one related to the problem of language and the speed of Americanization, and also to isolation and the relation to other Christians, was distance—geographically and culturally. It was a long way from western Michigan to New York or New Brunswick in the 1850s and, although the matter cannot be documented, it must have played a part in the thinking of the people. They felt far removed from the power centers of the church, and there was little of their kind of church life in between. "The East," found often in the literature, carried the connotation "far from us, distant, remote." Other than Van Raalte and a few others, the colonists must not have felt a real, inner connection with the church in the East. That is the strong impression that comes from a reading of the minutes of the congregations. The same is not conveyed in the minutes of classis, but Van Raalte was the clerk there, and it is his feeling that comes through. With that consciousness it was a short step for many to leave the Reformed Protestant Dutch Church, especially since there were also other reasons that made that decision appear desirable.

The geographical distance, however, was not as important as the cultural gap between East and West. Here were two groups, the one constituting the oldest church tradition in the country, the other a band of immigrants; the one speaking one language, the other a different one; the one the church of the Van Rensselaers, Livingstons, Roosevelts, and Martin Van Buren, the other living primitively in log houses struggling to get a start in the new world. The differences culturally were significant. Little wonder then that the two often felt far from each other, as is seen so clearly in the Freemasonry question, attitudes toward Americanization, and the singing of hymns. To think only of this last for a moment, one sympathizes with the bewilderment of some in "the East" who had heard about the stir incited by the use of hymns. In the Dutch Reformed tradition from the Synod of Wezel in 1568 up to the mid-nineteenth century, the General Synod had regulated church music, and synod had approved the use of hymns. With that in mind one appreciates the good sense—or impishness—of the comment: "Why a handful of Hollanders in the woods of Graafschap should dictate church music to the rest of the world is not clear."[62] The remark at least suggests the struggle necessary if co-existence were to be maintained within the one church.

Having considered non-theological factors that nudged people to division, it is necessary to note one or two theological concerns which played a role in the history under review. One was the need to distinguish fundamental from non-fundamental doctrine. Calvin had drawn that line earlier when he said that some doctrines are "necessary" whereas "there are other articles of doctrine disputed which still do not break the unity of faith."[63] That distinction is implicit in discussions at the Holland Classis and made explicit in the literature elsewhere.[64] Not all doctrinal error is of the same gravity. Baxter's weaknesses in sin and grace are not as serious as some other heresy. Belief in the triune God, in the biblical doctrine of redemption, and in the judgment to come are more basic in Christian understanding than Baxter's errors. When all doctrinal deviation is put on the same level, chaos ensues, for within a congregation there are various shades of understanding; not all understand everything aright. In fundamentals there must be agreement, at least implicitly; in non-fundamentals, as Professor N. M. Steffens of Western Seminary argued, there should be toleration and instruction. If that had been remembered, many family conflicts would have been avoided, and the *Kolonie* would have been blessed with a greater measure of peace.

A related consideration is the distinction between truth itself and our perception of it. Because we see through a glass darkly, humility is in order, as is the acknowledgement that we too may err. In the *Kolonie* this spirit was often lacking. Strong opinions were taken, and severe judgments were made which later reflection often showed to have been defective, but the damage had been done; children in Christ were injured and congregations were rent.[65] Much of this could have been avoided if the distinction mentioned above had been remembered.[66]

Having considered the theological and non-theological reasons for the secession from the Reformed Church in the 1850s, there remains the necessity of noting the later split in the colony over Freemasonry. Within a few years of their arrival in this country, some of the immigrants were disturbed over the rumors that were circulating about members of the Reformed Church, including office-bearers, being Freemasons. In evangelical and Roman Catholic church circles in America at this time there was considerable concern about alleged evils of secret, oath-bound societies in general and Freemasonry in particular. That concern found ready response in the hearts of Dutch immigrants whose European experience had predisposed them against such associations. In the Netherlands, Freemasonry was considered close to Deism and Unitarianism religiously and as existing outside the established church. Hence the rumors were disquieting to a growing number of people in the various communities. The matter came before classis in September of 1853 with the question "whether or not it is lawful for a member of the church to be a Freemason." The response was: "All look upon it [Freemasonry] as works of darkness, and thus unlawful for a [church] member." Although the matter was not to come before classis again for a period of years, it lay as a smoldering fire ready to burst into flames when the right winds would blow. Occasional puffs kept it alive, and in the late 1860s the sparks were fanned in both the Holland and Wisconsin classes. Overtures were sent to the General Synod requesting it "to deliver a distinct utterance of its disapprobation of the connection of the Lord's people with the Order of Freemasons, in order that the moral power of our whole Reformed Church may be against a great and growing evil." The response of the synod was agreement with a committee report which stated that "the uniform usage of the church has been to abstain from deliverance upon all abstract questions which are not purely ecclesiastical, or which may involve the exercise of consistorial discipline"; hence, no action. The vote was eighty-nine to nineteen.[67]

Dissatisfied by such evasion of an issue which was deeply disturbing its membership, the two classes repeated their overtures the next year. The response was given a year later and reads as follows:

> Our brethren are evidently sincere and earnest in their convictions. They are greatly perplexed on account of what they perceive to be a serious evil in the Church, and they have done well to state their difficulties. We cannot think, however, that they expect from Synod such a deliverance as would authorize Consistories to exclude Free Masons from church fellowship, for this would be to establish a new and unauthorized test of membership in the Christian Church, and would interfere with consistorial prerogatives.
>
> But at the same time your Committee believes that the path of prudence and safety lies outside of all oath-bound secret societies, in connection with which obligations may be exacted which conflict with the liberty of the individual Christian conscience.
>
> Moreover, they are convinced that the ordinances of the Christian religion, in connection with a divinely appointed ministry, if faithfully attended to, furnish all needful moral and spiritual culture, while the Christian Church possesses, in its holy teachings, and its pledges of mutual love, a far higher capacity for the development of practical benevolence than can be found in the moral lessons of any mere human organization.[68]

Although that answer failed to satisfy the petitioning classes, the matter did not come before synod again for a decade. In the meantime there were developments that served to heighten the tension between the two sections of the church. The church in the West was growing faster than was its ability to finance its operation, the college especially needing help from the older part of the denomination. Secondly, the Western classes became more vocal as they became stronger and began to feel at home in the new environment. Thirdly, an economic recession in the mid-1870s brought hardship to many, reducing revenues and fraying tempers. Fourthly, the fire that destroyed Holland in 1871 shook the entire *Kolonie* and set it back economically for more than a decade. Lastly, and most importantly, theological education in the West was discontinued. In order to understand the impact that this cessation of theological training had on the *Kolonie* it is necessary to understand the importance ascribed to such education by the immigrants. This could be demonstrated by references to memorials from the West, for that is where the want was felt, but let an eastern voice express the sentiment in the West for us. In a report to Synod by a special committee in 1879 the value of Hope College to the whole denomination is mentioned along with an appeal for more adequate funding for the school. Then the report states the importance of theology to the immigrants. David Cole is reporting:[69]

> The almost unanimous and deeply earnest desire of the Hollanders is for Theology. The whole colony had theological training for their young men before them as their supreme object in founding Hope College. It was not with the existence of Theology that they found fault in the past. They did not wish Theology removed. Their dissatisfaction was over matters entirely foreign to this. . . . With one heart they are anxious for the restoration of Theology. They do not want it *in* the College [as it had been from 1866 to 1877], but upon a separate foundation, so that no opening may be given for the entrance of discord. I am confident that signs of this will come out in some form of appeal to the present Synod.

The report goes on to make reference to the tension that has arisen within the church:

> Are the Hollanders loyal to the Reformed Church in America? I answer, Yes. A feeling has been engendered among them that our Church is not in sympathy with them, and they are in a sensitive condition upon this point. It is not difficult to understand how this has sprung up. The field is far from us at the East. Few of those who make our Eastern sentiment have seen it, and these have been bewildered for years by the conflicting reports they have heard and more especially still by the financial complications of the College. I myself recall the effect produced upon my own mind in back years by what I read and heard in reference to Hope College. Our Eastern men became tired of its very name. And our Holland brethren mistook the feeling that grew upon us. . . .

That same year irritation in the West reached a new high point and the ecclesiastical machinery of all four immigrant classes—Holland, Grand River, Wisconsin, and Illinois—was set in motion to petition the General Synod again concerning the old specter, Freemasonry. The overtures from the classes were supported by another from tbe Particular Synod of Chicago. Tension had reached a breaking point. Churches were represented as "disquieted and in danger of division"; their "condition is truly critical and intolerable"; rumors of imminent secession are denied; there is fear that Dutch immigrants will unite with another communion because of denominational hesitation in speaking out; and the difficulty of immigrant delegates at Particular or General Synods being "obliged to hear the Gospel preached and to receive the Communion from the hands of those whom we would disfellowship" [i.e., ministers who are Freemasons] is brought into the open.

Unlike the Synod of 1868 which had waved the issue aside as "abstract" and "not purely ecclesiastical," the Synod of 1880 declared the matter to be "not 'abstract,' but concrete" and that it touched "vital points of our faith and order and fellowship as a Church of Christ; and that it must needs be considered with the utmost circumspection and fidelity to all the great interest which it involves."

The rest of the report deserves full quotation:

> It must also be admitted that a subject which is so grave ought to have free and full discussion, and that no decision ought to be made upon it which does not respect the personal liberty, the rights of conscience and Christian obligations and privileges which are guaranteed to every minister and member of our Reformed Church by her Constitution, her doctrinal symbols, and her historic loyalty to freedom and to faith. Moreover, it is eminently proper and desirable for the Synod to declare that no other tests of church membership, and of Christian and ministerial fellowship should be applied than those which are set forth in our standards, and that church discipline, in all its shapes, must be taken in conformity with the Word of God and the established order of our Church. Your Committee believe, especially that in a matter which is so delicate and complicated as this, the ends which are sought for by the memorialists will be best secured by the power of Christian instruction and persuasion, and by Gospel principles faithfully applied, "with all longsuffering and meekness," and without strife or division, and without severity to those who may be 'out of the way.' Your Committee therefore recommend the adoption of the following resolutions:
>
> 1. *Resolved*, That this General Synod, after deliberate consideration of the memorials of the Classes of Holland, Wisconsin, Grand River and Illinois, do hereby recognize and appreciate with those bodies and the Churches which they represent, the practical difficulties and perplexities which are set forth in their respective papers.
>
> 2. *Resolved*, That while, on the *ex parte* evidence of the memorials now before it, this Synod cannot properly give its official testimony for or against Free Masonry and other oath-bound secret societies; and while it holds as sacred the indefeasible rights of all its ministers and members to their individual conscientious convictions and liberty of speech and action, subject only to their prior loyalty to Christ and to His Church, yet it hereby declares that no communicant member, and no minister of the Reformed Church in America ought to unite with or to remain in any society or institution, whether secret or open, whose principles and prac-

tices are anti-Christian, or contrary to the faith and practice of the Church to which he belongs.

3. *Resolved,* That this Synod solemnly believes and declares that any system of religion or morals whose tendency is to hide our Savior, or to supplant the religion of which He is the founder, should receive no countenance from His professed followers; and, furthermore, that no humane, benevolent or philanthropic, or reforming agency in this world can take the place of the Church of Our Lord and Savior Jesus Christ, whose principle is to 'do good unto all men, but specially to them that are of the household of faith,' and, therefore, that all who belong to this Church are induty bound to give it the preeminence over all orders or institutions, and to promote to the utmost of their power its unity, peace and prosperity, and especially its great charities and philanthropies.

4. *Resolved,* That this Synod also advises Consistories and Classes of the Church to be very kind and forbearing, and strictly constitutional in their dealings with individuals on this subject, and that they be and are hereby affectionately cautioned against setting up any new or unauthorized tests of communion in the Christian Church.[70]

Although the Synod of 1880 gave careful and courteous attention to the overtures on Freemasonry before it, the West remained dissatisfied and the classes of Holland, Grand River, and Wisconsin overtured the synod of 1881 in the same manner. That synod referred to the report of the previous year and then declared that the 1880 synod had gone "to the very extreme of its authority."

It must be borne in mind that the powers of the General Synod are limited; its jurisdiction and authority are a delegated jurisdiction and authority; the sources of which are primarily in the Churches, then with the Classes. The General Synod has no power to declare tenets of doctrine, nor to establish new tests of church membership; nor to effect any change in the Government or polity of the Church, save through the action of the constituency, in the manner prescribed in the Constitution.

The resolutions following reaffirm the actions of the synods of 1870 and 1880 "showing that the Synod, as such, does not sympathize with Free Masonry and other oath-bound secret societies," and that "it has neither the power nor the disposition to interfere with the prerogatives of the lower bodies in the exercise of discipline, except only in the manner prescribed by the Constitution." A third resolution, requesting that the issue be considered settled and warning against schims, failed.[71]

Synod had given clear reply on three occasions. It did not forbid local judicatories to use their own discretion in administering discipline, but it said that it had no right or power to do what the majority in the West wanted it to do, excommunicate Masons.

The result in the West was as might have been expected—some indifference, considerable disappointment, and some exasperation. The Classis of Holland alone lost 400 families by the time of the next synod.[72] Although the minutes of all the lower judicatories in the West tell the story, I select those of the two consistories with which my own life has been bound. At a consistory meeting in the Graafschap (now Central Park) Reformed Church on August 29, 1881, a resolution was adopted stating that if General Synod does not condemn Freemasonry "we shall be compelled to withdraw from being under the government of the Synod." When one recalls the numerous references to "independence" that appear in the literature,[73] the ominous character of that threat is seen. However, by February 6, 1882, a different judgment was rendered. There had been discussion of the rights of consistories and of the General Synod. Now one reads: "As long as we are not hindered in our leading of our congregation according to our conviction, we consider the threatened schism as a sin with which we can have nothing to do."

The story of the controversy over Freemasonry in Vriesland is the most dramatic in the *Kolonie*. Ever since the days of Haan, Dam, and Ulberg the community had been alerted to the dangers of affiliation with "the East." They had left in the earlier secession, but there were many in the Reformed congregation who wanted both to be faithful to the Old Dutch Reformed Church with its polity and teaching on church unity, and to hear a synodical condemnation of Freemasonry. Synod's repeated refusal to bar Masons from church membership by a synodical decree dispirited many in the congregation and angered others. Thus, on October 7, 1881, the consistory debated whether it would not "be better to break with the East so that in this way we may be spared a greater split." On October 18, at a special consistory meeting, a delegation from the congregation requested cutting ties with the East and letters of resignation from the consistory and congregation were received from two elders. On November 1 another elder left the church with his family. On December 16, three families requested that their names be struck from the roll. To all this the consistory responded that although it opposed oath-bound secret societies and raised its voice against them, "as long as we are not hindered in our congregational management in the carrying out of our calling according to our convictions, we view the threatened schism as sin, and we consider it an evil with which we may have nothing to do. Therefore, on the ground stated herein we do not break but preserve our affiliation with the Reformed Church and stir up all of our Holland Reformed Christians to preserve or to restore this unity with us in the same manner in the spirit of love." The consistory lamented the evils of Freemasonry and resolved to see the matter brought before synod yet again. At a meeting on December 23, when another family left, the illegality of a secret meeting of twenty-three members on December 10 was mentioned. A long resolution deplored the meeting and the secession of seventeen persons of those in attendance as "in conflict with Reformed Church government under which we stand." Members continued to leave monthly in 1882, with fifteen transferring to the Christian Reformed Church in Vriesland on August 18. At the same meeting the consistory petitioned the Board of Domestic Missions for a subsidy of $300 for 1883 because of the heavy loss of members and reduced income.

In taking the positions which they took with respect to honoring the judgment of the General Synod in its refusal to set conditions for church membership, the consistories of the Graafschap and Vriesland Reformed Churches—and other churches with them—were in accord with sound principles of Reformed church government. The admission, discipline, and dismissal of church members is committed to the elders of local congregations who fulfill their ministries under the constitution of the church. The addition of extra-biblical tests, or requirements, for church membership is possible but undesirable for, once a body of believers starts down that road, it is difficult to stop. Conditions for church membership set forth in Scripture are repentance toward God and faith in the Lord Jesus Christ, with subjection to the elders an implicit understanding. These should be the sole requirements for membership in any congregation of the one holy, catholic, and apostolic church.[74]

The Dutch Reformed Church in the Netherlands and in America had high appreciation for sound principles of church government. That is why the church order of 1816 in the Netherlands seems so out of character today. That is also why the secessions of the 1850s and 1880-82 were out of character for Reformed people and why using Wyckoff's "condition" of 1849 as at least partial justification for secession, as Graafschap did in 1857 and as other apologists have done later, is nonsense. It is true that Wyckoff told the colonists that if "at any time they found an ecclesiastical connection opposed to their religious prosperity and enjoyment," that they would be free to bid a "fraternal adieu, and be by themselves again."[75] The context of that remark, however, was the "galling chain of ecclesiastical domination" and the miserable "human rules . . . [and] oppression of tender consciences" from which they had just fled. Secession for the reasons given later was beyond the wildest imagination of the leaders of the *Kolonie* in 1850 and without justification.

After secession occurred, the new group limped along for a time. It received a leader of ability with the immigration of the Rev. D. J. van der Werp, who had been opposed to Van Raalte in the Netherlands and had been a member of a trio advocating a *new* secession within the seceding group there.[76] Not all immigrants were schismatics, however, and after the Synod of Zwolle—of 1882 in the Netherlands—favored the True Dutch Reformed Church, as the seceding group in this country, now known as the Christian Reformed Church, was called, most immigrants joined the latter and provided it with the leadership it needed. In adding their strength to the young church they gave it broader vision while retaining the ideal of "preserving Calvinism in a pure and undiluted form."[77] The inevitability of Americanization has wrought its changes in the new denomination as it has in its elder sister, and the future is bound to bring greater changes still. Whether those changes bring good or ill will depend on the faithfulness of both to their sovereign Lord who, by his grace, can fashion them according to his Word so that they are truly Reformed and, eventually—at the consummation, if not before—one.

V

Inspiration and Authority:
The Reformed Church Engages Modernity

Paul R. Fries

By chance, a bundle of cracked and yellow manuscripts had survived centuries of fire, flood, war, and revolution to allow a remarkable glimpse into daily life in a French mountain village. . . . The village was called Montaillou, and its local drama centered on the village priest. This tireless servant of the Lord appears to have construed his calling chiefly as ministering to the sexual needs of his female parishioners. Less literally carnal but equally worldly concerns preoccupied his flock. One thing strikes modern eyes as remarkable about this collection of rouges . . . Although they habitually flouted God's laws, wallowed in heresy, and thumbed their noses at God's Church, it never occurred to them to doubt His reality. The villagers faithfully performed the exercises of salvation, invoked Christ, the Virgin, and the saints, and sought absolution for their sins. By no stretch of the imagination did God obsess them, yet He framed their world.[1]

A generally accepted and therefore useful definition for the term "modernity" eludes even the most diligent reader of dictionaries, encyclopedias and scholarly books and articles. Yet without some grasp of what is meant by the word, any attempt to investigate the manner in which the Reformed Church in America has grappled with modernity must meet with frustration. Before turning to the principal task of this essay—which will be to analyze and evaluate the confrontation with modernity represented by two significant theological writings originating in the Reformed Church in America—a sketch of the manner in which modernity will be understood in the ensuing discussion need be provided. If a water tight definition is unavailable, an analytic description suitable for the purposes of this study can nevertheless be formulated.

The quotation standing at the head of this chapter concludes with a striking observation throwing considerable light on the concept of modernity. The sturdy peasants of Montaillou were irreverent and heretical and their priest immoral, yet the centrality of religion in their lives was beyond question for, as the author observes, God framed their world.

Modern women and men may be individually more pious, moral and orthodox than their medieval counterparts but ours is a different universe; religion no longer provides the structure, rhythms and boundaries of life. An anthropocentric frame has come to replace the theistic one which contoured human experience through the middle ages. The world now finds its definition and aspiration in itself rather than in that which transcends it; the *hominitas* (that which nature makes of us) and the *humanitas* (that which we make of ourselves) provide its horizon.[2] Modernity may be described as the progressive deconstruction on the basis of our given humanity (*hominitas*), through innumerable permutations, of a world configured by theistic faith and the corresponding attempts to achieve its reconstruction according to the visionary architecture of a truly human existence (*humanitas*). In modernity humanity has become both the standard and the goal.

Such an abstract formulation of the dialectics of modernity hardly captures the revolutionary character of this historical phenomenon. The term modernity describes a radical transformation in the western consciousness seeded at the time of the renaissance and reformation, coming to fruition through the cultural upheaval known as the enlightenment, and disseminated throughout the world in the 19th and 20th centuries. Today, virtually no nation or people remain untouched by its currents, especially those carrying its science, technology, and political theory. Modernity can be resisted and attempts made to escape it; such efforts will inevitably prove futile, however, for their outcome will be imprinted by the very cultural paradigm being repudiated. Those premodern elements which continue today are themselves shaped by their modern context. As our "epochal consciousness," to borrow Karl Jaspers' phrase, modernity is uniquitous and irresistible.[3] It *is* the social-cultural environment of our age.

Dietrich Bonhoeffer was perhaps the first theologian to recognize that modernity is not simply one current in twentieth century life but the river itself. The theology of secularization which was developed from his prison writings proved reductionistic and soon became outmoded, but Bonhoeffer's insights into the epochal consciousness of the age remain worthy of consideration. Employing a phrase introduced by the Dutch jurist, Hugo Grotius, Bonhoeffer recognized that in our time knowledge and value are no longer grounded in an appeal to some transcendent reality, but are established in such a way that they remain valid *etsi Deus non daretur* (even if there were no God). The world must make sense on its own, both in regard to understanding (epistemology) and action (ethics); other-worldly theories and constructs are strictly forbidden. The implications of Bonhoeffer's analysis suggest that

God has not become an *unnecessary* hypothesis for epistemology and ethics so much as an *impermissible* one. No longer can God be identified as a cause in the understanding of natural phenomena; his immutable will regarded as the foundation of jurisprudence; the biblical call to fear and honor him; the rationale for education; nor the decalogue claimed as the cement of social morality. Modernity does not dislocate God on the baiss of doctrinaire atheism or anti-religious polemic, but because women and men must be free from those religious encumberances which bind them if they are to take full responsibility for their world. Obedience, even to God, removes accountability. If modernity is functionally agnostic, it is so in the name of human hope (*humanitas*).

The deconstruction of the *Weltanschauung* shaped by faith could occur only through an early, persistant and perduring challenge to authority as it was understood and exercised in the old order. Where Roman Catholicism prevailed, the conflict centered on the authority of the church and its magisterium; when the ethos was determined by Protestant theology the classical understanding of the veracity and authority of scripture came under fire. While frontal attacks on the Bible by those committed to debunking "superstition" in the name of reason, nature or science gained considerable notoriety, more profound subversions of the Protestant doctrine of scriptural authority came through the application of overtly neutral critical methods expressing the presuppositions of modernity.

It can be no coincidence, for example, that the formulator of the *etsi Deus non daretur* mentioned above, Hugo Grotius (1583-1645), was also a poineer of the modern critical method. Grotius' commentary on the Bible, *Annotations*, strikes the modern reader as remarkable for a number of reasons, including its spurning of the favored allegorical method in the interpretation of the Song of Solomon, its expression of doubt concerning the historicity of Esther and its refusal of the Pauline authorship of Hebrews. The most arresting feature of Grotius' criticism, however, is found in the contention that the books of the Bible (at least the Old Testament) must be studied in the same manner and through the application of the same critical tools as any other ancient text. No theological *a priori* may be imposed on the study of scripture; the Bible must be allowed to speak for itself. The critical study of texts written by Moses would be no different in method from those written by Homer.

When Thomas Hobbes, another precursor of modern criticism, investigated the nature of biblical authority in his *Leviathan* (1651), he approached scripture with the freedom exhibited in Grotius' *Annotations* (which he had probably read), but with an even more penetrating exploration of their human composition. The scriptural texts themselves must yield answers to questions of date, authorship and purpose. Sounding more like a contemporary biblical scholar than a 17th century philosopher, Hobbes concludes that Moses could not have written the last six verses of Deuteronomy, and that, in fact, the entire pentateuch must have been composed after his death. Further, Hobbes determines, the book of Joshua appeared long after the warrior's demise, Judges was not produced until after the captivity and Samuel, Kings, and Chronicles were clearly post-exilic. Such radical judgments could be drawn because Hobbes denied that the Bible *per se* constituted revelation; it was rather the record of revelation. Approaching scripture armed with dogma, institutional authority, or prior determinative spiritual illumination was disallowed; only the exercise of reason, the common property of all human beings, could be permitted. Both the measure of the Bible and the instrument of its interpretation were located in the *hominitas*.[4]

The development of criticism since the pioneering work of Grotius and Hobbes has been long and complex, moving on many fronts and displaying myriad approaches, but the entire history turns on the two axes found in their writings, *viz.*, the Bible must be studied like any other ancient document and interpreted by the use of those critical tools which are given to humanity by nature. True, most critics believe the Bible to be inspired and confess that God's revelation is found in it. Such acts of faith, however, can no more play a substantive role in the critical method of scriptural investigation than can the belief in God the creator be allowed as a methodological factor in the physicist's explorations of a natural phenomenon. Modern criticism is both the child and mid-wife of modernity.

No indictment of biblical criticism is intended by the suggestion that it grew out of modernity. Indeed, the purpose of biblical criticism is to disclose the secrets of ancient texts, and this can occur only when the terms on which documents from the past are investigated and questions placed before them are formed from the substance of the modern consciousness. At the same time, the appearance of an analytical approach which categorically refused all theological *a prioris* obviously precipitated a crisis for those who regarded the human aspect of scripture incidental to the divine purpose. How can a book which according to the prescriptions of modern criticism must be viewed as the product of fallible human beings and which consequently contains faulty historical accounts, scientific impossibilities and internal incongruities yet be regarded as the infallible word of God? Little wonder that widespread alarm was registered in the second half of the 19th century when higher criticism migrated from the universities of the continent to the theological schools of America. The doctrines of verbal inspiration and biblical

inerrancy became the chief line of defense against the new criticism—
a strategy which would prove as effective as the construction of the
Maginot line in France after the first world war. Not all scholars and
theologians, of course, rejected the higher critical method. Increasingly
under fire for their views, these "modernists" were pressed to demonstrate how the revelational authority of scripture could withstand the
dissection of modern criticism. The lynchpin of the controversy came
to be the doctrine of inspiration, the conservatives claiming that the
doctrine of a verbally inspired Bible assured inerrancy and precluded
higher criticism; the liberals asserting that, to the contrary, the critical
method was fully compatible with the doctrine of an inspired Bible.
Controversialists on both sides of the question poured out their views
in a flood of pamphlets, articles, speeches and books.[5]

The Reformed Church in America was spared the violent upheavals
which shook many denominations during the period arching the turning
of the last century. Nonetheless, the problem of biblical inspiration was
before the church and could not be ignored. Two historically important
and theologically innovative essays appeared in the Reformed Church
in America during this period, each attempting, in its own way, to
articulate a doctrine of scripture demonstrating that the Bible viewed
through the analytical lenses of higher criticism could still be confessed
as the inspired word of God. The theologians whose writings will come
under examination in the following paragraphs—John de Witt and Albertus Pieters—represent both the older eastern church (De Witt) and
the younger congregations of the 19th century Dutch immigration to
the midwest (Pieters). The controversies surrounding the writings of
these theologians have grown obscure, but the fundamental question
each addressed, *mutatis mutandis*, remains consequential for those living in the final decades of the twentieth century: how can a doctrine of
biblical authority be developed which is not threatened by higher criticism? The question can be sharpened on the basis of the conclusion
drawn above that such criticism is a predicate of modernity: the issue
then becomes how an articulation of biblical authority can be achieved
which proves credible to the modern consciousness.

When John De Witt (1821-1906) wrote *What is Inspiration* (1893),
the fires of controversy had already been kindled in the Presbyterian
Church over the issue of the inspiration of the Bible. George Marsden
describes the turmoil erupting in that body:

> In the meantime conservatives counterattacked by bringing in succession
> formal action against three of the most famous of the progressive seminary
> professors, Charles A. Briggs, Henry Preserved Smith, and Arthur Cush-
> man McGiffert. By the end of the decade all three had left the Presby-

terian church as a result of these actions. Union Theological Seminary in
New York severed its ties with the denomination in 1892 in response to
the General Assembly's action against Prof. Briggs. Although some broad
issues of departure from Calvinist orthodoxy were involved, in each case
the specific allegations concerned the narrow issue of inerrancy. On several occasions during the decade the General Assembly declared that the
doctrine of inerrancy was a fundamental teaching of the church.[6]

Although not Presbyterian, De Witt's treatise was triggered in part by
the difficulties of Professors Smith and Briggs.[7] Written shortly after his
retirement from the faculty of New Brunswick Theological Seminary
(1892) in a florid homiletical style often obscuring the theological sophistication and acumen of the work, De Witt defends the critical method
by demonstrating that only by its employment can the true nature of
biblical revelation emerge. The higher critical method "has most to do
with the human element in the Bible" and its use demands that scripture
be examined "on such scientific principles as are commonly applied to
very ancient books. . . ."[8] When this method is put in effect, the errors
of scripture become evident and the historical conditioning of the writers—leading at times to the attribution of moral barbarism to God—
clearly perceived. Paradoxically, the mistakes and incongruities of the
Bible do not obscure but clarify its revelational purpose for they allow
a certain advance in teaching to be discerned. Accommodating the lim-
itations of primitive peoples, God revealed only as much as their simple
minds could grasp; future generations build on the crude articulations
found in the oldest texts until in the fulness of time the world was
prepared for the perfect revelation of God through the teachings of his
son, Jesus Christ. Higher criticism, then, exposes the historical evolution of God's work among his people and shows divine revelation to be
progressive: "historical progression, implying earlier insufficiency, is a
leading characteristic of the divine method of inspiration."[9]

Here De Witt shows his debt to 19th century thought with its at-
traction to evolution and the doctrine of progress. But he is also a son
of his age in the manner in which he understands the purpose of revelation and the *telos* of divinely guided evolution:

> God here, as everywhere, works from within in steadfast advance toward
> an ideal, not only in the outer world, but in man his living image. It all
> leads to a bright outshining in the far away future. We shall claim more
> distinctly by and by, that the production of a perfect humanity, at first
> in an individual, and afterward through him in the race—is the ruling
> purpose of the whole revelation and gives character and method to the
> inspiration that produced it.[10]

This historical movement toward perfection is not some sort of blind mechanical process, acting on a passive humanity, for "it is in accordance with all analogies in moral renovation by fresh communication of truth, that if man is thus restored, the renovating truth must first be grasped . . . by his intellectual and rational faculties. . . ."[11] By grasping the truth given progressively in revelation, the race gradually moves toward the full and perfect humanity exhibited by Jesus Christ and taught by his pronouncements.

De Witt's doctrine of progressive revelation suggests gradations of divine disclosure within scripture and he does not falter before this implication, bluntly labeling certain portions of the bible inferior to others.[12] The Old Testament receives particularly harsh treatment. He argues "that whatsoever in the Old Testament revelation, or in any professed revelation from God, is not in accord with the revelation of his righteousness, or purity, or love, or truth, in the words and life of Christ, has been annulled and superseded, and is practically no revelation for us."[13] This judgment, repeated at several points in his argument, does not apply only to the Old Testament, but to every part of the Bible excepting the words of Jesus and the witness of the gospels. These establish the norm. Indeed, all other parts of the Bible are gauged according to their congruity with the witness of the evangelists to Christ, but since the remainder of the New Testament reflects more perfectly (and is thus freer from crude and barbaric teachings, moral ambiguities and various kinds of errors) the life and teachings of the Lord, it receives gentler treatment. "The New Testament, in distinction from the Old Testament is *our own* revelation of God. . . . The revelations of the far past belong to us only partially and indirectly. . . ."[14] The Old Testament is revelation only to the degree it reflects Christ; it is not "self-luminous nor self-assertive. It shines with no dim luster, yet with light other than its own."[15]

What then is inspiration for John De Witt? The definition provided near the conclusion of the book strikes the modern reader as labored and fastidious—taking great pains to eliminate loopholes and loose ends.[16] Its quintessence, however, can be stated simply and in few words. For De Witt inspiration derives from revelation (and not the reverse). Those who provide faithful accounts of God's revelation leading to its culmination in Jesus Christ are inspired by the Spirit and their words provide sure guides—De Witt employs the word "infallible"—for faith and practice. Revelation, as has been shown above, points to and mediates the true humanity; the Bible presents the unfolding of the divine strategy for a genuinely human existence. By treating scripture like any ancient document, higher criticism allows for a separation of the kernel from the chaff and thus exposes God's progressive work in history. Apart from the critical method the grand design remains invisible. Those refusing higher criticism must remain blind to the configurations of the divine plan. The two elements of modernity identified above come into full dialectical relationship in De Witt's theology; the critique made possible by the *hominitas* discloses hope for the final emergence of the *humanitas*.

At first view, the theological topography of *The Inspiration of the Holy Scripture* seems to locate Albertus Pieters on a confessional terrain sharply dissimilar from that occupied by John De Witt. Delivered as a lecture in 1925, this essay is obviously occasioned by issues raised by higher criticism but makes no effort to deal with them directly. Its purpose is rather to elucidate and provide a modern apology for that article of faith which confesses the books of the Old and New Testaments as the inspired word of God. De Witt utilizes a theology of history by which human perfection is evolved to establish a critical principle for his doctrine of inspiration; Pieters' critical concern may be found in his more conservative objective of preserving those venerable doctrines (e.g., the atonement, resurrection, pre-existence of Christ, the second coming) which in his view are foundational to the Christian faith.[17] De Witt sought to establish the biblical basis for the moral transformation of humanity while Pieters, the former missionary, desired a solid footing for those doctrines necessary for the conversion of the race. In De Witt's writings everything aspires to the realization of the *humanitas*, a concern virtually absent from Pieters' explorations of inspiration. Pieters surely would have been suspicious of a theology like De Witt's heavily debted, as it was, to 19th century German thought. Indeed, the only strident note sounded in an otherwise irenic essay is elicited by Pieters' annoyance with modernists.

> But are there not at the present time . . . men who declare themselves to be Christians, and who yet reject the inspiration and authority, not to say, to a large extent, the historical truth, of the Bible? There certainly are. We call them "Modernists". . . . Without judging of any man's inward spiritual state, we may confidently say, in the light of history and logic, that such men are of two kinds;—first, those who think clearly and know where they are going and those who do not. The former will be found usually to have thrown overboard everything distinctive of Christianity as a historical religious system. The others, who do not think clearly, and do not know where they are going . . . are intellectual tightrope walkers. . . .[18]

A close reading of *The Inspiration of the Holy Scriptures*, however, discloses that Pieters too is playing on the fields of modernity. Indifferent to the *humanitas*, Pieters stands nearer to De Witt than might be expected in his employment of what is signified in this essay by the word *hominitas*. Biblical authority finds sure footing through the doctrine of inspiration; the doctrine of inspiration is established not by the critical method as in De Witt, but by a retrospective process of historical reason. In a key passage Pieters presents his method:

> We hold (inspiration) on various grounds both of experience and of evidence, but first of all by intelligently retracing the path by which this conception has come down to us; that is, by living over again, through historical study, the days in which the revelation appeared.[19]

Experience, evidence and historical study—all in the realm of natural capacity—but remarkably no mention of the testimony of the Holy Spirit which Pieters acknowledges to be the corner stone of the doctrine in the Belgic Confession,[20] but which he affords no better than "supplementary" status.[21] Pieters' interest centers not in divine confirmatory action, but in an *apologetic* for inspiration, and while no friend of modernism, his campaign draws him inexorably into the encampments of modernity.

Not that Pieters expected the use of historical reason to convict the unbelieving world. His apologetic is forged to serve the needs of the believing community. To his credit, implicit in the essay is the recognition that articles of faith must "make sense" to Christians in the same way as other things in their world. In a time when the methods of scientific and historical reason are regnant, this means the application of such reason to the Christian apologetic. The analogy employed is strained, but the use of retrospective historical reason is clearly defined when Pieters argues that to "live over again the historical process by which the faith arose, is as vital to an intelligent and reasonable faith in the inspiration of the Holy Scriptures as recalculation of the Newtonian formula is to an intelligent faith in the law of gravitation."[22]

How can the doctrine of inspiration be tested by entering "the historical process by which the faith arose?" Pieters provides detailed instructions. The allegedly inspired documents must be tested for authenticity, veracity, authorship, and date, using the resources of historical and textual criticism. When such an examination is impartially undertaken, Pieters believes, the verdict will be that the books of the Bible were written by honest men and that they are authentic and reliable. The next step in Pieters' apologetic prescription calls for the examination of the contents of the books of scripture. This investigation will reveal the prophetic claims made by Christ and his apostles. Jesus does not present himself as another Old Testament prophet speaking God's revelatory word; Jesus is presented by the New Testament as revelation. Pieters' comments that "the presence of such claims upon the pages of the gospels and epistles forces a choice of attitudes. We must either deny these claims or admit them."[23] There is no question where the author stands. "For myself, I can not get away from the conviction that the New Testament documents are true and reliable history; quite apart from and prior to any faith in their divine inspiration."[24] Remarkably, Pieters contends "It seems to me that only a man who on 'a priori' philosophical grounds is stubbornly resolved not to believe in a miracle can void the conviction of the truth of the resurrection."[25] If certainty is available on the basis of historical reasoning apart from the doctrine of biblical inspiration, one may ask if the doctrine is necessary in the first place. Be that as it may, the critical teaching of the New Testament concerning the resurrection is credible because scripture is historically reliable. Once the truth of the resurrection is established, the doctrine of inspiration becomes secure for both Old and New Testaments.

> If the resurrection of Christ is once admitted, everything goes with it. Then Christ is what he claimed to be, the Son of God and the Revealer of the Father. . . . No sooner do we accept Him in this way than two things become apparent: firstly, that He appointed the apostles to be the responsible and authoritative founders of the church . . . secondly, that both Jesus and the apostles point us back to the Old Testament as God's book. . . . Therefore, we cannot consider ourselves His disciples and yet reject the inspiration of the Old Testament.[26]

A retrospective process of reinactments, then, convinces the unbiased person that the books of the Bible are trustworthy. Since these books include testimony that Jesus Christ has been raised from the dead, thus confirming his divine nature and mission, it may be concluded that when he spoke, he spoke the truth. Since Jesus regarded the books of the Old Testament as inspired, then their inspiration can not be contested.

As unconvincing as this circular argument proves to be, there are two features of Pieters' work on inspiration worthy of note. The first is that he understood that Christians do not live in a vacuum; believers also imbibe the epochal consciousness and thus require that the grammar of faith be expressed through modern syntax. The second virtue of Pieters' effort appears in his respect for historic Christian doctrine. As noted above, he was concerned to preserve Reformed teaching on such matters as the atonement, resurrection, second-coming, and also on the inspiration and canonicity of the Old Testament.

On the debit side, Pieters lacked the hermeneutical sensitivity characteristic of De Witt. The mid-western theologian asserts that the discipline of historical research confirms the inspiration of the scripture but says nothing of the significance of that judgment for the articulation of faith in the modern age. De Witt has understood the cruciality of such an enterprise and in attempting to demonstrate that the critical method clears the way for an understanding of the message of the Bible which strikes the deepest cords of modern existence establishes the doctrine of inspiration. But De Witt's strength is also his weakness; he over-identifies with the cultural currents of the day, slighting a complex of doctrines foundational to the historic Christian faith. Both men, then, have failed in their efforts to produce arguments which are truly convincing. Pieters is unsuccessful finally not because of his contrived method and circular argument, but because of his failure to set the question of inspiration in a hermeneutical context. De Witt is unsatisfying for other reasons; his work for its intelligence and sophistication seems dated not only because his hermeneutic was too closely tied to the now repudiated belief in progress, but more importantly because it found no place for the seminal doctrines of the Christian faith. At the same time gratitude to both theologians is called for. They not only were courageous in tackling a difficult, complex and controversial subject, but both the success and failure of their works help define an issue which is yet before the church. How can a doctrine of scripture be formulated which retains the foundational doctrines of the faith (Pieters) and at the same time provides a hermeneutic which makes it credible to the modern mind (De Witt)?

This question can be fruitfully pursued only when it is recognized that behind the turn-of-the-century debates over inspiration stood a deeper and more strategic concern. The assumption, implicit in the writings of both De Witt and Pieters, that a sound doctrine of inspiration establishes and protects the authority of scripture was shared by most of their contemporaries. The investment of the doctrine of inspiration with this formidable responsibility was dubious from the outset; a world structured according to the *etsi deus non daretur* could hardly acknowledge the plausibility of a claim for biblical authority grounded in any understanding of divine intervention. Had the question of inspiration been by-passed and the problem of the authority of scripture directly addressed, a needless diversion could have been avoided and a more productive encounter between the Reformed Church and modernity achieved.

This conclusion finds confirmation in the history of the church since the "battle for the Bible" subsided. No longer does the Christian community hotly debate the doctrine of inspiration, and yet the problem of scriptural authority rises from every quarter. There would be no exaggeration in saying that the critical issue, *sine qua non*, for the church today is religious authority. The question framed at the conclusion of the previous section pertaining to the credibility of scripture in the age of modernity will necessarily resolve itself in the unraveling of the problem of authority. How can the Bible carry authority for the epochal consciousness of our time?

Discussions of authority in the church have often failed to recognize that through this epochal consciousness the understanding and function of authority has been transformed. Authority once found its ground in the divine being or will, and thus in a sacred order, holy law, or metaphysical system. The claims for authority were regarded as absolute. This conception of authority prevailed not only in religious systems but also undergirded law, government, values, morals and ethos. Modernity permits no such transcendent ground for authority; its claims too must be established *etsi Deus non daretur*. In the house modernity has built, authority must be constructed on "this worldly" foundations. Here too the new epochal consciousness has triggered a major shift in understanding. Any meaningful discussion of biblical authority must take this reorientation into consideration.

Like the term modernity, authority is more easily used than defined. For the purposes of this essay authority may be regarded simply as legitimated power. Power is the capacity to work some sort of change—in the material world, in the actions of people, or even in their thinking—and when that capacity carries with it legitimacy it may be designated as authority. A mugger with a gun exercises power; he can work change on his victims' thoughts, words and action. He, however, possesses no authority. A policeman can effect the same changes in a citizen, not because he carries a weapon (if the citizen is basically law abiding no weapon will be needed), but because within certain limits he has the right to command change—he possesses authority. His use of power has been legitimated by law and delegated through government. The authority of law and government, in turn, derive from a number of factors, the most fundamental of which is the consent of the people. Not all authority, however, is based on jurisprudence. In addition to *constituted* authority, possessed alike by policeman, senator and president, there is what might be designated *operational* authority.[27] Operational authority is discovered among those persons in our society who may have no legal charter, but who "make things work." The mechanic who warns a customer not to drive his automobile until the brakes are fixed, the cardiologist who advises her patient to change his diet and begin a program of exercise, the investment counselor who recommends the purchase of certain properties to a client—all these exercise operational authority. The legitimation of operational authority occurs through the consent of those who recognize the importance of such activities for the benefit of society. Yet a third type of authority, labeled *noetic*, may be identified. Our culture exhibits a large appetite for knowledge and values those who provide it. The psychiatrist who unravels the mysteries of human behavior, the astronomer tracing the enigmas of far-reaching galaxies, the poet or novelist fathoming the deepest recesses of the human heart—all provide instances of noetic authority.

Obviously these three types of authority overlap and are mutually supportive. But they are also linked in a more essential manner; they are not only congruent with the *etsi Deus non daretur*, but participate in the *hominitas* and *humanitas*. Our age no longer measures claims to authority by transcendental religious or metaphysical systems but gauges the use of power according to its engagement of the human enterprise. It values and legitimates that which provides an understanding of who we are and a promise of what we may become. Any authority which can not offer such will prove anemic no matter how strong its formal claims. This applies not only to secular expressions of authority but religious ones as well. The Pope can fulminate against the use of artificial means of birth control until his face is as red as a cardinal's mitre, but millions of the faithful will continue to ignore his strictures because even devout Roman Catholics can no longer accept an interpretation of sexuality based on a theory of natural law (*hominitas*), nor the vision of the ideal family constructed from it by their church (*humanitas*). Our age invests that which serves humanity with authority and denies it when convinced that no human good is advanced. The church possesses no immune system to protect it against the humanization of authority; religious authority, too, is a child of its age.

This suggests the need for what might be called a humanistic reading of scripture. De Witt was correct in recognizing that the hope for a transformed humanity (*humanitas*) shapes the modern consciousness and that a Christianity which could speak convincingly to this hope would speak with authority. But does such a humanistic hermeneutic "sell-out" to the secularism of our day, or at best compromise the fundamental teachings of the faith? As noted above, Pieters feared as much and De Witt's theology is clearly vulnerable at this point. Can a humanistic hermeneutic credible to the modern mind, and at the same time true to a confessional understanding of scripture, be developed?

The answer to this question is "yes" for the compelling reason that the concern for a truly human existence is not extraneous to the Bible, but stands at its very center. The Bible is the book of humanity *par excellence*. Writing in another context, the author of this article has attempted to frame those seminal issues of life which have occupied thoughtful men and women from the beginning of history: "if human existence is not what it might be, not what it *ought* to be, *what* in fact should it be, *why* is it not what it could be, *where* is its locus to be sought, *how* is it to be achieved or appropriated? In short, for what can mankind hope?"[28] The issues of human existence are precisely the concerns which occupy the scriptures and they are presented by the Bible in a manner which reveals both the fathomless mystery and the tragic ironies of life. But when speaking profoundly of the human situation the Bible also speaks of God. Absolutely no contradiction is contained in the assertion that the Bible is the Word of God and at the same time the book of humanity. The assumption that a "this-worldly-theology" must be purged of all transcendence owes more to Kant than to scripture or Christian tradition which acknowledge no such dichotomy. When biblical writers grapple with the human condition and struggle to find signs of hope, like Jacob they wrestle with God. And conversely, when the authors of scripture speak about God, unlike philosophers who play on the fields of pure ideas, they immediately fill their narrative with talk about humanity. Indeed, the Bible may accurately be described as a book 100% about humanity. But with equal truth, it may be represented as a book 100% about God. Biblical humanism, consequently, ought not be confused with the "secular humanism" of our times. It is *theonomous* and *trinitarian*.

A humanistic reading of the Bible will be unable to shrug-off the Old Testament in the easy manner of nineteenth century theologians such as Schleiermacher and Harnack (and De Witt who, as we have seen, stands in their company). Like some enormous stage extended in time rather than space, the Old Testament offers a prolonged drama with any number of acts and actors, the action illuminated by the light of Yahweh's presence which exposes the sins, vices and stupidities of the characters and yet at the same time heals those whom it searches. Existence in the Old Testament is played out in life's many arenas, and on its pages appear those myriad configurations which give structure, order, meaning and vitality to the human enterprise, e.g., law, government, politics, trade, business, economics, marriage, family, clan, education, and religion. Not just the individual, but all that comprises life must submit to the law and judgment of God and be claimed for his promise and purpose. If the puzzles of life remain unsolved something better than a solution is offered: the covenant fidelity of God pledged to bless first Israel and then the whole created order with the divine *shalom*. Not judgment but promise constitutes the final word of the Old Testament. Salvation will transform the earth, God's kingdom will be manifested and a new heaven and new earth will be created. The texts of the Old Testament sparkle with the promise of a new humanity.

The New Testament also proclaims God's promise for the salvation of the earth, but with concentration and enunciation found nowhere in the Old. The stage shrinks, time becomes compressed, but the action burns with an intensity previously unknown in scripture. The icon for the new and true humanity now is seen to be Jesus, the second Adam, who accomplishes through his crucifixion and resurrection what he images. On the cross he judges and redeems all that is sub-human and by his resurrection appears as the first fruits of the new age (humanity) and thus signifies the creation of a new heaven and a new earth. The broad promises of the Old Testament find their realization in Jesus Christ. The hope, "encapsulated" in the life and work of the Lord, dissolves in the medium of history through the working of the Holy Spirit. Thus, with Pentecost the action moves to yet a third stage—not the Israel of the Old Testament but the whole of the created order—as the Spirit brings the kingdom of Christ into time by creating signs of the Lord's salvific rule which not only point to, but *are* in anticipatory form, the new humanity.

A humanistic reading of the Bible which is both trinitarian and theonomous, then, represents no imposition of scripture, but an unfolding of its meaning *vis a vis* the epochal consciousness of our time. The modern yearning for the *humanitas* vibrates at the same frequency as the ancient proclamation of the *shalom* of Yahweh and the New Testament's hope in Christ. The hum of the biblical promise may even be discerned by those who listen carefully in the programs of secular humanism and the ideology of marxism. Indeed, as René Coste indicates, there is a certain convergence of Marxist and Christian hope:

> The ambition of Marxism . . . is to produce a new type of human being in full bloom, at least in the context of the classless society of its projected utopia. This ambition is shared by Christianity—and Christianity does not localize it in relation to the initial conversion to Jesus Christ and the sacramental experience of baptism, which together signify a radical transformation of existence. "You have put on a new nature," St. Paul wrote to the Colossians, "which is being renewed in knowledge after the image of its creator" (3:10).

> It could certainly be objected that there are radical differences in the levels of meaning and in the concrete goals of Marxist anthropology as compared with Christian anthropology. The overall goal remains nonetheless identical in purpose: the total fulfillment of the human being.[29]

Seeking the same objective, Marxism and Christianity nonetheless move on different trajectories. But let it be noted that the context between

Marx and Jesus does not center in the struggle between unbelief and faith. It turns rather on the question of the "total fulfillment of the human being." Which offers the best promise of a truly human world, the dictatorship of the proletariat or the Lordship of God in Christ through the Spirit? By arguing for God without contending for humanity the church has conceded the point and in so doing surrendered much of her authority.

Should modernity have run its course as some believe, and the world now have entered its post-modern phase, the same appeal for a humanistic reading of the Bible must be made. Gibson Winter, one of those who anticipates the demise of modernity has attempted to demonstrate the inherent contradiction in the paradigm showing that its excessive rationalizing of life (based on what is referred to as the *etsi Deus non daretur* in this essay) is a product of Augustinian theology which combines a fallen world with a sovereign God and leads not to the *humanitas* but its opposite. The restoration of the truly human in the mechanistic world of modernity may be achieved, according to Winter, by pursuing analogs to the process of artistic creation.[30] Exploring another area, the philosopher Stephen Toulmin discusses the appearance of post-modern science. Unlike other aspects of modernity, science in our time has defined itself in terms of an objectivity which cuts it off from human considerations; post-modern science, by contrast, attempts to "reinsert humanity into nature."[31] Instead of looking at the world of nature as outsiders, "we now have to understand how our own human life and activities operate as elements within the world of nature and the world of humanity. . . ."[32] This will bring with it the possible reunion of natural science and natural theology.[33] It is precisely at the point of the reintegration of religion with what has been regarded as secular that Harvey Cox's recent celebration of the post-modern finds its genesis. Writing in the Introduction to his *Religion in the Secular City,* Cox states "This is a book about the unexpected return of religion as a potent social force in a world many thought was leaving it behind."[34] But for the Harvey Cox of the 1980's, in contrast to the position he maintained in his first considerations of secularization, religion is not antithetical to the *humanitas,* but rather engenders it. Now it is no longer a religionless theology of secularization which offers the promise of a truly human existence, but a post-modern religious liberation theology.

While the author of this essay finds the post-modern return to religion for the sake of humanity congenial, having himself written on religion as the *conditio sine qua non* for a truly human existence,[35] the task of this study has been to inquire into the encounter of the Reformed

Church in America with modernity. We have traced the efforts of De Witt and Pieters to defend the authority of scripture by developing doctrines of inspiration compatible with the modern critical method and thus with modernity itself. While grateful for these efforts, we have also determined that the authority of scripture can not be established in the modern world (or post-modern, for that matter) by a doctrine pointing to the divine origin of the books of the Bible and have appealed for a scriptural hermeneutic which would "make sense" in terms of the regnant paradigm of the epoch. If in fact, the epochal consciousness is in the process of transformation, the need for a theonomous and trinitarian humanistic reading of scripture is not obviated, for every indication would suggest that post-modernity, like modernity, will be preoccupied with the question of a genuinely human existence. The medieval view in which God framed the world is gone forever. Now the *humanitas* provides its boundaries. Rather than lament this and live out of theological nostalgia, the church now may seek to discover God at the center of life. The church, including the Reformed Church in America, seems scarcely to have encountered modernity. Perhaps a happier verdict will one day be delivered concerning its engagement of post-modernity.

VI

Prose and Poetry:
Reformed Scholarship and Confessional Renewal

I. John Hesselink

While the Reformed Church in America has produced gifted scholars and teachers throughout its history, apart from a few notable exceptions it did not begin to make a significant impact upon the American theological scene until the 1960s. Prior to that time Reformed Church scholarship was directed more toward parochial concerns. Accordingly, it received little attention in academic circles.

In the 1960s, however, an unprecedented number of significant studies by Reformed Church authors appeared. Rather suddenly, a denomination known more for its preachers and missionaries began to make an impact on the scholarly world. This was enhanced in the next two decades by the increasing participation and leadership of RCA scholars in academic societies and in their contributions to scholarly as well as more popular national journals. Thus Reformed Church scholarship broke through the confines of local concerns and consumption (ethos) and began to touch and influence the larger world of scholarship (Oikumene).

Before highlighting those Reformed Church scholars and their contributions, several introductory remarks are in order. First, the narrow focus of this chapter will necessarily eliminate a wide range of publications which in their own way have been important to the Reformed Church in America, but which have not contributed either to the larger world of scholarship or to theological developments within the denomination. Second, although Samuel Zwemer (1867-1952) and Albertus Pieters (1869-1955) represent a previous generation of scholars, their output and reputation are not matched by any contemporary scholar in the Reformed Church, and I will comment briefly on their contributions. Third, it should clearly be stated that the Reformed Church had outstanding theological professors before the 1960s, although for various reasons these professors did not make a significant impact on the world of theological scholarship. I will, however, comment briefly on two of these professors, namely, John W. Beardslee, Jr. and Richard C. Oud-ersluys, because of their special significance within the Reformed Church. Finally, there is one "in-house" publication that is especially relevant to this chapter, and I will note it before moving to the primary focus of this chapter.

Samuel Zwemer was a distinguished missionary as well as a highly respected theologian in the Christian world.[1] For example, he wrote fifty books during his long career, and also founded and edited the influential quarterly, *The Moslem World*. His first book, *Arabia, the Cradle of Isalm*, was published in 1900;[2] his last book *Sons of Adam*, appeared in 1951, when he was eighty-four. His scholarly reputation was established primarily by his studies of Islam and the Arab world. His first book received very enthusiastic reviews in a host of journals including the London *Spectator*. The majority of his books were re-published several times, and many were translated into foreign lan-guages, nine in all. For example, his second book, *Raymond Lull: First Missionary to the Moslems*, was translated into Arabic, Spanish, Chinese, and Dutch.

Significantly, almost half of Zwemer's major works are on biblical and theological themes. Most of these books were written after he became professor of history and religion and Christian missions at Princeton Seminary in 1929.[3] Although during this period he continued to write books about the challenge of missions (*Into all the World*, 1943), world religions (*The Origin of Religion*, 1935), and Islam (*The Cross Above the Crescent*, 1941), increasingly he wrote on biblical and devotional themes, with his books being published both in Europe and the United States.

Although not nearly so widely known as that of Zwemer, the work of Albertus Pieters may also be mentioned here. A classmate of Zwemer's at Hope College (1857), he served for thirty-two years as a missionary in Japan before returning to this country to join the faculty of Western Seminary in 1926. His major works include *The Seed of Abraham*, the T.V. Moore Lectures at San Francisco Seminary, *Divine Lord and Sav-iour*, and *Can We Trust Bible History?* as well as numerous tracts and articles.

It is difficult to know how wide an audience these works had, almost all of them being published by Eerdmans which in the 1940s and 1950s did not have the distribution system and the reputation it now enjoys. Even so, Pieters' books must have been read far beyond Reformed Church circles, for they were reprinted frequently and were reviewed in standard theological journals.[4] In one case he was published by a New York firm (Revell), and *The Seed of Abraham*, as has been noted, resulted from lectures given at San Francisco Seminary. Albertus Pieters was unquestionably "one of the most illustrious sons of the Reformed Church in America,"[5] one who deserves far more attention than he has received thus far.

Although both men had international reputations, Zwemer was by far the more cosmopolitan of the two. Interestingly, he was also the more popular of the two scholars. Zwemer, for example, on three different occasions was one of the featured speakers at Keswick conventions in England. Pieters would probably not have felt at home in such gatherings. In fairness to Pieters, however, it should be pointed out that he was more the quiet scholarly type than Zwemer, who had the gift of being able to stir audiences of thousands of people.

John Beardslee, Jr. (1879-1962) taught at Hope College and Western Seminary before moving to New Brunswick Seminary in 1917, where he distinguished himself as a beloved professor. Extremely informed, incisive, and demanding, he was without peer as a teacher at New Brunswick during his career. He was also highly respected by those in the biblical field who knew him, but his circle of influence was limited because he published very little.

Richard Oudersluys taught at Western Seminary from 1942 until his retirement in 1977, and was an equally impressive teacher-scholar. Oudersluys' essays and reviews in the *Reformed Review* are outstanding examples of biblical scholarship: always cautious and conservative, but fully abreast of the latest research in the field, and written with grace and lucidity. His most solid scholarly effort, "The Theology of the New Testament," was an unpublished syllabus distributed only to students who took his course in New Testament theology during the 1950s.[6]

One volume in the "Historical Series," published by the denomination, namely, *Piety and Patriotism: Bicentennial Studies of the Reformed Church in America,* edited by James W. Van Hoeven, has become a source book on Reformed Church history in seminaries across the nation. The chapter on "theology" in that book, written by Eugene Heideman, has particular relevance for this essay. Heideman's chapter focuses largely on the period prior to the one being considered here and develops the point that "the central theological strands in the history of the Reformed Church . . . have been woven by a church determined to hold together two orientations," namely, a set of confessions inherited from the Netherlands, on the one hand, and a desire "to live under the sovereignty of God in America," on the other.[7] The early history of Reformed Church theological development, therefore, is one of tension between these two poles.

Although that point has been made by others, a later sub-thesis in the chapter is novel: Heideman maintains that since the 1950s Reformed Church theology has moved from an emphasis on predestination to that of eschatology.[8] Whether or not that is accurate, it is true that for the most part, Reformed theology has been decidedly pragmatic in recent years; the church has argued about biblical criticism and interpretation, especially in relation to issues such as the "historicity" of Adam and women in church offices, and has expended much effort—and money— on matters as divergent as church growth and issues of justice and peace.

This might seem to justify the conclusion that in the Reformed Church the American spirit, for better or worse, has won out over Calvin.[9] In many ways that is true, but at the same time there has been a very lively biblical and theological renaissance in the last twenty-five years which has not gone unnoticed in the wider theological world. This, then, sets the stage for a discussion of the central purpose of this chapter.

Because Reformed Church scholarship since the 1960s has been richly diverse, I have organized the material according to the following categories: Liturgical Renewal and Church Architecture; Biblical Studies and Commentaries; Historical Theology and Confessionalism.

Liturgical Renewal and Church Architecture

In these two closely related areas three Reformed Church scholars in particular have made distinctive and enduring contributions. In 1962 Howard Hageman's *Pulpit and Table* appeared;[10] it was followed three years later by a volume by Donald Bruggink and Carl Droppers, *Christ and Architecture.*[11] These two studies sparked the liturgical renewal within the Reformed Church and in wider Reformed and Presbyterian churches as well, quickly establishing for their authors a national, and eventually international, reputation.

Howard Hageman's reputation as a specialist in Reformed liturgics began with an important essay he wrote in *Theology Today* in 1958. Entitled "The Liturgical Revival," it documented the new interest in worship and hymnody in the American Church both on a practical and scholarly level. In particular, he notes the "amazing unanimity" in all these studies, whether American or European, Protestant or Roman Catholic.[13]

Subsequent work in the field resulted in Hageman being invited to give the prestigious Stone Lectures at Princeton Seminary in 1960. The result was a book which made a distinctive contribution to the study of Reformed liturgics: *Pulpit and Table: Some Chapters in the History of*

Worship in the Reformed Churches. Beginning with "A Tale of Two Cities" (Zurich and Geneva), where he clearly prefers Calvin's approach to worship over Zwingli's, Hageman traces the decline of Reformed liturgics in the Reformed Church in the "Gothic Age" (eighteenth and nineteenth centuries), to its revival first in the German-American Mercersburg theology, and then in the Dutch Reformed Churches after World War II.

Although the Bruggink and Droppers volume, *Christ and Architecture: Building Presbyterian and Reformed Churches,* is very practical in providing detailed structural designs, the book also contains a theology of the church and worship as well as a theology of church architecture. The thesis of the authors is expressed succinctly in the following passage:

> The Church is still built around the preaching of the Word, and nourished by the Sacraments, and it is therefore not at all inappropriate that in our architecture we should put first things first, and give primary expression to pulpit, font, and table. It is Christ who through his Word and Sacraments gathers the people of God, therefore one does not design around the congregation but around the symbols of Christ's presence. To begin in any other way is to deny the sovereignty of God and to deny God's initiative in the incarnation through which he calls men out of this world to be a people unto himself.[14]

Within the next two years at least fifty-two reviews of this work appeared, several in European journals and leading architectural periodicals. The responses were almost universally enthusiastic and encouraged the authors to produce a sequel which would focus on American rather than European churches. The result was *When Faith Takes Form: Contemporary Churches of Architectural Integrity in America.*[15] Much smaller in scope than their previous volume, and less explicitly theological, this book also has had significant impact on the American church.

These three writers profoundly influenced the shape of Reformed theology beginning in the 1960s, and rekindled interest in its Reformation roots. Reformed Church liturgy and architecture in the twentieth century had been largely congregational prior to that time, with each local church pretty much doing "what seemed right in its own eyes" on these matters. Indeed, many Reformed Church congregations reflected more the spirit and tone of fundamentalism in their worship and architecture, rather than the rich heritage of the Reformed tradition. Hageman, Bruggink and Droppers helped many in the church move beyond fundamentalism to an appropriate appreciation of Reformed liturgics, hymnody, and architecture.

The most recent and perhaps the most significant contribution of the

Reformed Church to the field of liturgy is *Rejoice in the Lord,* the first hymnal published solely by the denomination since 1869. Assembled under the guidance of the late Erik Routley, its editor, and under the supervision of a committee of scholars appointed by the General Synod, *Rejoice in the Lord* has already been hailed as one of the most important hymnals to be published in America in this century. Its conscious loyalty to the Reformed heritage in psalmody together with its ecumenical stance in hymnody, has already won for it an acceptance far beyond the confines of the Reformed Church in America.

Biblical Studies and Commentaries

The two Reformed church scholars in the biblical field who had already established national, if not international, reputations prior to the 1960s are J. Coert Rylaarsdam and E. Earle Ellis. Significantly, neither of them represents a mainline RCA stance, for Rylaarsdam has always been to the left of center whereas Ellis represented the more strictly conservative wing of the denomination. Both, however, in their own circles are recognized as first-rate scholars who have made significant and enduring contributions to the world of biblical scholarship.

Rylaarsdam, a Minnesota native and a Hope College and New Brunswick seminary graduate, served as a Reformed Church missionary in Arabia for three years before attending seminary. After a year of graduate study at Westminster College in Cambridge University, England, he began his doctoral work at the Divinity School of the University of Chicago. Completing that, he returned to New Brunswick Seminary in 1941 as a professor, but he was there only three years before he was invited to be Professor of Old Testament at the Divinity School of the University of Chicago. He taught there until his retirement in 1972.[16]

His reputation was originally established through the publication in 1946 of a single book, and that a rather modest one, *Revelation in Jewish Wisdom Literature.* For many years it was "the" book on this neglected subject and is still often cited in current discussions on wisdom literature. Five years later a larger world of non-specialists was to enjoy the fruits of his scholarship, this time in the exegesis of Exodus in the much-heralded *Interpreter's Bible.*[18] This represents a major breakthrough, for it was the first time that a Reformed Church scholar was asked to contribute a biblical commentary to a major series. This was followed by an invitation to write the essay on Hebrew Wisdom and the commentary on Proverbs in the new edition of *Peake's Commentary on the Bible,*[19] edited by Matthew Black and H. H. Rowley. Only two years later he contributed the volume *Proverbs to Song of Solomon,* in the popular "Layman's Bible Commentaries" series.[20]

Rylaarsdam continues to be very active in the area of Jewish-Christian dialogue. His essay on this subject, "Jewish-Christian Relationship: The Two Covenants and the Dilemma of Christology," first appeared in the *Journal of Ecumenical Studies*[21] and later in the *festschrift* for Lester J. Kuyper, *Grace Upon Grace.*[22] This essay puts in tension two key covenants of the Old Testament—the one with Israel, the other with David. That there may be tension between them is one thing; that the early Christians erred in their "one-sided view of the relation of the covenants to one another" is, however, problematic.[23] What is incontrovertible, however, is that J. Coert Rylaarsdam is one of the ablest biblical scholars the Reformed Church has produced.

The Reformed Church did not "produce" Earl Ellis. His roots are in the evangelical Baptist tradition. A native of Fort Lauderdale, Florida, he did his undergraduate work at the University of Virginia, received his B.D. and M.A. degrees from the Wheaton College Graduate School, and his Ph.D. from the University of Edinburgh. After teaching at Aurora College and the Southern Baptist Seminary in Louisville, Kentucky, he joined the New Brunswick Seminary faculty in 1962 where he remained until 1985, when he accepted a position at Southwestern (Baptist) Theological Seminary in Fort Worth, Texas.

Like Rylaarsdam, Ellis had already made a name for himself with the publication of his doctoral dissertation in 1957: *Paul's Use of the Old Testament.*[24] Four years later he produced a slight but important work titled, *Paul and his Recent Interpreters.*[25] This was followed by *The World of St. John: The Gospel and the Epistles.* This is also a small book (96 pages), but it would be quite false to conclude that Ellis is a lightweight in the scholarly world. For one thing, all three of these early works have been reprinted several times, indicating their usefulness and durability.

More importantly, whereas most of Ellis' earlier articles and reviews appeared in the Baptist journal, *Review and Exposition* and occasionally in the *Evangelical Quarterly,* his more recent writings have appeared in prestigious journals both here and abroad: *Interpretation, Journal of Biblical Literature, New Testament Studies, Theologische Literaturzeitung,* and *Zeitschrift für die Neutestamentliche Wissenschaft.*

Another indication of Ellis' scholarly reputation is seen in two other phenomena: the invitation to contribute essays to various types of dictionaries or encyclopedia as well as to *festschriften* in honor of retiring professors. In the former category Ellis has contributed essays to Baker's *Dictionary of Theology,* edited by Everett F. Harrison;[27] *The Biblical*

Expositor, edited by Carl F. Henry;[28] *The New Bible Dictionary,* edited by J. D. Douglas;[29] *Dictionary of Christian Ethics,* edited by Carl F. Henry;[30] *The Illustrated Bible Dictionary,* edited by N. Hillyer;[31] and the prestigious *Encyclopedia Britannica,* fifteenth edition.[32]

In regard his *festschrift* writings, Ellis has not only contributed scholarly monographs to volumes honoring some of the greatest New Testament scholars of our time, he has also edited several of these volumes. The following names represent a "Who's Who" in international New Testament circles for whom Ellis has written *festschrift* articles: Matthew Black,[33] B. Rigaux,[34] F. F. Bruce,[35] C. F. D. Moule,[36] L. Cerfaux,[37] Leon Morris,[38] Hans Conzelmann,[39] W. G. Kümmel,[40] Bruce Metzger,[41] and Oscar Cullman.[42] Something of Ellis' international contacts and reputation are evident here, for in this list are scholars from France, Germany, Switzerland, England, Scotland, Australia, and the United States. He has also contributed an essay—"Exegetical Patterns in 1 Corinthians and Romans"—to a *festschrift* for Lester J. Kuyper, an RCA scholar.[43]

In the midst of all this writing of reviews and essays Ellis also managed to produce two more books in the 1970s in the area of New Testament studies: *Eschatology in Luke* (1972),[44] and *Prophecy and Hermeneutic in Early Christianity* (1978).[45] The latter volume is a collection of previously published essays.

If Ellis did not write one more piece, his academic reputation would be permanently established. However, I have deliberately waited to mention his most signal achievement thus far, his commentary, *The Gospel of Luke* in the Century Bible Series (New Edition). Originally published in England in 1966,[46] it was subsequently published in this country by Eerdmans in 1981, reprinted in 1983, and is now available in a fourth edition. This volume is generally regarded as one of the most valuable commentaries in this distinguished series edited by H. H. Rowley and Matthew Black.[47]

In addition to Rylaarsdam and Ellis, there have been other biblical scholars in the RCA who have made impressive contributions to the larger church. Perhaps the most important of these is Lester Kuyper, emeritus professor of Old Testament at Western Seminary. Kuyper's earliest essays appeared in the *Western Seminary Bulletin,* and were probably not read beyond RCA circles. However, as early as 1947 he began to have articles published in the scholarly quarterly *Interpretation,* one of which, "Grace and Truth: An Old Testament Description of God. . . .",[48] is recommended by Raymond E. Brown in his *Commentary on the Fourth Gospel* in the Anchor Bible Series.[49] It is this kind of recognition that Reformed Church scholars rarely, if ever, received in an earlier era because they did not write for scholarly journals or participate in academic societies.

Kuyper's long and illustrious career was recognized on the occasion of his retirement with the presentation of *Grace Upon Grace: Essays in Honor of Lester J. Kuyper*, edited by his former student and colleague, James I. Cook.[50] Contributions to this volume included such internationally known scholars as James Muilenberg, Henry Gehman, G. Ernest Wright, and Th. C. Vriezen.

Historical Theology and the Emergence of Confessionalism

Before commenting on recent scholarly contributions of Reformed theologians, it might be helpful to provide some historical context for these studies. During much of the first half of the twentieth century, the Reformed Church's seminaries were generally dominated by pastoral systematic theologians who more or less quoted from the scriptures as a source book much as the older, nineteenth century orthodox theologians, quoted from here and there in history. This was especially true at Western Seminary where the teaching of systematic theology was little more than a pastiche of traditional Reformed dogmatics. Accordingly, it eschewed the historical-development approach to theology, was not very creative, and often was translated by students and clergy into static fundamentalist formulations. There were exceptions to this. We have already noted the contribution of Albertus Pieters at Western Seminary, whose scholarly writings represented traditional Reformed theology and to that extent were a polemic against the theology of the modernists, the dispensationalists, and the biblical literalists. At New Brunswick Seminary, Edward S. Worcester was the exception. Worcester was elected professor of theology in 1923 following a stormy challenge from some of the General Synod delegates concerning his views on the Canons of Dort. Worcester's historical approach to theology proved too extreme for many in the Reformed Church, particularly in the context of the modernist-fundamentalist controversy that was brewing in American Protestantism in the 1920s.

Worcester's appointment, however, was significant in that it seemed to signal a subtle change in both the style and substance of theology in the Reformed Church. This could be sensed in other areas as well, beginning in the 1920s. For example, Reformed seminary professors became less dogmatic toward the theory of evolution than a previous generation; Albertus Pieters, for example, set forth a defense of long ages of evolutionary development as being consistent with Genesis. In addition, these same professors became less sanguine about the future, particularly the future that included the dream of a Protestant Christian America moving toward the millenium. Most important, however, the change can be sensed in developments in the field of biblical theology, particularly in the scholarly historical and higher critical approach to the Bible. Lester Kuyper at Western Seminary, for example, showed that the language of the church's doctrinal standards needed modification to reflect that God is not the impassive sovereign of dogmatism, but the Holy One who "repents" and "grieves," and he also presented a literary-historical approach to Genesis 2-3 which challenged the more orthodox understanding of Adam and Eve rooted in "federal theology."

All of this challenged the traditional landmarks of Reformed dogmatic theology, as well as the method used by systematic theologians at Reformed Church seminaries. Because of this, however, another generation of theologians in the church began to rediscover the vitality and freshness of the Reformed tradition in new ways. For example, the liturgical and confessional renewal of the 1950s that we noted previously is the direct result of this. In addition, changes in the ordination of women, allowing elders to administer the Lord's supper, and defining the ordained ministry in terms of "function" rather than "status" can also be attributed to a more historical understanding of the church's classical doctrines.

Significantly, however, for the most part the church's professional systematic theologians did not participate in this renewal, preferring to hold solidly to both the methodology and the formulations of the older orthodoxy. The renewal in liturgy and confessionalism was brought about by seminary faculty in the fields of history, mission, liturgics, and especially biblical theology. Moreover, none of the church's professional theologians made any significant contribution to the scholarly world. Writing in 1947, an observer of Reformed theology stated the issue accurately:

> Perhaps the most outstanding characteristic of Calvinism that marks the [RCA] church today is its traditionalism. Its leaders are wont to boast of their blue-blood Dutch origin traced to colonial days, but this historic body has produced no outstanding theological thinking such as one would naturally expect from its famous Dutch theological and Calvinistic antecedents. Hardly a name of an outstanding systematic thinker in the field of Calvinist theology can be found on its rolls throughout the three centuries of its existence.[51]

Although this judgment was made of the eastern part of the church, the midwest fared little better:

Many of its ministers and parishioners have inherited something from the revival of Reformed theology which took place in the Netherlands in the previous century. Yet, even so, also among them one looks in vain, barring a few happy exceptions, for a virile, live, progressive testimony for the Reformed Faith in its distinctive expression and implications.[52]

M. Eugene Osterhaven, who began teaching at Western Seminary in 1953, is the first Reformed Church theologian to become internationally recognized as a scholar of the first rank. He also was one of the earliest to take the tradition seriously; Osterhaven was the first Reformed Church scholar to write a doctoral dissertation on John Calvin. He was followed in this by Justin Vander Kolk, who taught theology at New Brunswick seminary beginning in 1946. Although Vander Kolk did not publish any major works, both he and Osterhaven were the first theology professors in the Reformed Church to encourage the reading of Calvin in their courses, thus inspiring a new generation of Calvin scholars in the denomination. This meant, moreover, that at long last the church's professors of theology also began contributing to the church's liturgical and confessional renewal.

Osterhaven's contribution to this has been especially significant. For example, he worked with professors John T. McNeill and Lewis Battles on a scholarly new edition of Calvin's *Institutes*.[53] He also participated in a new translation of the Heidelberg Catechism. Most important, however, was his book *The Spirit of the Reformed Traditions*, which was published in 1971.[54] The title of the volume is significant; while sympathetic to the more static orthodoxy of previous periods, Osterhaven highlights the dynamic and even developmental character of Reformed theology. Significantly, the book also shows the growing influence of contemporary Dutch Reformed theology on Osterhaven's thought, especially that of Simon Vander Linde, Hendrikus Berkhof, and A. A. van Ruler. Osterhaven's latest book, *The Faith of the Church*, continues this emphasis.

At New Brunswick Seminary the confessional renewal has been carried on by Howard Hageman and John Beardslee III. We have already noted Hageman's work in the area of liturgics. Beardslee, who taught in the field of historical theology, has published major studies on seventeenth century Dutch theologians. His book, *Reformed Dogmatics*,[56] in the distinguished Oxford "Library of Protestant Thought" series, as well as his *The Doctrine of Scripture*,[57] both translate and interpret the writings of Johannes Wallebius, Gisbert Voetius, and Francis Turretin, theologians who significantly influenced Reformed thought in the seventeenth century.

An important achievement in the development of confessionalism in the Reformed Church in the last quarter century is the new confession, *Our Song of Hope*. [58] Written by Eugene Heideman, it is a creative and successful attempt to convey the Reformed faith in a modern idiom. In twenty-one brief stanzas Heideman does a remarkable job in expressing the tradition in language that should prove serviceable for many years.

Two motifs in *Our Song of Hope*, reflecting the influence of Heideman's mentor at Utrecht, A. A. van Ruler, are the frequent references to the work of the Holy Spirit and especially the work of the Spirit in the world. The subject of a majority of the affirmations—especially in Stanzas IV-VI—is neither the Father nor the Son but the Holy Spirit. Typical is Stanza IV: "The Spirit speaks through the Scriptures . . . The Spirit speaks through the Church . . . *The Spirit speaks in the world* . . ." (emphasis mine). Also in Stanza V: "As citizens we acknowledge the Spirit's work in human government . . ." and in Stanza X: "The boundaries of His [God's] love are not known, His Spirit works at the ends of the world before the church has there spoken a word." Basically, this is a salutary note, usually missing in traditional confessions, but one cannot help but wonder whether the classical Reformed linkage of Word and Spirit is here occasionally severed.

Such reservations notwithstanding, the Reformed Church should be profoundly thankful for Our *Song of Hope*. In the larger Reformed community it has been taken quite seriously. When the World Alliance of Reformed Churches convened a consultation in the summer of 1981 on the theme "Confessions and Confessing in the Reformed Tradition Today," Eugene Heideman was one of the twenty-five participants invited from around the world. In a booklet bearing the title of the theme published the next year, *Our Song of Hope* is the first confession cited in a section entitled "New Voices—A Few Examples." [59]

Another area where Reformed Church theologians have been productive and have made their mark is in the more general theological field. Eugene Heideman's doctoral dissertation was the first significant theological work to be published after World War II. Written under the supervision of A. A. van Ruler, *The Relation of Revelation and Reason in E. Brunner and H. Bavinck* [60] was an exceptionally perceptive work which showed promise that has come to rich fruition. It also represented a serious engagement with one of the leading theologians of our time. [61]

It was not until the 1960s, however, that RCA writers made much of an impact on the larger theological scene. In 1963 Howard Hageman wrote *Predestination,* a slim, popular volume for a series published by Fortress Books. [62] Here one sees already a smoothing of some of the sharper edges of Dort. The next year a more substantial work by a

Reformed Church author appeared, *Redemption and Historical Reality*,[63] by Isaac Rottenberg, then a young pastor in Shrewsbury, New Jersey. This is an excellent, sophisticated approach to *Heilsgeschichte* (redemptive history) in which Rottenberg analyzes the ways in which redemptive history affects historical existence. Rottenberg's knowledge of contemporary theology is impressive, yet he also utilizes the best of Dutch theology to illuminate his theses.

In the late 1970s the Reformed Church began to become known through two scholars who were specialists in the field of science and religion. The one, Eugene Klaaren, is a native son, who teaches at Wesleyan University in Connecticut; the other, Christopher Kaiser, is an adopted son who has taught at Western Seminary since 1977. Kaiser has doctorates both in astro-geophysics (U. of Colorado) and theology (U. of Edinburgh). His doctoral dissertation at Edinburgh was on *The Logic of Complementarity In Science and Theology* and he is now working on a major work on the history of science in the church. He has published scholarly essays on related themes in journals such as *Astrophysical Journal, Religious Studies, Crux*, and the *Patristic and Byzantine Review*.

In the meantime, Eugene Klaaren published *Religious Origins of Modern Science*.[64] The particular focus of the book is on the belief in creation in seventeenth century thought, the thesis being that "religion was conducive to the advent of modern science. . . ." Klaaren has also published in a variety of academic journals: *Zygon, Journal of American Academy of Religion, Union Seminary Quarterly Review*, and the *Journal of Presbyterian History*.

The decade closed with the publication of another excellent doctoral dissertation, this one by Paul Fries, *Religion and the Hope for a Truly Human Existence*.[65] The subtitle indicates the nature of the investigation: "An Inquiry into the Theology of F. D. E. Schleiermacher and A. A. van Ruler with Questions for America." This is a fascinating work but it is no longer available except in theological libraries. A shorter piece on a related theme is "God's Human Face: Reflections on Spirit, Kingdom and Culture," which appeared in the *Reformed Journal*.[66]

What Fries, Heideman, Rottenberg, and Osterhaven have in common in a broad knowledge of the Reformed tradition and contemporary theological literature, combined with an understanding of the Dutch theological scene. Their theological writings are ecumenical in the best sense of the word, but they contribute something special to theological scholarship which is impossible for most theologians in the world, namely, the benefits and insights of a vital Dutch theological tradition. Herein lies one of the distinctive gifts of the Reformed Church to the theological world.

The great strength of recent Reformed Church scholarship has been its return to its roots, both in the Netherlands and the Reformation. In this the writings of Dutch scholars such as G. D. Berkhouwer, Hendrikus Berkhof, and the late A. A. van Ruler have been particularly helpful. From these world-renowned scholars Reformed Church theologians have learned how to relate the distinctive features of Reformed theology to our own culture in an open, ecumenical fashion. Moreover, those Dutch scholars have helped Reformed Church theologians benefit from the best in contemporary theology, including the theology of Karl Barth, without necessarily becoming Barthians. Van Ruler has made his own special contribution by giving Reformed Church scholars a larger vision of the work of the Spirit in the world.

Interestingly enough, developments in the Netherlands have also been influential in liturgical development in the Reformed Church in America. Hageman's *Pulpit and Table* is greatly in the debt of the late Professor van der Leeuw; the RCA Liturgy of 1967 shows the influence of the *Dienstboek* of 1955, while many of the newer liturgical scholars in the RCA have studied at the *Liturgical Institute* in the University of Gronigen.

The net result has been a confessional renaissance that is not antiquarian but contemporary. The new critical study and use of our confessions and the reformers—especially Calvin—has helped the Reformed Church reclaim a more Reformed understanding of the Word and the sacraments, and has provided a way of theologizing that is more biblical and less scholastic than that of certain types of thinkers of an earlier age. At best this has resulted in a blending of reverent but critical biblical scholarship, liturgical reform, theological sophistication, sensitivity to social issues, and a healthy, well-rounded piety. At worst the Reformed Church has been both pragmatic and faddish, unconcerned about either the depths of its theological heritage or urgent world needs.

On balance, the last quarter century has been a good one for Reformed theology in the scholarly world; the Reformed Church has broken through many of its ethnic and parochial concerns and in the process discovered, paradoxically, that a particular ethos or confessional heritage need not limit nor stifle creative scholarship, but can actually enhance and stimulate it. James Bratt, in his brilliant study, *Dutch Calvinism in Modern America*, put it very nicely in his concluding paragraph: "The Reformed, as part of a faith with universal claims, cannot rest easy with ethnicity, but neither . . . can it rest easy without it."[67]

VII

Heidelberg and Grand Rapids:
Reformed Theology and The Mission of the Church

Eugene P. Heideman

The Reformed Church in America has made three fundamental shifts in its theology of world mission in the twentieth century. These shifts can be described by the following: from God's election of people to eternal security to his election of the church for mission; from confidence in providence to an expectant eschatology; from the doctrine of justification by faith alone to God's concern for justice in the world. These shifts are the result of the church's wrestling in its world mission task with classical themes in Reformed theology, especially God's election, God's sovereignty, and God's righteousness. How these shifts came about, and their consequences for the world mission task of the Reformed Church in the twentieth century, this chapter will attempt to make clear.

Reformation centers such as Geneva, Switzerland, and Heidelberg, Germany, faced three major tasks during the period 1550-1565. One was to state their confessional position and establish their church order clearly for their own citizens and others. The second was to maintain internal stability in the face of the threat of Anabaptists and others who seemed to be threatening public order by holding a position which rejected human authority as embodied in the church or the magistrates. The third was to help their people know how they were assured of salvation by faith alone, now that they could no longer hope to earn it by works.

The Heidelberg Catechism (1563) was written in the face of these three concerns. It focuses on the question of assurance of salvation. It informs believers that they are righteous only by faith in Jesus Christ (Question 60). It links this central affirmation with the Anselmic doctrine of the atonement and with the doctrine of election.[1]

In Question and Answer 18 the catechism says that all have trans-

107

gressed God's law and therefore are subject to the penalty of eternal death. God's righteousness consists in his upholding his law and punishing offenders fully. Ursinus commentary on the catechism plainly shows that righteousness here is understood in terms of Roman law. This contrasts with Old Testament usage where righteousness is considered in terms of God's concern of justice for the poor and oppressed.[2] If God did not exact the full penalty, he would not be just, according to the Anselmic view. It was Christ who then took the full penalty. We can therefore be assured of salvation because he is our mediator.

The second basis of assurance is the doctrine of election. Although the doctrine is not spelled out in the catechism itself, Ursinus' commentary, in an excursus on Question and Answer 54, links the doctrine of the church to election and to God's justice and mercy. God's election is (a) the basis of our assurance of salvation, and (b) together with reprobation the manifestation of God's mercy and justice. According to the doctrine of double predestination held by Ursinus, God's predestination of believers to salvation in Christ manifests his mercy; God's reprobation of others manifests in all eternity his justice in upholding the law by punishing the wicked.[3]

The catechism states further that the believer lives confidently not only because of election and justification by faith, but also because of God's providence, by which God rules over all details of life (Questions and Answers 27-28).

The doctrines of God's righteousness, election, and providence in the catechism served not only to reassure the believer, but also to preserve the good order of public life and respect for civil and ecclesiastical authorities. In Question and Answer 104, God's fatherly authority is directly related to the authority of parents and of civil and ecclesiastical authorities. As God has decreed all things and now rules through these authorities whom he has ordained, so the people must hear the decrees and instructions of magistrates and ministers with an attitude of "respectful obedience." Revolution or resistance to authority is ruled out, since it is God's will to govern us by their hand.

Where earthly authority is directly related to God's authority, it becomes the ruler's duty to fulfill God's righteousness by upholding the law and punishing evil-doers. The people are to hear the decrees of the rulers as being proper interpretations of the decrees of God. God's sovereign providence now works through the magistrates who are responsible for maintaining peace and order in the face of the trials and tribulations of life.

The major doctrines of the Reformation thus functioned to preserve the established order of society. Law and order in those tumultuous days were valued above social change and justice for the poor. Authorities were expected to be charitable and merciful, but these virtues were subordinate to strict righteousness. This emphasis on the established order was further strengthened by the doctrine of the changelessness of God in his sovereignty.

The phrase "the mission of the church" in this chapter's title does not occur in the Heidelberg Catechism. The duty of the church was to preach and teach the gospel to the people in the land, to administer the sacraments, and maintain ecclesiastical discipline (Questions and Answers 65-68). Believers were not asked to form mission societies or to seek mission opportunities. At their evangelistic best, believers by their "reverent behavior may win their neighbors to Christ" (Question and Answer 86). The commentary makes clear, however, that such soul-winning is to be carried out through obedient behavior such as is expected of wives in subjection to their husbands rather than by aggressive evangelistic outreach.[4]

The Reformed Church dates its official life in America from 1628. Its historic church order was formulated at the Synod of Dort in the Netherlands in 1618-19. Between 1628 and 1776 it existed under the supervision of the Classis of Amsterdam. Although there were several clergy who carried out ministries to the American Indians,[5] the Classis of Amsterdam was more influenced by world mission efforts in Indonesia than in America during the colonial period.

Neither the Reformed Confessions nor the church order adopted at the Synod of Dort spurred the church on to world mission. The Belgic Confession set forth the doctrine that the planting of the church throughout the realm was the duty of the civil authorities. Therefore, when the Dutch sailed to Indonesia or America, it was the duty of the East or West India Company also to provide for religious worship in the land. Article 36 of the Belgic Confession made very clear the duty of the civil authority to be responsible for public welfare, law and order, and the maintaining of public worship in their realm:

> Their office is not only to be concerned with and to watch over public policy, but also to maintain the holy worship of the Church, to prevent and remove all idolatry and false religion, to destroy the kingdom of the antichrist and to advance the kingdom of Christ, to see that the Word of the Gospel is preached everywhere so that God might be revered and worshipped by everyone, as he commands in his Word.

Prior to the Synod of Dort, in the period after 1595, the first Dutch Reformed missionaries went to Indonesia. Throughout the seventeenth century, a major effort in mission was carried out in that land. However, the role of both the church and the civil authorities left much to be desired. The civil authorities did assent to the sending of pastors and chaplains to Indonesia and did provide financial assistance. However, they were unenthusiastic about having the ministers there. First, a number of the East India Company authorities had taken mistresses and engaged in other forms of life-style not approved of by ministers. Second, they feared that preaching the Christian religion in Muslim and pagan centers could interfere with profit and trade, which was the company's primary interest. Third, in a time of conflict, the company's officers would simply transfer the ministry or missionary to another (and usually less desirable) location. Fourth, ministers were expected to care simultaneously for both Dutch and indigenous populations. Given the differences of language and culture, this was an impossible task.

From the side of the church, several classes, including that of Amsterdam did urge the company to send ministers and missionaries. The church also urged ministers to consider calls to Indonesia and provided training facilities for missionaries. It also at times raised small amounts of money for the support of missionaries. On the whole, however, these efforts were inadequate and not widely carried out.[6]

The church's response to the situation was consistent with the provisions of the Church Order of Dort, which still understood the primary responsibility for church planting to be with the civil authorities. The Church Order is introverted, concerned with the internal life of the church. Only one article out of eighty-six deals with mission outside the church. Article VII calls attention to the role of the missionary:

> No person shall be ordained to the ministry of the word, without settling in some congregation, unless he be sent as a *Missionary* to churches under persecution or employed to gather congregations, where none have been established.

The wording of Article VII clearly shows that such a missionary situation is abnormal, in contrast to the normal situation where the church has a fully developed structure of office bearers and official assemblies.

The Synod of Dort, which re-affirmed and strengthened the doctrines of God's righteousness, election, and sovereignty, reaffirmed the emphasis on law and order and the importance of obedience in the lives of believers and citizens. It was called together and underwritten by the civil authorities. In its section on ecclesiastical assemblies, the limited role of the church was made clear. Article XXIX provided that in ecclesiastical assemblies, "*ecclesiastical matters* only shall be transacted, and that in an ecclesiastical manner." With this provision, the Netherlands Reformed Church understood that under God the civil authorities were responsible for public justice and public welfare. The church in its deaconal work could carry out works of benevolence and mercy, but only within the general provisions of the law of the land.

The Reformed pastor and theologian, Gisbertus Voetius (1589-1676), felt the weakness of the Reformed theology of mission, and made several major contributions which influenced the Reformed Church in America. His central contribution was to establish three goals for mission. The first is that world mission is done to the glory of God, who is, as he recognized, the initiator of mission, rather than the individual, the church, or the missionary.

The second goal is the planting of the church. Voetius was able to give a clear place in the church order to mission, since Article VII on the missionary had spoken of the planting of churches. It also indicated that the individual convert is not to be left to his or her own devices, but is to be incorporated into the life of the church.

A third goal of mission is the conversion of the individual. Although Voetius linked conversion closely with church-planting, he did give it a distinct place and thereby opened the door to later pietistic attitudes which made conversion of the individual the central goal for mission.

Apart from his statement of the goals of mission, Voetius made two other contributions to a Reformed understanding. John Calvin and others had understood the Great Commission in Matthew 28:16-20 to be limited to the twelve apostles. It was not a "missionary text" for post-apostolic times. Voetius said that this passage must be understood as a command to the church, not only to the first-generation apostles.

This new interpretation of the passage led to a second contribution. Voetius maintained that the church as such is called to mission activity. Rather than looking first to the civil authorities to place ministers and churches everywhere in their realm and then giving the church a supporting role, Voetius held that it was the church which had the primary responsibility. The civil authorities had to play a supporting role, in accord with Acts 13:1-5. Moreover, by "church" he meant that one must begin with the work of the local congregation, rather than wait for a decision from a synod or classis before taking action.

The history of world mission in the Reformed Church in America really began in 1787 with the formation of the Committee on Church Extension and in 1792 with the adoption of the *Explanatory Articles* which adapted the Church Order of Dort to American conditions. John Livingston, the "father of the Reformed Church," believed that it was possible to retain intact the Reformed theology of Dort and Heidelberg even while changing the character of the Reformed Church from a national established church to a voluntary membership American denomination.

Livingston was a post-millenialist. He believed that Christ would come in about the year 2000 A.D. and that the Spirit of God was at work in the world, preparing it for the coming of Christ who would set up the peaceable kingdom. He trusted God to lead the nation as well as the church.

At the beginning of the nineteenth century, the Reformed Church accepted the idea that benevolent and mission work should be carried out by voluntary societies, organized for a specific task to be done by committed people. Tract and Scripture distribution, welfare projects, and foreign and domestic missionary work were furthered by such societies, operating outside the direct control either of the church or the state. These organizations were non-sectarian and non-political in nature. They tried not to threaten the theology or the polity of the churches. They were able to get things done when the civil authorities and the church did not yet have sufficient agreement to act.

In the American situation, no one said very much about the fact that these societies were more threatening to Reformed theology than first met the eye. Voluntary societies do not wait to hear a decree from the ordained authorities. They are ready to seek change and even to challenge established order. In any case, Reformed Church interest in mission began with voluntary societies which tended to move into the denominational orbit and to a large extent under denominational control after 1850.

The domestic and foreign mission boards of the Reformed Church did not challenge the theology of Heidelberg and Dort throughout the whole period 1800-1960. The goals of Voetius were the Reformed Church's goals. In the overseas situation, the central point of concern became the issue of how to know when the missionary task would be finished in one place and allow the missionary to move on to a "region beyond."

Rufus Anderson pointed the way for Reformed Church mission strategy.[8] He said that when a church is formed in a foreign country and has developed to a point where it is self-propagating, self-governing, and self-supporting, then the mission has come to an end. The missionaries should move on and begin work in another place.

Anderson's theory was in accord with Dort. "Church" carried responsibility for believers and for lands which were already more or less Christianized. "Mission" was responsible for those regions which were not yet evangelized. The church could focus on serving the believers. The missionary society would enlist those members of the church who felt called to support the missionary enterprise.[9]

Throughout the nineteenth century, the doctrine of providence played a great role in giving confidence for world mission. In the United States, the Reformed Church believed in the manifest destiny of the nation under God. In spite of reservations about colonialism, missionaries were able to enter many countries following the flag of Britain. It was felt that the English-speaking nations were the more moral and benevolent. The church could take care of the needs of people to be justified by faith alone; the civil authorities could be depended on to seek "liberty and justice for all."

At the outbreak of World War I, Reformed Church world mission personnel were still defenders of the traditional doctrines of Heidelberg and the Church Order of Dort. They were still optimistic about God's providence, although somewhat less sure of inevitable progress than those of a generation earlier. Albertus Pieters was typical to the extent that as a missionary in Japan he wrote more on mission strategy than on theology.[10]

In his 1912 book, *Mission Problems in Japan,* Pieters expressed his trust that in the providence of God, the Asian countries were ripe for the gospel. His real concern was the relation of the missionary to the church in Japan. In agreement with Dort, he made a distinction between the work of the church *ad intra* and the work *ad extra.* Nine-tenths of the time, talent, and financial strength of the church are devoted to its internal or *ad intra* labor. The remaining tenth is devoted to work outside itself. The missionary is an emergency person, like a soldier sent out on a temporary mission until the warfare ends.

Pieters attacked the three-self theory of Anderson, which by 1912 had become standard mission theory in the Reformed Church. He maintained that the Reformed Church mission was present in Japan independently from the issue of whether or not there was a mature church there. If the mission left when the church became mature, then growth would cease because the *ad intra* activity by definition dominates the life of the church. The mission had to continue even though the church was present, since the two represented different types of activity.[11]

Samuel Zwemer, missionary in the Arabian Gulf, was a contemporary of Pieters.[12] He also held to the doctrines of Heidelberg and Dort. He stated repeatedly that there could be no compromise with Islam on these matters and aggressively debated with the Muslims. He too trusted in the providence of God and was ready to admit that under England's flag, great educational and cultural progress was being made in the Middle East.[13]

From the writings of Pieters, Zwemer, and others one can conclude that at the time of World War II, the Reformed doctrines of God's righteousness, election, and providence were so securely established that they were taken for granted rather than discussed. The focus of mission discussion was on the relation of church to mission, on mission strategy, on evangelism, and works of charity.

World War II and its aftermath constitute a watershed for Reformed theology and its understanding of the world mission of the church. In Europe, the new era began earlier with the Reformed theologians surrounding Karl Barth, who confessed at Barmen in 1934 that one could not have any confidence in general providence or natural theology.[14] In Europe, people began to talk once again of martyrdom. The church no longer felt it could keep silent simply because the government had spoken. The spirit of the times was more often felt to be pessimistic than optimistic.

In the 1960's the full extent of the changes in the world and nation were being felt by North Americans. Civil rights controversies, rumors of the "ugly American," the apparent decline of American power in the world, and the Supreme Court's decisions about religion shook public confidence that the United States is a "Christian nation." In 1970, Dr. John Piet, missionary for twenty years in India and professor at Western Theological Seminary, published his book, *The Road Ahead: A Theology for the Church in Mission.* He called for change and gave five characteristics of our age which raise issues about election and the church. He listed the rise of secularism, the resurgence of national religions, divisions among Christians, the increase in world population, and the spectre of famine.[15]

Piet then went on to attack the doctrine of election as stated in the Belgic Confession. His basic point was that the Reformed confessional statements do not give adequate attention to the Old Testament background of the doctrine of election. Election is not simply a matter of security or assurance. It is election to a purpose. Israel was elected to be a blessing to the nations. The Christian church is elected to be God's instrument in mission.[16]

Piet's re-direction of the doctrine of election has been accepted in Reformed Church world mission. Election is a dynamic concept related to the life of the church in the world as well as a static concept that fixes the eternal salvation of the believer. It means that mission is central to the being of the church rather than peripheral in the church order.

By the end of the 1960's the faith in providence which looks optimistically to the future had been severely shaken. The morality of the nation was being called into question. People were less sure about the supremacy of their own culture and technology. They began to sense that the church which understood itself as mission would as often have to speak prophetically to its times as Nathan and Amos had to criticize the kings of their days. The Word of the Lord is not so much mediated through the progress of history as it is the Word of the Lord which comes from the Bible against the movement of history and culture.

The sovereignty of God came in the 1970's to be stated in eschatological language, which reads the present in terms of God's future, rather than in providential or decretal terms. The Reformed Church accepted a new confessional statement, *Our Song of Hope*, as a supplement to the older statements. Its language is clearly eschatological in nature in that it does not rely on a doctrine of common grace or providence to understand the changes taking place:

> God will renew the world through Jesus.
> He will put all unrighteousness out,
>   purify the works of men's hands,
>   and perfect their fellowship in Himself.
> He will wipe away every tear;
>   death shall be no more.
> There will be a new heaven and a new earth,
>   and His creation will be filled with His glory.[17]

This shift in emphasis led the Reformed Church to place the concept of the Kingdom of God central in its understanding of world mission. In that kingdom, God encounters both the church and the culture with the Word and calls them to live according to his will. World mission was not understood to be the doing of the will of God wherever one was in any of the six continents. The cities of North America became focal points for mission. Congregations discovered many opportunities for mission in their own backyards. They recognized that they had ignored many people whom God loved. They developed counseling ministries, singles ministries, ministries with the disabled, street ministries and institutional ministries as specific callings in the world mission of the church.

The shift of perspective regarding God's election and God's sovereignty could not fail to be related to the doctrine of justification by faith alone. The Heidelberg Catechism still says "God wills that his righteousness be *satisfied*" (Question and Answer 12). *Our Song of Hope* remains Anselmic in its doctrine of the atonement, but it also insists that in Christ's death, "the justice of God is *established*."[18] In using the word, "established," it linked the atonement of Christ to the righteousness and peace of God in the Old Testament. It recognized that Christ came not simply for the sinners but also for the poor, the widows, and the orphans. He came to give sight to the blind, to heal the sick, and to set the captives free.

In *The Ad Hoc Report on World Mission* adopted in 1980, the General

Program Council of the Reformed Church re-affirmed the three goals for world mission and commented, in the section on the manifestation of the glory of God in his kingdom, that justice and justification by faith alone cannot be separated from each other:

> Translated into contemporary language, our ultimate goal is that God's will be done everywhere on earth as it is in heaven. Although the evangelization of peoples and individuals cannot wait until the justice of God is established throughout the world, one cannot offer a truncated Jesus to the world. Justification by faith cannot be separated from justice on earth. Jesus in his own lifetime manifested the unity of purpose and action of God who both heals the sick and forgives the repentant, who converts the woman at the well, and who calls for justice in the temple. The gospel today as always is caught up in the great movements of events in the world and the church ignores these at its peril. Ultimately, there is no non-political Christian.[19]

The linkage between justice and justification by faith alone proved to be disturbing to the life of the church and the world. The Heidelberg formulation valued law and order above change; peace and tranquility took precedence over justice for the poor. In the troubled and war-torn world of the sixteenth century there was good reason to place a high value on tranquility. In the Germany of the 1930's, however, the church recognized that the separation of justification by faith alone from justice led to "cheap grace" as Dietrich Bowhoeffer called it, to support for a regime which was exterminating the Jews, and to world-wide violence and war. Order in society purchased at the cost of injustice is ultimately oppressive and self-destructive.

So long as the church trusted the civil authorities to maintain justice in society, it could be content to accept the separation between justice and justification by faith. In the past several decades, that confidence has waned. Governments today are much more likely to be seen as insensitive, bureaucratic, and even oppressive. As a result, the world mission of the church is now understood to include not only evangelism and charitable works, but also the affirmation of human and civil rights, non-violent support of oppressed peoples, and protests against unjust government policies such as the racially segregating laws of the Republic of South Africa.

From its beginning, the Reformed tradition has confessed that God rather than anything or anyone else is always the first and the last word. Historically, however, the understanding of that confession has shifted as the Reformed Church in each century attempted to live out the meaning of God's election, sovereignty, and righteousness in its own cultural context. In the nineteenth century, part of that shift can be seen in the birth of the church's commitment to world mission; the Reformed Church in America had no program of world mission before that time. In the twentieth century the shift has been equally fundamental and has changed the church's theology of mission in three important ways: from understanding election as security to election to service; from faith in providence to eschatology; from justification by faith alone to God's concern for justice in the world. These shifts have been disturbing to many in the church; they have challenged old assumptions and required difficult and sometimes courageous action on the part of Reformed Christians. Undergirding these changes, however, has been the firm conviction that God is the sovereign and faithful Lord of the universe, and that world mission must follow the command of Christ to "seek first God's kingdom and his righteousness, and all these things will be yours as well" (Matt. 6:33).

VIII

Piety and Patriotism:
Reformed Theology and Civil Religion

Dennis N. Voskuil

Eager to lay claim to an early stake in the New Zion, the Reformed Church in America has traced its ecclesiastical origins back to 1628 when Domine Jonas Michaelius organized a congregation of fifty Dutch communicants on Manhattan island. Hence, the somewhat misleading but oft-heard assertion that The Reformed Church is "the oldest Protestant denomination on the North American continent."[1] Without doubt the Reformed Church is an institution with a venerable New Netherlands rootage but it is probably more accurate to trace its beginnings to June, 1772, when leaders of the Dutch Reformed Church in the American colonies formally approved the "Articles of Union." Drafted by John H. Livingston, "the father of the Reformed Church,"[2] these Articles not only brought together the *coetus* and *conferentie* factions, but officially severed the legislative and judicial ties with the Classis of Amsterdam. Thus began the process of decolonization for the American Church—a process which continued during the Revolutionary War and its aftermath. By 1792, the independent denomination had drafted and adopted a new constitution and liturgy. The first meeting of the General Synod of the Reformed Protestant Dutch Church in North America was held two years later, in 1794.

The fledgling American Reformed Church of the late 18th century was not merely a reconstitution of the Dutch Reformed Church on American soil. While confessions, liturgy and constitution were virtually identical to those employed by the church in the Netherlands, these religious traditions were transposed in a new nation—one in which there was an official policy of disestablishment. The "Preface to the Explanatory Articles of the Constitution of 1792" noted that the document had omitted all references to "the immediate authority and interposition of the Magistrate in the government of the Church," such as had been "introduced more or less into all the national establishments in Europe." In America "a fair trial" would be given as to whether "the

Church of Christ will not be more effectively patronized in a civil government where full freedom of conscience and worship is equally protected and insured to all men, and where truth is left to vindicate her own sovereign authority and influence, than where men in power promote their favorite denominations by temporal emoluments and partial discriminations."[3]

This paper will explore the manner in which Reformed faith and thought have developed in the context of American culture. Though important, the constitutional arrangement of church and state is not the exclusive issue. Our concern will be broader. We will attempt to examine the ways in which members of the Reformed community came to terms with the American culture—its history, values, political processes, national identity and constitutional arrangements. It will be demonstrated that Reformed thought was transformed but not reduced by the American experience. In general, the basic principles of Reformed theology and polity were reinterpreted as they were worked out in the context of a non-European culture.

As one examines the history of Reformed thought in America during the past 200 years, it becomes apparent that Reformed Christians have been comfortable citizens of this nation. The constitutional arrangement has been accepted, indeed, even applauded, for it has been interpreted as disestablishment of a particular state church, the European model, but never as the disestablishment of religion, especially the Christian religion. In fact, during the nineteenth century Reformed thought assumed that America was a quasi-established Protestant country; the concerns expressed and battles waged were in terms of preserving a Protestant version of public morality. Buttressed by a magisterial theological heritage which gave divine origin to nations and kingdoms and divine sanction to governmental authorities, it is not surprising that Reformed Christians were loyal citizens in times of crisis and tranquility. When Rufus Clark wrote during the centennial year of 1876 that he regarded "Patriotism with an American citizen as next to his religion, if not part of it,"[4] he was expressing the sentiments of the majority of Reformed Christians. While there have been numerous expressions of concern about the evils of American society, few have doubted that church and nation were working in tandem to carry out God's will on earth. Seldom have Reformed Christians felt out of step with the pervasive sway of culture. Few the prophets who have pronounced a counter-cultural message. Patriotism and piety have so often and nearly converged in public Reformed thought that one can in fact identify a pervasive form of "civil religion."

While the term "civil religion" can be traced back to the writings of

Rousseau, it was popularized in this country during the late 1960's in an article by sociologist Robert A. Bellah, "Civil Religion in America." Bellah wrote quite positively about "an elaborate and well-institution-alized civil religion in America" which "has its own seriousness and integrity and requires the same care in understanding that any religion does."[5] Bellah identified some of the points of this religion with certain motifs of traditional Christianity, but insisted that it was neither sectarian nor specifically Christian. It was a national religion which drew Americans together around national experiences, national saints and martyrs, a national creed, national holy days, and a national God.

Bellah's interpretation has elicited a barrage of responses. Few scholars wholly agree with Bellah's clearly positive position, but the term "civil religion" has gained great currency in the market of ideas. Today it is a malleable term which includes such diverse notions as "the transcendent universal religion of the nation," "folk religion," "religion of democracy," "religious nationalism" and "Protestant civic piety."[6] It is not necessary here further to elaborate these versions of civil religion, but only to underscore the fact that in one form or another Reformed Christians seem to have participated in and contributed to American civil religion. But the Reformed embrace of any form of civil religion (even Protestant civil piety) has been cautious and somewhat self-critical. Again and again, expressions of patriotism have been tempered by the vigorous Reformed assertion that all human authorities and institutions fall under the sovereignty of God. In the end, Paul's conviction that Christians must obey their governing authorities, for these have been instituted by God (Romans 13:1-2), has been interpreted through Peter's dictum that "we must obey God rather than men" (Acts 5:29).

The foundations for an American civil religion were laid during the period of the Revolutionary War when thirteen disparate colonies united against a common foe, and began the tentative process of forming a federal union. The Revolutionary War provided the nascent nation with a unifying experience, with a common history of martyrs, saints, heroes, and heroines. Almost immediately, Americans began to romanticize and glorify the Revolution, and common national identity began to coalesce around the patriotic myths which were related to the war period. The revolution became the American "Exodus," the root experience which succeeding generations of the "Chosen People" could remember and appropriate as their own heritage.[7] It is little wonder, then, that Reformed Church chroniclers have tended to identify the war as a holy cause and the Dutch Reformed colonists as heroic patriots. John W. Beardslee III has noted that while later generations have tended to provide divine sanction to other wars, for the "purposes of membership in the American community" it has been necessary to identify the Revolutionary War as a holy event. "To deny that divine providence provided the American Revolution" has been the "most unthinkable kind of un-American behavior."[8]

In one of the "Centennial Discourses" commissioned by the Reformed Church for the centennial celebration of 1876, John A. Todd documented the Dutch Reformed role in the Revolutionary War. In an introductory statement, Todd assured his readers "that of all the Christian denominations in the land there was not one that surpassed the staunch old Dutch Church in her unflinching devotion to the country's cause. She was loyal to the nation, if she was rebellious to the King, and she believed herself to be justified in the maxim that 'Rebellion to tyrants is obedience to God.' " What followed was an account which documented the abuse and desecration of Reformed churches by the British, and glorified the patriotic activities of its laity and ministry such as Jacob R. Hardenbergh and Dirck Romeyn. Included in the accounts are patriotic pronouncements of the embattled General Synod which met sporadically during the war. Especially noted was the memorial presented by the Synod of 1780 to the state government of New York. One of the paragraphs of this memorial was particularly lauded by Todd. It read:

> That the unwearied exertions of these United States, and of this State in particular, and especially the unparalleled perseverence of the American army exhibited in the prosecution of the present *Just* and *Necessary War*, from whatever personal motives it might otherwise proceed, cannot but be considered as *National virtues*, such as have been usually owned and accepted of by the Deity in the issue.

Todd enthused over the fact that the synod had explicitly sanctioned the war as a just cause during one of the darkest periods of the conflict for the Americans. "That," Todd concluded, "was enlightened Christian patrioism, and in this Centennial year of rejoicing every member and friend of the Reformed Dutch Church in America can look back upon her sturdy and unflinching steadfastness with a glow of laudable, honest pride. Thank God, no son or daughter of hers has need to blush for her record!"[9]

Todd's article is a prime example of the sort of selective memory which buttresses the myths of American civil religion. While he was fully aware of the fact that certain representatives of the Dutch Church had long been identified as Tories, Todd chose to ignore such examples of "unpatriotic and unchristian conduct,"[10] for it was his concern to engender patriotic pride among members of the Reformed Church. Recent historians of the American Revolution have begun to tell the whole story of Dutch Reformed involvement. Indeed, we are learning now that there were a number of Dutch Tories who overtly resisted the Revolution, as well as a larger number of "neutrals" or "secret Tories." Indeed, it may be that in some areas of New York and New Jersey, between one-third and one-half of the Dutch could be considered Tories.[11]

The concern here is not to review the history of the Revolutionary war but to indicate how the selective memory of Reformed Church historians reflected the prevailing ethos of American civil religion. This does not mean that Dutch Reformed Christians were not *actually* expressing patriotic sentiments during the Revolutionary era. Indeed, there is strong historical evidence that most of the Reformed laity and the large majority of the Reformed ministers were supportive of the Revolution.[12] This was especially true of the English-speaking wing of the Dutch Church. In an article written during the second American centennial, Earl William Kennedy took note of the manner in which three prominent ministers of the collegiate churches in New York City marshalled strong biblical and theological support for the Revolutionary cause in their sermons. Beyond that, according to Kennedy, Archibald Laidlie (1727-1779), John H. Livingston (1746-1825), and William Linn (1752-1805), had begun to identify America as God's chosen and blessed land by the close of the Revolutionary era. Linn's sermons most clearly echo the themes of America's uniqueness, virute and manifest destiny.[13] The colorful pulpiteer delivered a Fourth of July message in 1791 entitled "The Blessings of America," which glorifies both the religious liberties and economic opportunities available in America. Linn extended an invitation to the oppressed of Europe:

> . . . Here is an asylum for you, our brethren of the old world, whose labors go to support lazy priests and luxurious princes; who though you rise early and late take rest, obtain only scanty subsistence for yourselves and families. Forsake your hard taskmasters. Refuse to dig an ungrateful soil which will not yield you bread. Haste you to the fertile plains of America. Fill her new, and as yet, uninhabited territory. She opens wide her arms to embrace millions, and waits to crown all the industrious and virtuous with plenty and happiness.[14]

Like many of those who contributed to the expressions of an emerging cultural nationalism, Linn drew a very clear contrast between the vices of Europe's monarchies and the American republic, which he once identified as "the last noblest work of God." Kennedy identified these statements as expressions of Linn's "nationalistic self-admiration," his price in being an American. Such enthusiastic Americanism, avers Kennedy, approximates civil religion "in both its active and its passive forms."[15]

Kennedy further suggests that Linn's "political religion reached . . . its apogee"[16] in a eulogy on George Washington which he delivered during February, 1800, in which he compared the father of this country to the great heroes of the Old Testament:

> If we compare him with characters in the Sacred records, he combined the exploits of *Moses* and *Joshua,* not only by conducting us safely across the Red Sea and through the wilderness, but by bringing us into the promised land; and like *David,* he conquered an insulting Goliath, and rose to the highest honors from a humble station; like *Hezekiah*, he ruled; and like *Josiah* at his death, there is a mourning 'as the mourning of Hadarimmon in the valley of Megiddon.'

It is not enough for Linn to compare Washington to religious giants of Judeo-Christian history, he goes on to identify him as "God's servant" who attended church and acknowledged "a Providence" and honored God in "all his public documents."[17] In his veneration of Washington, Linn lays the foundation for the sort of patriotic piety which would find expression in Reformed churches in succeeding decades. Early in the nineteenth century, for instance, a Reformed Church pastor would pronounce the following benediction at a Fourth of July service:

> The God of Abraham, the God of Issac, and the God of Washington bless you all.[18]

The cult of the American Revolution has been nurtured to considerable degree by those Christian citizens who participate in the most sacred of national holy days—the annual Fourth of July celebrations. The strength of civil piety in the Reformed Church becomes wholly apparent when one remembers the July Fourth sermons which have consistently engendered patriotism. Furthermore, a survey of the denominational magazines and newspapers reveals that almost annually editors rehearsed sacred events and ideas of the Revolution and encouraged the readership to honor America. With amazing consistency, these Independence Day editorials have perpetuated the notion that America was founded upon distinctly sacred principles. In 1889, for instance, the *Christian Intelligencer* printed an editorial, "The Birthday of Liberty," which stated that the Declaration of Independence held significance far beyond that of establishing a new nation. "It was the proclamation of the true and abiding principle underlying Government and Society. It formulated the Christian idea of the State . . . it incorporated for the first time in the foundation of a nation, principles which had been the slow fruitage of the teaching of Christ." The editorial suggested that the Declaration providentially evolved through the centuries, and that it marked an epoch not only for our nation but for the entire world:

> Though it named not Christ or His Gospel, it founded the nation on a central and essential idea of Christianity, and made it necessary . . . that we should be a Christ-honoring and Christ-obeying people.

The editorial encouraged the readers to celebrate the national event in the context of the churches and sabbath schools. "Of all the anniversaries, the Fourth of July should be *religiously* observed."[19]

During the centennial celebration of 1876, the editor of *The Christian Intelligencer* reflected upon the then evident results of the grand experiment of the constitutional separation of Church and State—an experiment which diverged from European customs. He thought it ironic that in this country where church and state were not united and where religion and government have little direct legal connection, "religion and patriotism, natural allies, were never more intimately related nor more essential to each other." The common verdict of the religious history of the United States would ultimately conclude that under the impartial protection of a free government, individual denominations have been enabled to use their resources to adapt "to the spirit of the times, to the wants of the people, and to the genius of our republican institutions." The proof was in the pudding:

> With honest pride Americans may ask the world to study the results of her voluntary religious system—to behold her churches and their benevolent and educational agencies, their home and foreign missions, their support of the ministry, their church buildings and parsonages, their universities, colleges, schools for both sexes, their Sabbath-School system, their charities, and their perfect liberty to preach their doctrines, develop their ecclesiastical polities, and to spread their agencies wherever men and money and Christian enterprise can carry them.[20]

The mutual blessing of civil and religious liberty—again and again this theme is echoed by Reformed thinkers during the 19th century. As if to answer potential critics of the American system, evidence was marshalled to demonstrate that both church and state benefitted from the arrangement. The church has been lively, strong, and mission-oriented; the state has been infused by an educated, alert, and patriotic citizenry. In his contribution to the collection of Centennial Discourses (1876), Rufus Clark reminded his Reformed readers that their political and religious duties were inseparable because America was essentially a Christian nation:

When we remember that the Bible is the source and guardian of our
civil institutions and national blessings; when we have reason to believe
that the interests of freedom, civilization and Christianity are largely
involved in the perpetuity and prosperity of our republic, when we look
upon the streams of influence for good or evil that flow from us, far
beyond the boundaries of our own land, we cannot but regard it as a
Christian duty to do all in our power to elect men of principle to office,
and to preserve the purity of all departments of our government.

Clark was hopeful that Christian citizens could purify the governmental
system and realize the divine destiny of the nation. "If we are faithful
to the trusts committed to us, a hundred millions may in the future
thank us, and unite in giving glory to God for widespread national
blessings, that flow from the union of liberty with a pure national
religion."[21]

Despite the legal separation of church and state these writers believed
that ours was "a free and Christian government."[22] Throughout the
nineteenth century (and perhaps the twentieth century) there was an
implicit assumption among Reformed thinkers that America was essentially a Christian country, founded by Christians and established upon
Christian principles. In fact, ours was viewed not merely as a Christian
nation but as a Protestant nation. Those who have studied American
religious history tend to agree that the nineteenth century was one of
great Protestant influence. Robert Handy's *Christian America* illustrates
how dominant Protestant influence was during this era, and Martin
Marty's *Righteous Empire* demonstrates that a form of Protestant hegemony existed during much of the nineteenth century. Even a cursory
reading of the *Intelligencer* reveals that the leaders of the Reformed
Church tended to equate Protestant piety with public morality. The
contributors to the paper during this period consistently advocated Sabbath laws, temperance laws, and immigration laws.

The latter concern went hand-in-hand, of course, with a scarcely-
veiled anti-Catholicism. There was great fear that the dramatic influx
of Roman Catholic (and Jewish) immigrants would vitiate public morality. The real or imagined Protestant hegemony seemed to be disinte-
grating. To effect such a religious influence upon public policy during
the early nineteenth century, members of the Reformed Church helped
to erect what has come to be known as the "benevolent empire," a host
of independent Protestant agencies which were dedicated to single-issue
social concerns. Reformed Christians were often prominent in the
founding of such agencies as The American Bible Society (1816), The
American Education Society (1816), the American Colonization Society
(1817), The American Tract Society (1825), The American Temperance

Society (1826), The American Peace Society (1828), and The American Antislavery Society (1833).[23] Later, because of interdenominational squabbles and tensions, the Reformed Church, like most other Protestant groups, organized its own denominational boards and agencies. But even when mission activities became fragmented and disjointed, Reformed Christians believed that they were participants in a providential program for the moral transformation of America. At times, great confidence was expressed that these efforts would result in a truly Christian Society. In an 1861 *Intelligencer* article, "America for Christ," Anson Dubois urged his fellow Reformed Christians to labor more arduously in bearing their part "in the great enterprise of making this whole country truly a Christian country."[24] The 1876 report of the General Synod on the state of religion urged a similar goal: "to make this country the land of the schoolhouse, of the Bible, of the Sabbath, and of the Sanctuary."[25]

While it is clear that Reformed Christians sought the amelioration of certain social ills, it is also clear that they addressed social problems in generally conservative and individualistic ways. In his important study of the history of the Reformed Church's response to social concerns, John De Jong has shown that the nineteenth century church stressed personal conversion and nurture rather than efforts to effect change in the fundamental structures of society. De Jong believes that this individualistic approach to social change which epitomized the evangelical approach was reinforced by a pervasive Culture-Protestantism, "a willingness on the part of the church to embrace the prevailing social values and institutions and assign to them a religious significance." Reluctance to call for penetrating social change was predicated upon the conviction that this constituted a lack of support for national values and institutions. Patriotic piety seemed to predicate a social conservatism.[26]

De Jong suggests that the Reformed Church's strong opposition to the abolitionist movement before the Civil War was predicated at least in part upon this pervasive Culture-Protestantism. Abolitionism was identified as a dangerous radicalism which would lead to a rupture of American society. The evil of slavery could be eradicated most effectively through the conversion of the slave-owner. Considering the Reformed Church's reluctance to attack social evils at the structural level, it is not surprising that the denomination was hesitant to embrace the social gospel movement which emerged during the late nineteenth and early twentieth century. Like the evangelicals who erected the benevolent empire earlier in the century, the social gospellers sought to Christianize America; but while the former group tended to concentrate upon such moral concerns as Sabbath observance and temperance, the latter group concentrated upon such structural social concerns as labor conflict, living conditions, poverty, business abuses, and political corruption. As De Jong points out: "These were problems that demanded new tactics." Instead of relying upon individual conversion, moral nurture, and benevolence, the social gospellers launched direct attacks on inhumane social institutions and practices.[27] Many in the Reformed Church were certainly suspicious of the social gospel because most of its adherents were deeply influenced by the form of theological liberalism which became such a powerful force from 1890-1930. But the social gospel, as we have learned from many evangelicals in our own era, is not the exclusive domain of liberal theology. The reluctance to embrace the social gospel is also related to the inherent cultural conservatism of the Reformed Church, a general support of American values as these were manifested in social, political, and economic structures.

Considering the Reformed Church's general disdain for the social gospel, it is ironic that two of its most prominent proponents, Graham Taylor and Abraham J. Muste, were sons of the denomination. Born a decade before the Civil War, Taylor attended Rutgers College and New Brunswick Seminary, before serving as the pastor of a Reformed Church in Hopewell, New York. Dismissed to the Congregational Church in 1880, Taylor became an important social gospel activist and theoretician as a teacher at Hartford and Chicago theological seminaries, and founder of a social settlement in Chicago. A. J. Muste was born in the Netherlands in 1885, grew up in Grand Rapids, Michigan, and attended Hope College and New Brunswick seminaries. After serving in the Fort Washington Collegiate Church in New York City, he was also dismissed to the Congregational Church in 1915. Deeply concerned about many social issues, Muste became one of America's most consistent and articulate pacifists. Before he died in 1967, Muste had a profound influence upon three generations of peace activists. It is significant that both of these men felt constrained by the Reformed Church and early in their ministries left the denomination to pursue their broad interests in social concerns.[28] The cultural Protestantism of the Reformed Church did not provide a congenial climate for an expansive and penetrating social gospel.

While the Reformed Church never came to embrace the social gospel movement it is true that during the twentieth century the church became more deeply involved with controversial social concerns. During World War I the General Synod brought together committees on temperance and Sunday observance to form the Committee on Public Morals, which then dealt with a broader range of social issues. By the time of the Great Depression, the name had been changed to the Committee on Social Welfare, and the synod was willing to endorse the committee's determination to address and ameliorate contemporary problems by "correcting those conditions in our social life which are immediately responsible for them."[29] By 1955, the social welfare committee was succeeded by the Christian Action Commission, which has since investigated such problems as poverty, unemployment, women's rights, homosexuality, prison reform, and abortion. Generally in front of the church on these issues, the commission has not always been successful in gaining the endorsement of the General Synod for its proposals. Most of the papers and position statements prepared by the commission have been endorsed by the synod for review and consideration by the churches, but few have had a salutary impact upon the churches. Many of the statements have been benignly neglected or consciously ignored. In general, the Reformed Church of the twentieth century has acknowledged that there is a social dimension to the gospel but has been cautious about proposing structural remedies for social ills.

The Civil War was the second great event in the melding of an American civil religion. The revolution of the previous century had been our exodus experience as George Washington, the American Moses, has led his people from the bondage of old world pharaohs, while other fathers of the republic such as Thomas Jefferson and James Madison wrote the Declaration of Independence and the Constitution, our sacred scriptures. But the Civil War, "the center of American history,"[30] posed the most significant challenge to the national unity and self-identity which this country would face during its first two centuries of existence. It was an intensely tragic war as fraternal blood was spilled on American soil. In the end, the Union would be preserved under the leadership of Abraham Lincoln, the martyred president who has become the very embodiment of the American ideal. As Robert Bellah points out, with the Civil War, "a new theme of death, sacrifice and rebirth enters the civil religion." This theme is symbolized in the life and death of Lincoln, and it is stated most poignantly in the Gettysburg Address, "the 'New Testament' of Civil Religion Scriptures."[31]

While the Reformed Church generally recognized slavery as an evil institution, it did not support the cause of abolitionism, for it was considered a radical remedy which was disruptive to American society.[32] The proper Christian response to slavery was to proclaim the liberating gospel of salvation to both slaves and slave owners. Once the Confederate states seceded from the Union, however, the Reformed Church gave unwavering support to the cause of the North. Already during the early months of 1861, the readers of the *Intelligencer* were informed that it was their "patriotic duty" to support the newly elected president.

On the left column of the front page of this paper was affixed a small American flag with the following verse:

> Tis the star-spangled banner.
> O! Long may it wave
> O'er the Land of the Free
> And the home of the brave.
> For right is right, since God is God
> And right this day must win:
> To doubt would be disloyalty
> To falter would be sin.[33]

This expression of patriotism was to be reprinted in every issue of the paper throughout the war years.

By 1862, the *Intelligencer* had become strongly anti-slavery, and now identified the cause of the Republic as that of preserving freedom for all mankind:

> We are fighting today for liberty for the World; for the power, influence, and example of a Christian nation of self-governing freemen . . . The fate of nations hangs on our heroism, our fidelity, and our devotion. Beyond the wide domain we call our own; beyond the mighty breadth of waters that separates us from other lands, millions of men are watching us, as they pray for the safety of the Republic. Rising out of dark abodes, and soaring upward on wings of prayer, from the hearts of the struggling and toiling millions, their hopes, their aspirations, and their sighs mingle with our own. In this mighty contest, involving not alone our wide territory, or our mighty rivers, or our crowded States, but involving freedom, and the great problem of virtuous, intelligent, and Christian self government, we have an issue to decide which is full of awful responsibility. . . . Stand, then, by the Government in the solemn hour of its trial. Stand by the Union in the day of storm and fear. Give all that you can give, of hope, of zeal, of wealth, of life. For we are doing battle for the world and for humanity.[34]

Having identified the war as a holy and righteous case, the *Intelligencer* gave unqualified support to the employment of the weapons of destruction. Only a military solution to civil strife would be acceptable. "The sword is the peacemaker," insisted the editor in early 1864. "The true conciliations are our rifled guns and minnie balls." More well-armed soldiers were needed to bring an end to the horrible strife. Indeed, the paper insisted that it was the duty of Christians to encourage enlistments and "to lend moral support to the Government in executing the conscription."[35] When spirits flagged before the tide turned toward the Unionists, the *Intelligencer* provided an unambiguous description of the actors in this tragic drama. The Northern soldiers were opposed to "the vilest, meanest, most godless despotism the world ever saw—a despotism engendered by the most malignant and selfish passions, that ever fired the human breast with an accursed lust of power." If the cause of the rebels was malicious and despicable, the cause of the Unionists was pure and noble. "Much of the best blood that ever coursed through the throbbing arteries of freemen has been willingly shed, in as holy a cause as ever devoted its martyr's to sacrifice."[36]

On April 13, 1865, the *Intelligencer* announced that the war was finished and that 'the powers of darkness' had failed to "dismember the Republic." Not only had the Republic been saved but "exalted as a witness for the rights of man and the truth of God before all nations."[37]

A few days later the paper wrote of the assassination of President Lincoln, and of the anguish of a nation in mourning. The editor bemoaned the fact that at the moment of personal victory, when Lincoln had begun to disarm his critics and when his administration was being hailed for its successes, he had been felled by "a cowardly hand, sealing with a martyr's blood the sacred principles to which his life had been devoted." How quickly Lincoln's life was embroidered with hagiography![38] Within days of his death, he had become an American saint, fallen martyr of America's civil religion. A resolution adopted by the General Synod of 1865 further canonized the assassinated President:

> We bless God for the incalculable service that our late beloved president rendered to the cause of Union and liberty, and for the testimony for Christianity which he left behind him; and over his new-made grave we consecrate ourselves afresh to the country and the cause for which he lived and died, and to the Savior whom he honored."[39]

The patriotic piety expressed by the eastern church through the pages of the *Intelligencer* was matched by those in the western church. Although the Dutch settlers had arrived in Michigan, Wisconsin, Illinois and Iowa as recently as the late 1840's and 1850's, these immigrants were very supportive of the cause of the Union in their adopted country. In his article on the Dutch churches in Michigan during the Civil War, Wynand Wichers indicates that there were patriotic appeals in the Dutch newspapers of western Michigan colonies even before the attack on Fort Sumter. The Reverend Albertus C. Van Raalte, founder and guiding force in these colonies, is described as one who actually recruited young men to serve in the Union army. Among the many Dutch youngsters who served in Michigan regiments and fought the Confederates in the major battles of the War were two of Van Raalte's own sons. Most of the Dutch soldiers, including Van Raalte's sons, returned home from the war having contributed significantly to the preservation of the

Union.[40] Undoubtedly, this involvement helped to strengthen the patriotism and loyalty of these recent immigrants. These Dutch settlers now "owned" the nation's experience, and were bona fide members of the American civil religion.

The lessons of patriotism and piety would not be lost on the offspring of these nineteenth century Dutch colonists. In the first issue of *The Leader* (October 31, 1906), the first English-language newspaper serving the Western churches, Evert J. Blekkink noted: "A religious weekly must be patriotic. Next to the love of God is the love of country." In a trial run of the same issue John H. Kleinheksel reminded the readers that the Dutch immigrants who left their homes, friends, and fatherland "in quest of a larger liberty," quickly assumed the duties of citizenship and gave evidence of loyalty to the new flag "by enthusiastically offering to go as volunteers" in the Civil War. "They were now no longer strangers and aliens, for their own sons had sealed with their life-blood the right to the proud title of American Citizen."[41]

Many of the early editorials of the *Leader* espoused a vital patriotism and linked it with Reformed piety. In an editorial titled "America First," Evert Blekkink called for genuine patriotism and gratitude to God for America. "As Christians and loyal citizens," it was necessary to render full devotion to the church of Christ and to "the characteristically American institutions which by common grace and in the divine providence are our glory." Blekkink concluded that the true Christian patriot was able to say, "America First." This did not mean "America right or wrong" for there were evils to be overcome and good to be established. "Beloved America must be made more beloved so that it may continue to be in the future what it has been for more than three-hundred years to millions, the promised land."[42]

In the twentieth century the issues of war and national security have continued to provide a sharp focus for the relationship of piety and patriotism in the Reformed Church. In general, the Reformed Church in America has followed the theological tradition of other Reformed Churches in supporting what have been described as "just wars."[43] Unlike the "peace churches" which have consistently resisted Christian involvement in wars, the Reformed Church has sometimes cautiously, but other times incautiously, endorsed America's involvement in international conflicts. The general tendency has been to rally around the flag with a theological rationale which supports the thesis that peace and justice can be secured through war.

The Reformed Church appears to have supported the neutralist policy of Woodrow Wilson during the early months of World War I. However, once the United States was drawn into the conflict, the church tended to support the war with patriotic enthusiasm. An April 11, 1917, issue of the *Intelligencer* editorialized that America had become involved in a "righteous war," a war to preserve the principles of justice and liberty. It was considered the duty of the then present generation to enlarge and enrich the freedoms fought for by "the fathers of '76, the patriots of '61," and "the heroes of '98 who contended to free the slaves of an old world despotism." How could Americans turn deaf ears to new cries of suffering in the world? "God knows we want no war, but God help us if we accept the pusillanimous peace merely to escape the burdens of conflict. In no such way can we save ourselves nor fulfill our destiny as a nation that loves its fellowmen and the God-given principles of liberty and right."[44] In the West, Evert Blekkink provided an equally ringing endorsement of the war for the readers of *The Leader*. In an Independence Day editorial which focused upon "Love of Country," Blekkink concluded that America had entered the war "on the side of Democracy." There was therefore no choice under the supreme rule of God but to resist evil. "When Imperialism dictated where we should go and what we should do on the high seas, torpedoed our ships, and sent cargo and passengers mercilessly to the bottom, there was no alternative than to resist unto blood." Taking its cue from the *Intelligencer* during Civil War days, *The Leader*, during World War I, emblazoned its editorial page with an unfurled American flag, and the following verse:

Since God is right, His right is might
Such right the day shall win.
To doubt would be disloyalty,
To falter would be sin.[45]

Desiring "to affirm its loyalty and pledge its support to the President and Government of the United States, in this hour of National Crisis," the General Synod of 1917 passed a resolution commending the churches and their members to offer financial support to the government. To set a patriotic example representatives to the synod contributed $500 for the purchase of Liberty Bonds to be given as a gift to various mission agencies of the church. Furthermore, the synod sent a letter to President Wilson "affirming its loyalty to a patriotism which has become sacred in this world-testing time."[46] The synod of 1918 renewed this pledge of loyalty to the president, the country, and "the righteous and Christian cause" for which "the government and her Allies are contending."[47]

Following World War I, which so many Christians had identified as a holy war for democracy, a surge of pacifism began to sweep through many protestant churches. It was during the twenties and thirties that the Fellowship of Reconciliation became so prominent. Much of this pacifist fervor was a reaction to the war fever which had been fanned by many church leaders.[48] Reinhold Niebuhr, for instance, confessed this sin of militarism and joined the Fellowship. While it is difficult to determine how many members of the Reformed Church reacted in a similar way, some may have been influenced by A. J. Muste who was Secretary for the Fellowship during the late 1930's. There is, however, little evidence that the church confessed collective guilt for its blatant support of war, although there were undoubtedly individuals who were driven toward pacificism.

There is certainly evidence that the Reformed Church became increasingly interested in the concern for international peace. In 1922, the General Synod established the Committee on International Justice and Goodwill, which took as its mandate the drafting of a statement of support for such concerns as the Washington Conference on arms limitation, the Kellogg Peace Pact, and the League of Nations and the Court of International Justice. Over the next decades, this committee and others dealing with peace issues, recommended synodical opposition to compulsory military training, the establishment of peace committees throughout the church, and cooperation with other churches to strengthen peace efforts.[49] Again it is difficult to determine whether these peace concerns were truly heeded in the churches during the twenties and thirties. Articles in the church papers during this period reveal that if there was some concern for international peace, this was not accomplished through a softening of the rhetoric of nationalism. Editors still enthused that America was God's country and that Christians should be proud patriots. For example, a Memorial Day editorial in the *Intelligencer-Leader* (1939) reminded the readers to be thankful for national blessings and encouraged them to adopt "a true Christian patriotism," which was described as "a deep and enduring faith, faith in the idea and ideal upon which the nation was founded and builded— liberty; faith in the nation's worth to the world; faith in the nation's future."[50]

As World War II approached, there were some in the Reformed Church who warned against the close association of religion and patriotism as well as against the militarization of Christianity. One who argued consistently for the position of pacificism was B. D. Dykstra. Permitted to voice his views on the pages of the *Intelligencer-Leader*, Dykstra was a courageous and irrepressible critic of militarization. If not a doctrinaire pacifist, Luman Shafer also gave eloquent support to international peace efforts.[51] In 1940, as the war ripped through Europe, the report of the Committee on International Justice and Good Will produced a statement which sharply warned against nationalism. "Nations have set themselves up as objects of supreme devotion and demand that loyalty and sacrifice of their subjects that should be given only to God. Individual life has lost its value before the demands of race and nation."[52]

In the end, Dykstra, Shafer, and others were lonely prophets who faced a long tradition of support for national military activities in the cause of justice. In June, 1941, as the nation was gearing up for another world-wide conflict, the General Synod passed a resolution affirming its "loyalty and devotion" to the country during a "time of unlimited national emergency," while expressing "concern, encouragement, support and interest" for the young men of the church who were being called into the armed forces.[53] As the nation became actively involved in World War II, there was little need to pass other patriotic resolutions in support of the war effort. Relatively little is said about the war at the General Synod or in the pages of the denominational papers because there was little debate as to whether this was a just war. Concerned about those in the church who may have genuine reservations about personal involvement in war, the synod did recognize and minister to conscientious objectors, even setting up a fund in 1941 to help them pay for the costs of participation in the Civilian Public Service Corps. During the late 1960s and 1970s when the United States was engaged in the Viet Nam conflict, the synod provided tacit approval for the nation's involvement, but again demonstrated concern for conscientious objectors who could not support the war.[54] In 1969, the General Synod voted to repeal the Selective Service act of 1967 in favor of a system of voluntary enlistment and, in 1971, the synod heard the concerns of draft-resistor Glenn Pontier. While it did not vote to receive the draft cards of Pontier (and others who were conscientiously opposed to the war), it did express "support for his right of Christian conscience," embraced him "in Christian love," and promised "to maintain the fellowship of Christ."[55]

In terms of practice, Reformed Christians of the twentieth century have continued to believe that patriotism and piety are interrelated—to be a good Christian is to be a "good American." To be sure, there are those like B. D. Dykstra and Glenn Pontier who have argued that there is an inherent tension between the demands of the nation and the demands of the Gospel. By and large, however, the American flag has found a rather comfortable home in the sanctuaries of Reformed Churches. In fact, this powerful symbol of nationalism has at times received prominent display. On special occasions, some churches have decorated their sanctuaries with the flag and with red, white and blue bunting, demonstrating unreserved loyalty to the nation and to the civil religion which provides a unifying ideology.[56]

Our review of patriotism and piety appears to demonstrate that the Reformed Church has embraced, almost uncritically, the forms of civil religion which have found expression in this country during the 200 years of its nationhood. In terms of the paradigms provided by H. Richard Niebuhr,[57] the Christ of the church has often been the Christ of culture. It is important to point out, however, that despite some obvious evidence of cultural identity and even cultural captivity, there has always existed an inherent theological tension between the nation and the church. It is a tension which arises from the very pinion of Reformed thought—the doctrine of the sovereignty of God.

It is unnecessary here fully to elaborate the Reformed doctrine of the church and state, but it is useful to provide an outline of the doctrine, especially as it has been interpreted by theologians associated with the Reformed Church in America. Nearly all such discussions begin with an examination of Romans 13, the *classicus locus* of the state-church question. There is agreement in Reformed circles that the governing authorities have been instituted by God, not merely to restrain evil but to further his divine purposes in the world. In an article concerned with "Theocracy and the Reformation," Eugene P. Heideman points out that Calvin recognized a positive role for the government which went far beyond that recognized by Luther or the Anabaptists. In fact, the civil government as well as the church was understood as a vehicle for true peace and justice. Christians, then, are not to view the state as merely a neutral force or as a negative, restraining influence, but as a partner in furthering the cause of the gospel of Christ. Heideman does not advocate the sort of theocracy which has been associated with Calvin's Geneva; he simply argues that those who follow Calvin will acknowledge the positive functions of the state in the divine order.[58] Isaac Rottenberg tends to reinforce such a view when he suggests that both the church and state must be envisaged as "divine institutions, which each according to its own nature, and therefore in its own way, fulfill a function in the overarching reality of the kingdom."[59]

When they assign a positive role to the governing authorities, Heideman and Rottenberg seem to be direct intellectual descendants of the Apostle Paul, John Calvin, and Guido de Bres, who probably framed the Belgic Confession. Article 36 of this standard of faith for the Reformed Church states not only that God ordained earthly authorities "in order that the unbridledness of men might be restrained, and all human affairs might be conducted in good orderly fashion," but their office is also

> To maintain the holy worship of the church, to prevent and remove all idolatry and false religion, to destroy the Kingdom of the anti-Christ, to see that the Word of Christ is preached everywhere so that God might be revered and worshipped by everyone, as he commands in His Word.

This statement, of course, was drafted during the 16th century in Europe, when the state was explicitly Christian and given the responsibility of supporting and protecting the churches. When the Reformed Church in America established its constitution in 1792, it was well aware that it would be functioning in a new "secular" order. Hence, Article 36 has been qualified to accommodate the disestablishment of a state-supported church.[60] While the state is officially separated from the church in the United States, it is not to be viewed as an institution wholly separated from God. Rottenberg, for example, argues from Romans 13:1 that "the governing authorities find their ultimate ground in the will of God, and not the will of man."[61]

Rottenberg realizes that the powers that be may not know or acknowledge their divine origin and purpose. Indeed, the powers may "seek the source of their authority even in their own divine nature instead of their institution by God," and therefore become "demonic." At this point, of course, the church must confront the state with the proclamation that "the state is not ultimate, only God and His Kingdom are."[62] This means that a tension, real and potential, will exist between the church and the governing authorities, even if those authorities have been elected by a majority of the citizens, of whom many will be Christians. The sovereignty of God brings judgment upon any human institution which will claim sovereignty for itself.

With its "high" view of the state (or government), Reformed theology provides an ideological counterweight to the sort of patriotism which merges into nationalism. While definitions of the term "nationalism" vary somewhat, the two recognized authorities on the subject tend to agree that nationalism has become a modern religion. Hans Kohn has defined nationalism as "a state of mind, in which the supreme loyalty of the individual is felt to be due to the nation-state," while Carlton J. Hayes argues that when the national state becomes "a paramount, a supreme loyalty," and when "national emotion is fused with religious emotion . . . nationalism itself becomes a religion or a substitute for religion."[63] It must be acknowledged that Reformed Christians generally have not understood or resisted the dangers of nationalism. But the Reformed principles of the sovereignty of God have served at least to goad the church in the right direction. In a discussion of the civil rights struggle in the 1960's, when resistance to unjust laws was being advocated, Charles Kamp acknowledged that Christians should obey the laws of the state, but he went on to insist that "we have a higher law, the Law of God." To obey God's law it may be necessary to break human law.[64] Addressing himself to the same issue, Winfield Burggraaff suggested that while government is usually a means of grace, Caesar is not always to be viewed as an ally of Christ. "That is why Christians who profess to stand under the lordship of Christ, and not of Caesar, give to Caesar no more than is absolutely necessary, so that they may give to God all that He demands."[65]

In a trenchant article which was published by the *Church Herald* in 1971, Isaac Rottenberg wrote that the gospel of Christ sets believers free from the cultural captivity which has held so many Christians in bondage. He suggested that while the church attempted to proclaim a "non-political and a-cultural" gospel, it had actually nurtured an insidious form of cultural bondage—including the bondage of nationalism. He concluded that the Gospel is a message of grace which cures us of cultural astigmatism and allows us to see clearly the political implication of the kingdom of Christ.[66]

Most recently, in a discussion of the nuclear arms race, nationalism has come under attack as a cultural bondage which prohibits us from understanding that our ultimate security comes not from nuclear arms but from trust in God. In a paper produced in 1979, the Theological Commission of the Reformed Church insisted that "we must recognize the demonic power of nationalism," for in making claims of sovereignty "the state oversteps the boundaries provided for it in God's order. It pretends to be God." The Commission cited Oscar Cullmann's biblical verdict on nationalism: "It is just this religious claim of the state that constitutes the Satanic."[67] A study guide intended to assist the church in efforts at peacemaking helps its readers to gain a biblical perspective on Christian citizenship. While acknowledging the importance of national citizenship, Reformed Christians are reminded of the higher citizenship mentioned in I Peter 2:9:

> Christians are citizens of God's Kingdom first. This allegiance comes before any other. Our first loyalty is to God and the 'holy nation,' his chosen people, the Church. No earthly state or political party is more important than the new community we share in Christ.[68]

Piety and patriotism have been closely related for Reformed Christians in America. Properly so, for church and nation are both agents for God's peace. But the church has too often failed to recognize that the kingdom of God and the kingdom of America are not one and the same. When the church has too uncritically accepted the claims of the nation it has verged toward an unhealthy nationalism. But when the church has stepped away from culture and asserted God's sovereignty, it has been a prophetic voice calling the nation back to its appointed task. In the present nuclear age, may God continue to raise up such prophets of justice and peace in the Reformed community.

NOTES

Introduction

1. *The Acts and Proceedings of the General Synod, Reformed Church in America,* 1984, p. 29 (Hereinafter cited as *Minutes,* General Synod.)
2. *Ibid.,* p. 28.
3. *Ibid.*
4. For an excellent study of the persistence of the Dutch Reformed culture in North America, see James D. Bratt, *Dutch Calvinism in Modern America: A History of a Conservative Subculture* (Grand Rapids: Eerdmans Publishing Co., 1984).
5. Maurice G. Hansen, *The Reformed Church in the Netherlands* (New York: Board of Publication of the Reformed Church in America, 1884), p. 21. For additional information on the history of the Reformed Church in the Netherlands, see Howard G. Hageman, *Lily Among the Throns* (New York: Reformed Church Press, 1975), and M. Eugene Osterhaven, "The Founding of a Church," in *Reformed Review,* Vol. 34, No. 3 (Spring, 1981), pp. 186-192.
6. Maurice G. Hansen, *op. cit.,* p. 63.
7. *Ibid.,* p. 65.
8. *Ibid.,* p. 105.
9. *Ibid.,* p. 75.
10. *Ibid.,* pp. 147-148.
11. Leroy Nixon, *Reformed Standards of Unity* (Grand Rapids: Society for Reformed Publications, 1952), p. 20.
12. A classic study of the Synod of Dort, representing the orthodox perspective, is Thomas Scott, *The Articles of the Synod of Dort, and the Rejection of Errors: with the History of Events Which Made Way for that Synod, as Published by the Authority of the States-General; and the Documents Confirming its Decisions* (Utica: William Williams, 1831).
13. J. L. Neve, *A History of Christian Thought,* Vol. 2 (Philadelphia: The Muhlenberg Press, 1946), p. 23.
14. Maurice G. Hansen, *op. cit.,* p. 118.
15. *Ibid.,* pp. 166-170.

Chapter I
Orthodoxy and Piety:
Two Styles of Faith in the Colonial Period

1. [Students interested in Dutch Reformed theological history during the colonial period will find the following sources helpful: John Romeyn Broadhead, *History of the State of New York: First Period, 1609-1644* (New York: Harper, 1853); Thomas J. Condon, *New York Beginnings: The Commercial Origins of New Netherland* (New

York: New York University Press, 1968); Edward Tanjore Corwin, *Ecclesiastical History of the State of New York*, 7 vols. (Albany: J. B. Lyon, 1901-1916); Edward Tanjore Corwin, *Manual of the Reformed Church in America* (New York: Board of Publication of the Reformed Church in America, 1902); Gerald F. De Jong, *The Dutch Reformed Church in the American Colonies* (Grand Rapids: Wm. B. Eerdmans, 1978); Herman Harmelink III, "Another Look at Frelinghuysen and His Awakening," *Church History*, XXXVIII, V. 4 (December, 1968), pp. 423-438; Alice P. Kenney, "Religious Artifacts of the Dutch Colonial Period," *de Halve Maen*, LIII, vol. 4 (Winter, 1977-78); Adrian Coulter Leiby, *The Revolutionary War in the Hackensack Valley: The Jersey Dutch and the Neutral Ground, 1775-1783* (New Brunswick: Rutgers University Press, 1962); Adrian Coulter Leiby, *The United Churches of Hackensack and Schraalenburgh, New Jersey, 1686-1822* (River Edge: Bergen County Historical Society, 1976); Joseph Anthony Loux, ed. and trans., *Boels' Complaint Against Frelinghuysen* (New Brunswick: Historical Society of the Reformed Church in America, 1979); John Pershing Luidens, "The Americanization of the Dutch Reformed Church," Unpublished Ph.D. Dissertation, University of Olkahoma, Norman, Oklahoma; George L. Smith, *Religion and Trade in New Netherland: Dutch Origins and American Development* (Ithaca: Cornell University Press, 1973); James Robert Tanis, *Dutch Calvinistic Pietism in the Middle Colonies: a Study in the Life and Theology of Theodorus Jacobus Felinghuysen* (The Hague: Nyhoff, 1967); James Robert Tanis, "Frelinghuysen, The Dutch Clergy, and the Great Awakening in the Middle Colonies," *Reformed Review* vol. 38, No. 2 (Winter, 1985), pp. 109-118; James W. Van Hoeven, ed., *Piety and Patriotism: Bicentennial Studies of the Reformed Church in America, 1776-1976* (Grand Rapids: Wm. B. Eerdmans, Publishing Co., 1976, pp. 1-33; Arnold J. F. Van Laer, ed., *Documents Relating to New Netherland, 1624-1626*, in the Huntington Library (San Marino: Henry E. Huntington Library and Art Gallery, 1924); M. G. Van Rensselaer, *History of the City of New York in the Seventeenth Century*, 2 vols. (New York: Macmillan Co., 1909).—Ed.]

2. Gerald F. De Jong, "The Ziekentroosters or Comforters of the Sick in New Netherland," *New York Historical Society Quarterly*, LIV (Oct., 1970), pp. 339-359.

3. [Gisbertus Voetius (1589-1676) served as professor of theology and "oriental" (i.e. Semitic) languages at the University of Utrecht, from 1634 to 1676. His writings on piety ("Precisionism") and orthodoxy made him a dominant and often controversial figure in seventeenth century Dutch theological circles. For an excellent introduction to Voetius, as well as a translation of some of his works, see John W. Beardslee III, ed. and trans., *Reformed Dogmatics: Seventeenth-Century Reformed Theology Through the Writings of Wollebius, Voetius, and Turretin* (New York: Oxford University Press, 1965)—Ed.]

4. [Johannes Cocceius (1603-1669) held the chair of theology at the University of Leiden from 1640 to 1669. Expert in biblical languages, Cocceius' "covenant theology" became a critique of Voetian "Precisionism" and divided the church in the Netherlands in the seventeenth century.—Ed.]

5. [The term "Arminian" has roots in the seventeenth century conflict in the Netherlands over the doctrine of election. Jacobus Arminius (1560-1609), a professor of theology at the University of Leiden, opposed the orthodox position on election. His supporters were called "Arminians" or "Remonstrants."—Ed.]

6. [Johannes a' Marck (1655-1731) was a disciple of Voetius. His dogmatic and exegetical writings gave Voetian thought further theological underpinnings.—Ed.]

7. [The "five points" of Calvinism that emerged from the Synod of Dort are total

depravity (inability), unconditional election, limited atonement, irresistible grace, and perseverence of the saints.—Ed.]

8. [Supralapsarianism and infralapsarianism were opposing theological positions regarding God's eternal decrees. The former (supralapsarianism) argued that God's decrees concerning election or reprobation occurred before creation, while the latter (infralapsarianism) held that God's election decrees came after the Fall, even though the Fall was foreseen. These two positions were hotly debated at the Synod of Dort.—Ed.]

9. Gerrit Vander Lugt, trans., *The Liturgy of the Reformed Church in America* (New York: Board of Education of the Reformed Church in America, 1968), p. 517.

10. *Ibid.*, p. 518.

11. John W. Beardslee III, ed. and trans., *op. cit., p. 332.*

12. *Maurice G. Hansen*, op. cit., p. 218.

13. [Willem a' Brakel (1635-1711) was a Dutch pietist whose three volume study, *The Reasonable Service of God*, was very influential in shaping the piety of Frelinghuysen.—Ed.]

14. [Gijsbertus Bonnet (1723-1805) was professor of theology at The University of Utrecht. See Bonnet's *Ecclesiastes: Schetswyze opheldering van Salomons Prediker*, 2 vols. (Utrecht: n.p., 1781-1783) and *Verzemeling van Leerredenen*, 4 vols. (Utrecht: n.p., 1774-1792).—Ed.]

15. See Jack Klunder, "The Sermons of Dutch Clergy During the Colonial Period," Unpublished Doctoral Dissertation, Westminster Theological Seminary, Philadelphia, Pa., 1984. Klunder's dissertation stresses the place of covenant theology in eighteenth century Dutch colonial preaching. Of similar spirit to these theologians and pastors was Johannes vander Kemp (1664-1718), whose sermons on the Heidelberg Catechism were translated in 1810 by John M. van Harlingen (New Brunswick: Abraham Blaure, 1810).

16. [The Rev. Henricus Selyns (1636-1701) served Dutch churches in and around New York (New Amsterdam), and "was the most eminent of the ministers who came from Holland" in the seventeenth century. See Charles Corwin, *A Manual of the Reformed Church in America, 1628-1922* (New York: Board of Publications of the Reformed Church in America, 1922), pp. 495-497.—Ed.]

17. See, for example, his Latin poem to Cotton Mather in Charles Corwin, *op. cit.,* pp. 735-740.

18. [See, for example, John W. Beardslee III, *op. cit.,* pp. 1-25; James Tanis, "The Heidelberg Catechism in the Hands of the Calvinist Pietists," *Reformed Review*, vol. 24, no. 3 (Spring, 1971), pp. 154-161; M. Eugene Osterhaven, "The Experiential Theology of Early Dutch Calvinism," *Reformed Review*, vol. 27, no. 3 (Spring, 1974), pp. 180-189; and M. Eugene Osterhaven, *The Spirit of the Reformed Tradition: The Reformed Church Must Always be Reforming* (Grand Rapids: Wm. B. Eerdmans Publishing Co., 1971), pp. 110-143.—Ed.]

19. [See Howard Hageman, "William Bertholf: Pioneer Domine of New Jersey," in *Reformed Review*, vol. 29, no. 9 (Winter, 1976), pp. 73-80, for an excellent brief study of Bertholf.—Ed.]

20. [The Rev. Bernardus Freeman (1662-1743), emigrated from Westphalia in 1700. He served as a missionary to the Mohawk Indians near Schenectady, New York, and subsequently ministered in Dutch churches in and around New York City.—Ed.]

21. [The best study of Frelinghuysen is James R. Tanis, *op. cit.* See also Herman Harmelink III, *op. cit.*—Ed.]

22. [The Rev. Theodorus Frelinghuysen, Jr. (1723-1774) served the Dutch Church in Albany before his untimely death at sea.—Ed.]
23. [The Rev. John Henry Goetschius (1717-1774) served Dutch churches in Long Island and northern New Jersey.—Ed.]
24. [The Rev. Johannes Leydt (1718-1783) served Dutch churches in northern New Jersey.—Ed.]
25. [The Rev. Eliardus Westerlo (1738-1790) served for thirty years the Dutch church in Albany.—Ed.]
26. See a summary of this teaching in Marck's *Christianae Theologogiae Madulla* (Amsterdam: n.p., 1721), p. 416.
27. Joseph Anthony Loux, *op. cit.* Loux' work is a translation of *Klagte.*
28. [In this context, the term *coetus* represents a more pietistic "style of faith," and the term *conferentie* the more orthodox. In broader terms the *coetus-conferentie* schism split the Dutch Church from 1747-1772.—Ed.]
29. [See Joseph Anthony Loux, *op. cit.*, pp. 126-127, and *passim.* —Ed.]
30. [Jean de Labadie (1610-1674), a convert to Calvinism from the Roman Catholic priesthood, became a leader of the experiential pietist movement in the Netherlands in the seventeenth century. His followers were often called "Labadists."—Ed.]
31. [The Rev. Johannes Ritzema (1710-1796) served Dutch churches in New York city and Kinderhook, New York. He was an important leader of the *conferentie* side of the *coetus-conferentie* schism.—Ed.]
32. Edward Tanjore Corwin, *Digest of Synodical Legislation* (New York: Board of Publication of the Reformed Church in America, 1906), pp. v-vi.
33. James R. Tanis, "Reformed Pietism and Protestant Missions," *Harvard Theological Review,* 67 (1974), pp. 65-73.
34. James R. Tanis, *Dutch Calvinistic Pietism in the Middle Colonies, op. cit.*, p. 86. Tanis also notes that the Classis of Amsterdam showed concern for the failure to reach the indigenous people of North America and attributed the absence of missionary accomplishment to controversy. *Ibid.*, p. 73.
35. [René Descartes (1596-1650), a French philosopher-theologian-mathematician, was part of the phalanx of "Enlightenment" scholars who challenged orthodox Christian thought in the seventeenth century.—Ed.]
36. Charles E. Corwin, *op. cit.*, p. 335.

Chapter II
Dort and Albany:
Reformed Theology Engages a New Culture

1. *The Magazine of the Reformed Dutch Church,* III (June, 1828), p. 95.
2. Perry Miller, *Life of the Mind in America* (New York: Harcourt, Brace & World, 1965), p. 7.
3. John De Witt, *A Funeral Discourse, Occasioned by the Death of the Rev. John H. Livingston* (New Brunswick: William Meyer, 1825), p. 11.
4. For additional information on Livingston's contribution to Reformed thought, see Eugene Heideman's essay, "Theology," in James Van Hoeven, ed., *Piety and Patriotism, op. cit.*, pp. 96-98.
5. John De Witt, *op. cit.*, p. 19.
6. James Spencer Cannon, *Lectures on Pastoral Theology* (New York: Charles Scribner, 1853), p. 17.

7. *Christian Intelligencer,* IX (Sept. 8, 1838), p. 25.
8. *Ibid.*
9. *Ibid.,* IX (Aug. 25, 1838), p. 17.
10. John F. Schermerhorn, "Letters to the Editor," in *Ibid.,* IX (Oct. 6, 1838), p. 29.
11. *Minutes,* General Synod, I (May, 1791), pp. 217-219.
12. See "Preface to the Entire Constitution, Embracing Doctrines, Liturgy, and Government, 1792," in Edward Tanjore Corwin, *op. cit.,* pp. v-vii.
13. *Minutes,* General Synod, IIA (June, 1814), p. 35.
14. *Ibid.*
15. *Ibid.,* p. 36.
16. *Acts and Proceedings of the Classis of Montgomery, New York* (May 26, 1819).
17. *Minutes,* General Synod, III (Oct., 1820), p. 27.
18. *Ibid.,* p. 31.
19. *Ibid.*
20. *Ibid.*
21. The True Reformed Dutch Church in the United States of America remained in existence as a separate body until 1865, when it merged with the newly organized Christian Reformed Church, a body which had also seceded from the Reformed Dutch Church. For information on the secession of the Christian Reformed Church, see pp. 83-124, this volume.
22. *The Christian Intelligencer,* II (Sept. 17, 1831), pp. 26-27.
23. *Ibid.,* II (Sept. 24, 1831), p. 31.
24. *Ibid.*
25. *Ibid.*
26. *Ibid.,* II (Sept. 3, 1831), p. 17. See also *Ibid.,* p. 13.
27. *Minutes,* General Synod, III (June, 1831), p. 16.
28. See Eugene Heideman's chapter titled "Theology," *op. cit.,* p. 102.
29. Philip Schaff, *The Principle of Protestantism as Related to the Present State of the Church.* Translated by John W. Nevin. (Chambersburg: Publication Office of the German Reformed Church, 1845), p. 37.
30. *Ibid.,* pp. 113-114.
31. *Ibid.,* pp. 128-131.
32. Rev. William Craig Brownlee, who emigrated from Scotland to North America in 1807, led the Reformed Church in its opposition against the Roman Catholic Church.
33. See *The Christian Intelligencer,* IV (Aug. 7, 1845), p. 14, (Aug. 28, 1845), p. 26, and *passim.*
34. John W. Nevin, "The Dutch Crusade," *Mercersburg Review,* VI (1854), p. 74.
35. *Ibid.,* pp. 92-93.
36. See Berg's defense of Reformed orthodoxy in his *Old Path's, or a Sketch of the Order and Discipline of the Reformed Church Before the Reformation* (Philadelphia: J. B. Lippincott & Co., 1845).
37. N. H. Dosker, *De Hollandsche Gereformeerde Kerk in Amerika* (Nijkerk: C. C. Callenbach, 1893), p. 168.
38. Howard G. Hageman, *Pulpit and Table: Some Chapters in the History of Worship in the Reformed Churches* (Richmond: John Knox Press, 1962), p. 85.
39. Theodore Appel, *The Life and Work of John Williamson Nevin* (Philadelphia: Reformed Church Publication House, 1889). See especially chapter 33, pp. 396-409.
40. *Ibid.,* p. 409.
41. *Ibid.*
42. Edward Tanjore Corwin, *A Manual of the Reformed Church in America, 1628-1878* (New York: Board of Publication of the Reformed Church America, 1879), p. 507.

43. See Franklin D. Steen, "Tayler Lewis on Scripture: A Defense of Revelation and Creation in Nineteenth Century America," Unpublished Th.D. dissertation submitted to the faculty of Westminster Theological Seminary, Philadelphia, Pennsylvania, 1971.

44. Philip Schaff, "Preface of the General Editor," in Johann Peter Lange, *A Commentary on the Holy Scriptures* (New York: Charles Scribner, 1868), p. vi. For a good account of Lewis' life and work see Eliphalet Nott Potter, *Discourses Commemorative of Professor Tayler Lewis, LL.D., L.H.D., Delivered at Commencement, 1877* (Albany: J. Munsell, 1878).

45. Tayler Lewis, *The Six Days of Creation: or the Scriptural Cosmology, With the Ancient Idea of a Plurality of Time-Worlds, in Distinction From Worlds in Space* (Schenectady: G. Y. Van Debogert. London: John Cahpman, 1853).

46. Franklin D. Steen, *op. cit.*, pp. 115ff. An example of Lewis' ideas in regard creation is the following: ". . . A development theory in the sense of species from species . . . may be as pious as any other . . . It may be regarded as a method of God's working." See Tayler Lewis, *The Six Days of Creation, op. cit.*, pp. 219ff.

47. *The Christian Intelligencer*, XXXIV (July 17, 1862), p. 2.

48. *The Christian Intelligencer*, XXXII (April 18, 1861), p. 2. Lewis wrote numerous articles in *The Christian Intelligencer*. See, for example, his "Interpretation of Exodus 21:20, 21:35," in XVIII (May 5, 1864), p. 1; "Interpretation of Job 42:7," in XXXV (Jan. 21, 1864), pp. 1ff; "Interpretation of Matthew 5:22—A Tract For the Times," in XXXV (Feb. 11, 1864), p. 1; "The National Oath," in XXXII (Nov. 14 and Dec. 26, 1861), pp. 1ff.

49. Franklin D. Steen, *op. cit.*, p. 93.

50. *Ibid.*, p. 94.

51. *Ibid.*

52. Gregg Alan Mast, "The Eucharistic Service of the Catholic Apostolic Church and its Influence on Reformed Liturgical Renewals of the Nineteenth Century," Unpublished Ph.D. dissertation submitted to the Graduate School of Drew University, 1985. See especially pp. 175-205.

53. See Gerald F. De Jong, "The Controversy over Dropping the Word Dutch from the Name of the Reformed Church," *Reformed Review*, vol. 34, no. 3 (Spring, 1981), pp. 158-170.

54. Herman Harmelink III, *Ecumenism and the Reformed Church* (Grand Rapids: Eerdmans Publishing Co., 1968), pp. 38-69.

Chapter III

New York and Holland:
Reformed Theology and The Second Dutch Immigration

1. *The Christian Intelligencer*, VIII (Sept. 24, 1848), p. 26; VIII (June 4, 1849), p. 17; and *passim*. See also William O. Van Eyck, *The Union of 1850: A Collection of Papers by the Late Wm. O. Van Eyck, Esq. on the Union of the Classis of Holland With the Reformed Church in America, in June, 1850* (Grand Rapids: Wm. B. Eerdmans Publishing Co., 1950), p. 93.

2. *Minutes*, General Synod (June, 1847), p. 196. See also *Ibid.* (June, 1848), pp. 425-427.

3. *The Christian Intelligencer* (Sept. 20, 1849), pp. 24-25.

4. *Ibid.*, p. 24.

5. *Ibid.*, p. 25.

6. *Ibid.*

7. The General Synod apparently decided it was not appropriate for the Classis of Holland to join the Classis of Michigan, which had been organized by the Board of Domestic Missions in 1841.

8. As reported by Professor Charles Scott of Hope College, Holland, Michigan, in an address at New Brunswick Seminary, New Brunswick, New Jersey, and printed in *Centennial of the Theological Seminary of the Reformed Church in America, 1784-1884* (New York: Board of Publication of the Reformed Church in America, 1885), p. 252. Scott remarked that Van Raalte was unable to remember the exact year of his visit.

9. *Minutes*, General Synod (June, 1834), pp. 301-319. This material contains Mc-Clelland's sermon and gives a full acount of the issues in the conflict.

10. *Ibid.*, p. 306.

11. *Ibid.*, p. 308.

12. *Ibid* p. 314.

13. *Ibid.*, p. 319.

14. *Ibid.* (June, 1817), p. 48.

15. *Ibid.*, p. 49.

16. *Ibid.* (June, 1824), p. 52. [Samuel Hopkins (1721-1803) was a New England theologian in the tradition of Jonathan Edwards, under whom Hopkins studied. Hopkins went farther than Edwards, however, in allowing greater freedom of the will. The term "Hopkinsian" refers more to the spirit of theological liberalism, particularly as it relates to the question of the freedom of mind and will, than to the actual theological position of Samuel Hopkins. For an excellent brief statement on "Hopkinsianism," see George M. Marsden, *The Evangelical Mind and the New School Presbyterian Experience* (New Haven and London: Yale University Press, 1970), pp. 34-46.—Ed.]

17. [The Rev. Henrick Scholte led the Dutch immigration to Pella, Iowa, in 1847.]

18. Henry E. Dosker, *Levensschets van Rev. A. C. Van Raalte, D. D.* (Nijkerk, Netherlands: n.p., 1893), p. 162.

19. The term is imitative of the earlier "Catholic Scholasticism," which refers to the ponderous theological systems created by Thomas Aquinas and other Catholic theologians in the medieval period.

20. See my "The Place of the Covenant in Calvin's Thinking," *Reformed Review*, vol. 10, no. 4 (June, 1957), pp. 1-22.

21. Cocceius did not originate "federal theology," although he gave it its first systematic statement in Dutch Reformed thought.

22. [Gisbertus Voetius (1589-1676) served as professor of theology and "oriental" (i.e. Semitic) languages at the University of Utrecht.—Ed.]

23. [Abraham Hellenbroek's (1658-1731) writings received broad distribution in America during the eighteenth century, especially his catechism, titled *Specimen of Divine Truths*, and *A Sermon . . . from Canticles*, which was a strong attack on "unregenerate" clergy.—Ed.]

24. [Willem a' Brakel (1635-1711) was a Dutch pietist whose three volume study, *The Reasonable Service of God*, was very influential in shaping the piety of eighteenth century Dutch Reformed church life.—Ed.]

25. [Joducus van Lodensteyn (1620-1677), was a pietist pastor who served in Utrecht in the seventeenth century.—Ed.]

26. [Hermannus Witsius (1636-1708) was a Dutch pietist whose writings were very influential in the colonies.—Ed.]

27. A helpful source is Heinrich Heppe, *Geschichte des Pietismus und der Mystik in der Reformirten Kirche, namentlich der Niederlande* (Leiden: E.J. Brill, 1879).

28. Henry S. Lucas, *Netherlanders in America* (Ann Arbor: The University of Michigan Press, 1955), p. 493. Lucas notes that Thomas a' Kempis *Imitation of Christ* was among those volumes prized most by the Dutch immigrants.

29. Henry S. Lucas gives an engaging account of this story in *Dutch Immigrant Memoirs and Related Writings* (Assen, Netherlands: Van Gorcum, 1955).

30. The Heidelberg Catechism, Question 26.

31. *Ibid.,* Questions 27 and 28.

32. [See especially Calvin's *Institutes of the Christian Religion,* Book III.—Ed.]

33. Gordon J. Spykman, *Pioneer Preacher: Albertus Christianus Van Raalte* (Grand Rapids: Heritage Hall Publications, 1976).

34. *Ibid.,* p. 54.

Chapter IV
Saints and Sinners:
Secession and the Christian Reformed Church

1. *The Belgic Confession,* XXVII, XXVIII, Calvin writes that there is only one church and it "is called 'catholic' or 'universal,' because there could not be two or three churches unless Christ be torn asunder—which cannot happen" (*Institutes,* IV,i,2). Calvin believed this so strongly that he wrote it into a catechism for children. In answer to the question why the church is called "catholic" or universal, the Geneva Catechism reads: "This signifies that as there is only one head of the faithful so also all ought to be united in one body; so that there are not many churches, but only one, which is spread throughout the world." Baum, Cunitz, and Reuss, eds., *Corpus Reformatorum, Ioannis Calvini Opera Quae Supersunt Omnia,* (Brunswick: n.p., 1863-1900), pp. 34, 39.

2. In describing the reluctance of the leaders of the *Afscheiding* (secession) of 1834, and later, to leave the Netherlands Reformed Church, H. E. Dosker writes, "They were Hollanders and the Old Testament ideas of the *peoples' church* [*volkskerk*: the church for all the people] is instilled in every Hollander." Italics his. *Levensschets van Rev. A. C. Van Raalte, D.D.* (Nijkerk: C. C. Callenbach, 1893), p. 15. Cf. p. 30.

3. In his report Wyckoff mentions that "on Monday the Classis met," and that "Rev. Van Raalte deemed it would be expedient to assemble the ministers and the elders of the churches. Accordingly he dispatched letters and messengers to the several ministers and consistories, inviting them to a conference with me on Monday, June 4th." Wm. O. Van Eyck, *The Union of 1850*: A Collection of Papers on the Union of the Classis of Holland with the Reformed Church in America, in June, 1850. Selected and Edited by the Permanent Committee on History and Research of the General Synod of the Reformed Church in America (Grand Rapids: Wm. B. Eerdmans Publishing Co., 1950), p. 76. It is important to note this because of later charges that the meeting on June 4 was not a properly constituted meeting of the Classis of Holland and that therefore its actions were illegal. Henry Beets, among others, who claims this, also says that that assembly decided on union (*besloot tot vereenigen*). *De Christelijke Gereformeerde Kerk: Zestic Jaren van Strijd en Zegen* (Grand Rapids: Grand Rapids Printing Company, 1918), pp. 74-75. Rather, the vote on union in the classis took place over a month later, on July 10.

4. H. E. Dosker, *op. cit.,* p. 323; Wm. O. Van Eyck, *op. cit.,* p. 73.

5. The minutes of the consistories of Holland, Graafschap, and Overisel of that period are lost. Elder J. G. Van Hees of Zeeland reported that Rev. Van der Meulen "rang

the changes" on the matter even in his sermons during 1849, and Elder T. Ulberg of Vriesland, who left the RCA, reported that Van Raalte insisted that the congregations be brought into the discussion (Wm. O. Van Eyck, *The Union of 1850*, p. 33). The later claim that the union was engineered "by about twenty men," that "the congregations were not consulted," and that "not a single consistory" discussed the matter is preposterous. (Beets states this: *Zestig Jaren*, pp. 77f. Cf. Wm. O. Van Eyck, *op. cit.*, pp. 32f, 39.) *De Grondwet*, (June 27), 1911.

6. *Classis Holland—Minutes A.D. 1948-1958* (Grand Rapids: Wm. B. Eerdmans Publishing Co., 1950), pp. 36f.

7. Beets declares the union of 1850 to have been illegal (*onwettig*) and to have been effected in an unchurchly (*onkerkrechterlijk*) manner, whereas the secession of 1857 is said to have been "legal, obligatory, and justified" (*wettig, plichtmatig, gerechtvaardigd*) in a chapter bearing that caption (*Zestig Jaren*, pp. 72-75). In another work he refuses to call the events of 1857 a secession, but speaks of the "Return of 1857." *The Christian Reformed Church* (Grand Rapids: Baker Book House, 1949), p. 35. In a more accurate presentation John H. Kromminga writes that "the formal legality of the union of 1850 is beyond serious question," and he calls the event of 1857 a secession. *The Christian Reformed Church* (Grand Rapids: Baker Book House, 1949), p. 35.

8. Aleida J. Pieters, *Grand Rapids: A Dutch Settlement in Michigan*, (Grand Rapids: The Reformed Press, 1923), pp. 23-30.

9. H. E. Dosker, *op. cit.*, p. 9.

10. J. C. Rullmann, *De Afscheiding* (Kampen: J. H. Kok, 1930), pp. 261-291; D. H. Kromminga, *The Christian Reformed Tradition* (Grand Rapids: Wm. B. Eerdmans Publishing Company, 1943), pp. 93-97; N. H. Dosker, *De Hollandsche Gereformeerde Kerk in Amerika* (Nijmegen: P. J. Milborn, 1888), p. 192.

11. H. E. Dosker, *op. cit.*, p. 52.

12. Wm. O. Van Eyck, *Landmarks of the Reformed Fathers*, (Grand Rapids: The Reformed Press, 1922), p. 132.

13. At the first meeting of classis on April 23, 1848, these subjects had been considered and resolved unanimously. At the meeting of April 30, 1851, the retirement of elders was reconsidered. The same subjects were to reappear at classis on April 28, 1852 and April 28, 1853.

14. D. H. Kromminga, *op. cit.*, p. 110. Beets, who characterizes Haan as "a pronounced Calvinist of the Van Velzian [i.e., strict] type, with bulldog tenacity," says that "there would, humanly speaking, have been no return in 1857 to the standpoint left in 1849, without Gijsbert Haan." *The Christian Reformed Church*, p. 70.

15. *Classis Holland—Minutes A.D. 1848-1858*, pp. 62, 79ff., 91ff.

16. *Ibid.*, pp. 35, 117f.

17. *Ibid.*, p. 129.

18. *Ibid.*, p. 126. The final minute about the difficulty with Smit runs for 16 pages, pp. 122-138.

19. D. H. Kromminga, *op. cit.*, p. 107.

20. H. E. Dosker, *op. cit.*, p. 145.

21. Twice the reading of Baxter's works was raised at Holland Classis, on September 26, 1853, and Septebmer 5, 1855. The general attitude toward the book in question was that it contained much good material. "However, the ministers declare(d) that there are a few expressions in the little work of Baxter which they themselves do not dare to defend or to employ." *Classis Holland—Minutes 1848-1858*, p. 144.

22. H. E. Dosker, *op. cit.*, p. 245.

23. In addition to the minutes of consistory, see H. E. Dosker, *op. cit.*, pp. 242-248.

24. H. E. Dosker states that, inasmuch as Van den Bosch had been an opponent of Brummelkamp in the church in the Netherlands, it is not surprising that from the time of his arrival in the colony he opposed Van Raalte. *op. cit.*, p. 263.

25. *Classis Holland—Minutes 1848-1858*, pp. 240-243.

26. *Minutes of the Highest Assembly of the Christian Reformed Church, 1857-1880* (Grand Rapids: Mimeographed, Calvin Seminary, 1937), Preface.

27. *Ibid.*, p. 1; John H. Kromminga, *op. cit.*, p. 34.

28. *Classis Holland—Minutes 1848-1858*, pp. 252-254.

29. *Minutes of the Highest Assembly of the Christian Reformed Church, 1857-1880*, p. 122.

30. *Minutes of the Highest Assembly of the Christian Reformed Church, 1857-1880*, pp. 12, 62, 66, 72, 77f., 97f., 104, 109, 111f., 120.

31. Henry Zwaanstra demonstrates this concerning the Christian Reformed Church in his dissertation: *Reformed Thought and Experience in the New World: A Study of the Christian Reformed Church and its American Environment*, 1890-1918 (Kampen: J. H. Kok, 1973). In the struggle between Confessional Calvinism, Separatist Calvinism, and American Calvinism, it was the last which prevailed. *Tempora mutant et nos mutamur in illis*: times change and we are changed in them.

32. Beets gives the complaints within the colony against the Reformed Church in the East in his *Zestig Jaren*, pp. 87ff. These complaints were based on the observation of immigrants on their way West and show weaknesses in the life and practice of the Reformed Church. A similar, or equivalent, list could be drawn of any denomination. A generation earlier there had been charges of "Hopkinsianism" within the Reformed Church in America. For this and other doctrinal disputes at that time, see James W. Van Hoeven, "Salvation and Indian Removal: The Career Biography of The Rev. John F. Schermerhorn, Indian Commissioner." Unpublished Ph.D. Dissertation submitted to the faculty of the graduate school at Vanderbilt University, 1971, pp. 67-69; 84-86; 93-96.

33. Volume VII, pp. 379-392 gives a summary of these concerns voiced during the period under consideration.

34. Wm. O. Van Eyck, *The Union of 1850*, p. 23.

35. *Ibid.*, p. 21.

36. N. H. Dosker, *op. cit.*, p. 168. In 1847, the year of the Dutch migration, John W. Nevin gave a similar judgment saying that the Reformed Church was "accustomed to glory also in its orthodoxy; which is of the high Calvinistic order, according to the measure of the Belgic Confession and the Articles of the Synod of Dort. He places a high value of course on catechetical instruction, and cherishes a special veneration for the Heidelberg Catechism." *History and Genius of the Heidelberg Catechism* (Chambersburg: Publication Office of the German Reformed Church, 1847), p. 106.

37. Van Vranken's *Socinianism Subversive of Christianity* (New York: Robert Carter, 1841), demonstrates his own doctrinal stance and the futility and apostasy of Unitarianism.

38. *Classis Holland—Minutes 1848-1858*, pp. 53, 144, 202, 204f. An elder delegate to synod, Van Hees, also reported to classis that "he could say with full certainty that he knew her to be the old pure Reformed Church. . . . They adhered to the Reformed confessional standards . . . the delegates to the meetings of synod had found [there] and among the professors the strongest attachment to the Reformed doctrine." *Ibid.*, pp. 204f.

39. *Centennial of the Theological Seminary of the Reformed Church in America,*

1784-1884 (New York: Board of Publication of the Reformed Church in America, 1885), p. 252.

40. I knew a layman in Grand Rapids, a member of the Protestant Reformed Church, who said that he thought that he had read all the theological writings of Abraham Kuyper, Herman Bavinck, and Benjamin B. Warfield. Although the amount of his reading was unusual, the interest in theology was not among those of his generation. Numerous instances could be cited.

41. Rullman, *De Afscheiding*, pp. 261-291. Those able to read Dutch should read the account by N. H. Dosker of the strife at Dutch synods engendered by this party spirit, *De Hollandsche Gereformeerde Kerk in Amerika*, pp. 191-193. Dosker had attended all the synods from 1849-1872. Cf. Wm. O. Van Eyck, *Landmarks of the Reformed Fathers*, pp. 301ff.

42. *Partijzucht, partijschap, partijstrijd* (love of dissension, factionalism, party strife) are words used by historians of this period to describe the mood of some of the immigrants.

43. "Van Raalte and Union With the Reformed Church," *Calvin Forum*, XII (June-July, 1947), p. 239.

44. *N. H. Dosker, op. cit.*, p. 199.

45. *Ibid.*, p. 229. Yet, Beets compares "the leaders of the movement of 1857" to Luther, Zwingli, and Calvin! *The Christian Reformed Church*, p. 61.

46. John K. Kromminga, in his balanced appraisal of the secession of 1857, calls attention to Haan's misquotation and inaccurate charges even though some of what he said was correct and carried weight. *The Christian Reformed Church*, pp. 32f.

47. E.g., pp. 15-18b in which thirty-one members of the seceded Grand Rapids congregation petitioned their classis to have him removed from his office as elder. The minutes are in Dutch.

48. *Classis Holland—Minutes 1848-1858*, pp. 244f.

49. H. E. Dosker, *op. cit.*, p. 295ff. Cf. A. J. Pieters, *op. cit.*, pp. 171-179, Beets, *Zestig Jaren*, p. 94f., Hyma, *Albertus C. Van Raalte* (Grand Rapids: Wm. B. Eerdmans Publishing Co., 1947), pp. 145, 215f., 253f.

50. The Hon G. VanSchelven, "Historsche Schetsen," *De Groudwet*, Feb. 9, 1915, quoted by Beets, *Zestig Jaren*, p. 85. Cf. Hyma, *Albertus C. Van Raalte*, pp. 145, 215f, 253f; John H. Kromminga, "Albertus C. Van Raalte," *Calvin Forum*, XII (June-July, 1947), p. 211.

51. Albertus Pieters, whose father, as Van Raalte's successor at the First Reformed Church in Holland, conducted the funeral of the leader, once told me that it was his conviction that the reason for the secession lay in the quarrelsomeness of the people—Pieters said, "They were that way in Europe, and they were that way when they came here—and Van Raalte himself." My recollection leads me to believe that he meant Van Raalte's strong leadership which sometimes tended to be domineering.

52. *Minutes of the Highest Assembly of the Christian Reformed Church, 1857-1880*, p. 15.

53. H. E. Dosker says that the language question was "the great, all-dominating concern in the history of our Dutch people in America." *Levensschets*, p. 199. John H. Kromminga shows the truth of Dosker's observation and how linguistic isolation helped shape the Christian Reformed Church. *The Christian Reformed Church*, pp. 91-101. For a congregational case study of Americanization see Elton J. Bruins, *The Americanization of a Congregation* (Grand Rapids: Wm. B. Eerdmans Publishing Company, 1970).

54. Henry Zwaanstra, *Reformed Thought and Experience, op. cit.*

55. *Classis Holland—Minutes 1848-1858*, p. 203.
56. *Ibid.*, pp. 248, 246.
57. For the missionary interest in the *Kolonie* see Samuel M. Zwemer, "The Influence of the Dutch Emigration of 1847 on Foreign Missions," in *Historical Souvenir of the Celebration of the Sixtieth Anniversary of the Colonization of the Hollanders in Western Michigan*, Zeeland, Michigan (August 21, 1907), pp. 40ff.
58. John H. Kromminga, *The Christian Reformed Church*, chapter IV, "Deliberate Cultural and Ecclesiastical Isolation," and *In the Mirror* (Hamilton: Guardian Publishing Co. LTD., 1957), pp. 49-64; 91-96.
59. B. DeBeij and A. Zwemer, *Stemmen uit de Hollandsche-Gereformeerde Kerk in de Vereeigde staten van Amerika* (Groningen: G. J. Reits, 1871), p. 126.
60. *Classis Holland—Minutes 1848-1858*, pp. 227, 242, 248.
61. *Ibid.* The singing of hymns at public worship was approved in the Christian Reformed Church in 1934. The controversy over hymn-singing among the Seceders in the Netherlands is given in Rullmann, *De Afscheiding*, index, under *Gezangen*.
62. Wm. O. Van Eyck, *The Union of 1850*, p. 100.
63. *Institutes of the Christian Religion*, IV, i,12.
64. E.g., N. M. Steffens, *Gereformeerde Maandschrift* (Grand Rapids: D. J. Doornink, 1880), pp. 56ff.
65. A case in point is the Haan-Daalman controversy in Grand Rapids. *Classis Holland—Minutes 1848-1858*, pp. 187-197.
66. Cf. N. H. Dosker, *De Hollandsche Gereformeerde Kerk in Amerika*, p. 230.
67. *Minutes, General Synod*, 1868, p. 461.
68. *Minutes, General Synod*, 1870, pp. 96f.
69. *Ibid.*, 1879, p. 359. Cf. N. H. Dosker, *De Hollandsche Gereformeerde Kerk in Amerika*, pp. 87, 207. Dosker reports having heard, after the cessation of theological work at Hope College in 1877, "That is the work of the Freemasons."
70. *Minutes, General Synod*, 1880, pp. 535f.
71. *Ibid.*, 1881, pp. 733f.
72. *Ibid.*, 1882, p. 68.
73. E.g., *Classis Holland—Minutes 1848-1858*, pp. 50, 60, 81f., 135. Reference is even made to "a certain passion for independence." p. 50. H. P. Scholte, founder of Pella, Iowa, was an independent who did not unite with the Reformed Church in the East. C. Vorst, main author of the Brochure of 1869 in defense of the secession, later became an Independent in Grand Rapids.
74. Abraham Kuyper's agreement in 1882 with the stand of the Synod of the Reformed Church on Freemasonry came as a surprise to many. See H. E. Dosker, *op. cit.*, pp. 334f, for Kuyper's statement.
75. Wm. O. Van Eyck, *The Union of 1850*, p. 77.
76. H. E. Dosker, *op. cit.*, p. 54; N. H. Dosker, *op. cit.*, p. 201.
77. Cf. Henry Zwaanstra, *op. cit.*, p. 36.

Chapter V
Inspiration and Authority:
The Reformed Church Engages Modernity

1. James Turner, *Without God, Without Creed*, quoted in the *New York Times Book Review* (May 19), 1985.
2. Paul R. Fries, *Religion and the Hope for a Truly Human Existence* (Ph.D. dissertation, University of Utrecht, 1979), p. 1.

3. Karl Jaspers, *Man in the Modern Age* (Garden City: Anchor Books, Doubleday and Co., 1957), p. 4.
4. This summary of the contribution to the development of criticism made by Grotius and Hobbes is based on K. Grobel's article under the heading "Biblical Criticism" in *The Interpreter's Dictionary of the Bible* (New York: Abingdon Press, 4 vols., 1962), V. 1, pp. 409-410.
5. For a superb treatment of "the battle for the Bible" see George Marsden, *Fundamentalism and American Culture* (New York/Oxford: Oxford University Press, 1980), especially pp. 102-108. See also James D. Bratt, *Dutch Calvinism in Modern America* (Grand Rapids: Wm. B. Eerdmans Publishing Company, 1984), pp. 105-107.
6. George Marsden, *op. cit.*, p. 117.
7. John DeWitt, *What is Inspiration* (New York: Anson D. F. Randolph & Company, 1893), pp. iv-v.
8. *Ibid.*, pp. 33-34.
9. *Ibid.*, p. 85.
10. *Ibid.*, p. 112.
11. *Ibid.*, p. 113.
12. *Ibid.*, p. 168.
13. *Ibid.*, pp. 181-182.
14. *Ibid.*, pp. 152-153.
15. *Ibid.*, p. 152.
16. *Ibid.*, pp. 163-164.
17. Albertus Pieters, *The Inspiration of the Holy Scriptures* (Grand Rapids: The Church Press, n.d.) p. 3.
18. *Ibid.*, p. 5.
19. *Ibid.*, p. 9.
20. *Ibid.*, p. 12.
21. *Ibid.*, p. 19.
22. *Ibid.*, p. 12.
23. *Ibid.*, p. 10.
24. *Ibid.*, pp. 10-11.
25. *Ibid.*, pp. 10-11.
26. *Ibid.*
27. Both the terms operational and noetic are borrowed from Roger Shinn. I employ the word operational in a way differing from Shinn's, however, who uses it to describe the authority of government. My use of the concept of noetic authority is the same as Shinn's. Roger Shinn, "The Locus of Authority: Participatory Democracy in the Age of the Expert," in *Erosion of Authority*, ed., Clyde L. Manschreck (Nashville/New York: Abingdon Press, 1971), pp. 93-104.
28. Paul Fries, *op. cit.*, p. 1.
29. Rene Coste, *Marxist Analysis and Christian Faith* (Maryknoll: Orbis Books, 1985), p. 102.
30. Gibson Winter, *Liberating Creation* (New York: The Crossroad Publishing Company, 1981), pp. 111-115.
31. Stephen Toulmin, *The Return to Cosmology* (Berkeley: The University of California Press, 1982), p. 210.
32. *Ibid.*, p. 155.
33. *Ibid.*, p. 254.
34. Harvey Cox, *Religion in the Secular City* (New York: Simon and Schuster, 1979), p. 20.
35. Paul Fries, *op. cit.*, p. 2.

Chapter VI

Prose and Poetry:
Reformed Scholarship and Confessional Renewal

1. For a full-scale biography of Zwemer, see Christy Wilson, *Apostle to Isalm* (Grand Rapids: Baker Book House, 1952); see also the essay by Herman Harmelink III, "World Mission," in *Piety and Patriotism: Bi-Centennial Studies of The Reformed Church in America, 1776-1976,* pp. 77-94.

2. His first publication was a booklet written in Dutch while he was a middler at New Brunswick Theological Seminary! Entitled *Zendings-Woorden* (Missionary Worlds), it contained a miscellany of missionary hymns, a chart showing the various religions of the world, and other information about the mission situation in that day.

3. This was his second invitation to join the Princeton faculty. In 1928 he was invited to teach at Princeton after spending part of his furlough there as a visiting professor, but he declined and returned to Cairo where he spent seventeen years training Christian workers and doing research and writing for the Nile Mission Press. On this period see Chapter 15 in Wilson, *op. cit.*

4. See, for example, the review of *Notes on Genesis* in *The Evangelical Quarterly* (Jan., 1946), pp. 41-42.

5. "A Tribute to Albertus Pieters," *Reformed Review,* Vol. 9, No. 3 (January, 1956), p. 42. No author is listed, but it was written by M. Eugene Osterhaven.

6. He had originally thought of having this published, but felt that works like Moltmann's *Theology of Hope,* which appeared in the mid-1900s, preempted the field. This was an unfortunate judgment, for this single-spaced 139-page manuscript contains a wealth of material which is still remarkably fresh and helpful. The two foci are the redemptive-historical event of Jesus Christ and the Kerygma as developed in the gospels and epistles.

7. *Piety and Patriotim, op. cit.,* p. 95.

8. *Ibid.,* p. 105. Heideman's principal support for this thesis is a quotation from an essay by Elton Eenigenburg, "The Christian Hope," written for the *Western Seminary Bulletin* in 1953. The essay was written in response to the World Council of Churches Assembly of that year and its theme, "Jesus Christ the Hope of the World." Heideman may be projecting his own shift in outlook resulting from his study in the eschatological theological atmosphere in post-war Netherlands. This comes to fruition in his *Song of Hope* as he acknowledges in the conclusion of his essay (p. 110).

9. For example, books that are on the borderline between psychology and theology, such as *Making It to Adolescence: The Emerging Self* (Philadelphia: Westminster Press, 1972), by Arthur J. DeJong, for many years an administrator at Central College and now the president of Muskingom College; and the various works by the Hope College professor of psychology and a Reformed Church layman, David G. Meyers, especially *The Human Puzzle: Psychological Research and Christian Belief* (San Francisco: A Harper/CAPS Book, 1978); and *The Inflated Self. Human Illusions and the Biblical Call to Hope* (New York: The Seabury Press, 1980); or books in the area of Christianity and literature, e.g., the studies of C. S. Lewis by Peter Schakel. One of the leading Lewis interepreters in the world, Schakel has produced three books on the great English writer: *The Longing for a Form,* editor (Kent State University Press, 1977; reprinted by Baker Book House, 1977); *Reading with the Heart: The Way into Narnia* (Grand Rapids: Wm. B. Eerdmans Publishing Co., 1979); and *Reason and Imagination in C. S. Lewis. A Study of "Till We have Faces"* (Grand Rapids: Wm. B. Eerdmans Publishing Co., 1984).

10. Richmond: John Knox Press, 1962.
11. Grand Rapids: Wm. B. Eerdmans Publishing Co., 1965.
12. Vol. 6, No. 4, pp. 490ff.
13. *Ibid.*, p. 492. On pp. 493 he points out four areas of common agreement which emerge from these liturgical studies.
14. *Op. cit.*, p. 285.
15. Grand Rapids: Wm. B. Eerdmans Publishing Co., 1971.
16. For a full *vita* and a listing of all of his publications until 1977, see *Scripture in History and Theology. Essays in Honor of J. Coert Rylaarsdam*, edited by Arthur L. Merrill and Thomas W. Overholt (Pittsburgh: The Pickwick Press, 1977).
17. Chicago: The University of Chicago Press, 1946.
18. The exposition was done by J. Edgar Park, both being only one part of Volume 1 of *The Interpreter's Bible* (New York/Nashville: Abingdon Press, 1952). This volume received mixed reviews, but it was generally agreed that Rylaarsdam's contribution was one of the best parts of it.
19. London: Thomas Nelson and Sons, 1962.
20. Richmond: John Knox Press, 1964. Also published by SCM Press in London.
21. Volume 9 (1972), pp. 249-70.
22. Edited by James I. Cook (Grand Rapids: Wm. B. Eerdmans Publishing Co., 1975), pp. 70-84.
23. *Ibid.*, p. 83. The argument is a very complicated one, as is Rylaarsdam's conclusion: "If both Judaism and Christianity continue to revolve around the same two covenants that are paradoxically related to each other [the one being more historical, the other more eschatological, according to Rylaarsdam], then their relationship, whatever its tensions, is forever mutually interdependent; and their separation from each other is rooted in the paradoxical character of the interrelationship of the two covenants in which both participate. If that be the case, there is a basis for dialogue, something not located hitherto" (*Ibid.*).
On this important question cf. *Christ in the Light of the Christian-Jewish Dialogue* by John T. Pawlikowski, O.S.M. (New York: Paulist Press, 1982), especially pp. 26ff. where Rylaarsdam's position is analyzed and critiqued.
24. Edinburgh: Oliver and Boyd, 1957; Grand Rapids: Wm. B. Eerdmans Publishing Co., 1957. Eerdmans published a paperback version in 1981 and reprinted it in 1984.
25. Grand Rapids: Wm. B. Eerdmans Publishing Co., 1961. Reprinted in 1967, 1973, and 1979.
26. London: Lutterworth Press, 1965; New York/Nashville: Abingdon Press, 1965, as a part of the "Bible Guides" series. This was reprinted by Eerdmans in 1984.
27. Grand Rapids: Baker Book House, 1960.
28. Philadelphia: Holman, 1960.
29. London: InterVarsity Fellowship, 1962; and Grand Rapids: Eerdmans, 1962.
30. Grand Rapids: Wm. B. Eerdmans Publishing Co., 1975.
31. Leicester: InterVarsity Press, 1980; and Wheaton: Tyndale House, 1980.
32. Chicago: The University of Chicago, 1974.
33. *Neotestamentica et Semitica. Studies in honour of Matthew Black,* (Edinburgh: T. & T. Clark, 1969), editor.
34. "Midrashic Features of the Speeches of Acts," *Hommage au Professeur B. Rigaux,* ed. A. Descamps, (Gembloux: J. Duculot, 1970).
35. "The Role of the Christian Prophet in Acts," *Apostolic History and the Gospel.* Essays Presented to F. F. Bruce, ed. W. W. Gasque, (Exeter: Paternoster; and Grand Rapids: Eerdmans, 1970).

36. "Christ and Spirit in I Corinthians," *Christ and Spirit in the New Testament. Studies in honour of C. F. D. Moule*, ed. B. Lindars (Cambridge: University Press, 1973).

37. "La fonction de l'eschatologie dans l'evangile de Luc," *L'evangile de Luc. Memorial L. Cerfaux*, ed. F. Neirynck (Gembloux: T. Duculot, 1973.)

38. "Christ Crucified," *Reconciliation and Hope. Presented to L. L. Morris*, ed. R. Banks (Exeter: Paternoster; and Grand Rapids: Wm. B. Eerdmans Publishing Co., 1974).

39. "New Directions in Form Criticism," *Jesus Christus in Historie und Theologie. Festschrift für H. Conzelmann*, ed. G. Strecker (Tübingen: J. C. B. Mohr, 1975).

40. "Weisheit" und "Erkenntnis" im I. Korintherbrief," *Jesus und Paulus. Festschrift für W. G. Kummel*, ed. E. E. Ellis and E. Grässer, (Gottingen: Vanderhoek and Ruprecht, 1975).

41. "The Silenced Wives of Corinth," *New Testament Textual Criticism. Essays in Honour of B. M. Metzger*, ed. E. J. Epp (Oxford: Clarendon Press, 1981).

42. "Oscar Cullmann and Reformed Circles," *Testimonia Oecumenica*, ed. K. Froehlick (Tübingen: Hans Vogler, 1982).

43. Grand Rapids: Wm. B. Eerdmans Publishing Co., 1975.

44. Philadelphia: Holman, 1972.

45. This originally appeared as Vol. 18 in *Wissenschaftliche Untersuchungen zum Neuen Testament* (Tübingen: J. D. B. Mohr, 1978); and was published in the United States by Eerdmans the same year and reprinted again in 1980.

46. By Thomas Nelson and Sons, Ltd. in London. A revised edition was published by Nelson in 1974.

47. As in the case with any book—especially a commentary—some reviewers have their reservations. Hugh Anderson, for example, reviewing this commentary in the *Scottish Journal of Theology* (February, 1971), complains that the exegesis is too brief, but still concludes that there are "many stimulating and illuminating observations on the text" and compares this work favorably with recent commentaries by A. R. C. Leaney and G. B. Caird.

William Neil expresses a consensus viewpoint when he concludes his review in *The Expository Times* (September, 1967) with the words, "Dr. Ellis takes the measure of the latest scholarship and has given us a first-class commentary. . . ."

48. *Interpretation* 18 (1964), pp. 3-19.

49. The Gospel According to John I-XII (Garden City, New York: Doubleday, 1966), p. 14. Concerning the key words "grace and truth" in John 1:14, Brown closes his own comments with, "Kuyper gives a complete treatment."

50. Grand Rapids: Wm. B. Eerdmans Publishing Co., 1978.

51. "Calvinism in American Theology Today," in *Calvinism in Times of Crisis. Addresses delivered at the Third American Calvinistic Congress* (Grand Rapids: Baker Book House, 1947), pp. 83-4.

52. *Ibid.*, p. 84.

52. Philadelphia: Westminster Press, 1960.

53. Philadelphia: Westminster Press, 1960.

54. Grand Rapids: Wm. B. Eerdmans Publishing Co., 1971.

55. Grand Rapids: Wm. B. Eerdmans Publishing Co., 1972.

56. Published in New York in 1965. This was reprinted by Grand Rapids: Baker Book House, 1977.

57. Published by Grand Rapids: Baker Book House, 1981.

58. Grand Rapids: Wm. B. Eerdmans Publishing Co., 1975. *Our Song of Hope* was approved "as a provisional standard" by the General Synod of 1974 and adopted as a contemporary statement of faith by the General Synod of 1978.

59. Geneva; World Alliance of Reformed Churches, 1982, p. 6.

60. Assen: Van Gorcum and Co., 1959.
61. At the time Eugene Heideman was writing *about* Brunner I was studying *with* him in Tokyo. I have written several smaller articles about Brunner, most of which appeared in Japanese journals. Cf. "Encounter in Japan-Emil Brunner, and Interpretation," in *The Reformed Review*, IX. 2, (January, 1956).
62. Philadelphia: Fortress Press, 1963.
63. Philadelphia: Westminster Press, 1964.
64. Grand Rapids: Wm. B. Eerdmans Publishing Co., 1977. This is a revision of his Harvard Divinity School doctoral dissertation.
65. Published by the author in 1979.
66. October, 1980.
67. *Dutch Calvinism in Modern America. A History of a Conservative Subculture* (Grand Rapids: Wm. B. Eerdmans Publishing Co., 1984), p. 221. This is a revised version of Bratt's doctoral dissertation done under the supervision of Sydney Ahlstrom of Yale University.

Chapter VII
Heidelberg and Grand Rapids:
Reformed Theology and The Mission of the Church

1. [Anselm (1033-1109) was a monk who was born in Italy, educated in France, and ended his life as Archbishop of Canterbury. His famous book, *Why God Became Man*, became the classic statement on the doctrine of atonement for orthodox Christianity.—Ed.]
2. Zacharias Ursinus, *Commentary on the Heidelberg Catechism*, G. W. Williard, trans. (Grand Rapids: Wm. B. Eerdman's Publishing Co., 1954), pp. 69 and 325. [Zacharias Ursinus (1534-1583) and Caspar Olevianus (1536-1587) were the principal writers of the Heidelberg Catechism, which was written in 1563.—Ed.]
3. *Ibid.,* pp. 295, 298, 303.
4. *Ibid.,* p. 466.
5. [The Rev. Bernardus Freeman (1662-1743) and Johannes Megapolensis (1603-1706) were two Dutch Reformed ministers who did missionary work among the Indians in North America.—Ed.]
6. H. D. J. Boissevain, *De Zending in Oost en West* (The Hague: N. V. Algemeene Boekhandel voor Inwendige en Uitwendige Zending, n.d.), Vol. I, pp. 21-69.
7. *Ibid.,* pp. 54-57. Voetius preceded William Carey who made the same point. See William Carey, *An Enquiry into the Obligation of Christians to Use Means for the Conversion of the Gentiles* (London: The Carey Kingsgate Press, 1961), pp. 7-13.
8. [Dr. Rufus Anderson (1796-1880) served as secretary of the American Board of Commissioners for Foreign Missions, from 1826 to 1856.—Ed.]
9. For a fuller treatment of the historical development and impact of Anderson's theory in Reformed Church missions, see my *A People in Mission: The Surprising Harvest* (New York: The Reformed Church Press, 1980), pp. 29-34.
10. [Albertus Pieters (1869-1955), served as a Reformed Church missionary to Japan from 1891 to 1923, professor of religion at Hope College, Holland, Michigan, from 1923 to 1926, and professor at Western Theological Seminary, Holland, Michigan, from 1926 to 1939.—Ed.]
11. Albertus Pieters, *Mission Problems in Japan* (New York: The Board of Publications, Reformed Church in America, 1921), pp. 8-10.
12. [Samuel Zwemer (1867-1952), served as a Reformed Church missionary to the Mid-

dle East from 1890 to 1929, and as a Professor at Princeton Theological Seminary, New Jersey, from 1929 to 1952.—Ed.]

13. Samuel Zwemer, *Dynamic Christianity and the World Today* (London: The Inter-Varsity Fellowship of Evangelical Unions, 1939), p. 74.

14. [The Barmen Declaration (1934) emerged in the German church struggle (*Kirchenkampf*), when the Confessing Church in Germany courageously declared its opposition, based on Christian convictions, against the existing German Church which was then loyal to Hitler.—Ed.]

15. John Piet, *The Road Ahead: A Theology for the Church in Mission* (Grand Rapids: Wm. B. Eerdmans Publishers, 1970), pp. 11-17.

16. *Ibid.*, pp. 38-47.

17. Eugene Heideman, *Our Song of Hope: A Provisional Confession of Faith of the Reformed Church in America* (Grand Rapids: Wm. B. Eerdman's Publishers, 1975), p. 10.

18. *Ibid.*, Stanza 4, p. 6.

19. The *Ad Hoc Report on World Mission* was commissioned by the General Program Council of the Reformed Church in America.

Chapter VIII
Piety and Patriotism:
Reformed Theology and Civil Religion

1. Various authors have repeated this assertion, and for many years gave it semi-official sanction by printing it on the Credits Page of its journal publication. While the issue begs a careful study, there can be little doubt that the Episcopalians and Congregationalists have cause to dispute the claim that the RCA is the oldest Protestant denomination in North America with a continuous ministry. The Episcopalians trace their origins to Virginia in 1607 and the Congregationalists to Plymouth, Massachusetts in 1620. While the Anglicans and Pilgrims did not have an ordained ministry functioning early on the RCA cannot claim a continuous ministerial presence since 1628.

2. See Elton J. Bruins, "The Father of the Reformed Church, John H. Livingston," *The Church Herald* (January 2, 1959), pp. 4-5.

3. Edward Tanjore Corwin, *A Digest of Constitutional and Synodical Legislation of the Reformed Church in America* (New York: The Board of Publication of the Reformed Church in America, 1906), p. vi.

4. Rufus W. Clark, "The Relation of Religion to Our Civil Liberties," in *Centennial Discourses: A Series of Sermons Delivered in the Year 1876 by the Order of the General Synod of The Reformed (Dutch) Church in America* (New York: Board of Publication of the Reformed Church in America, 1877), p. 16.

5. Robert A. Bellah, "Civil Religion in America," in Russell E. Richey and Donald G. Jones, eds., *American Civil Religion* (New York: Harper and Row, Publishers, 1974), p. 21. The now famous article was originally printed in the Winter, 1967 issue of *Daedalus, Journal of the American Academy of Arts and Sciences*, p. 1-21.

6. These five meanings of civil religion were elaborated by Russell E. Richey and Donald G. Jones in the introduction to *American Civil Religion* (New York: Harper and Row, Publishers, 1974), pp. 14-18.

7. Various Biblical motifs have been employed to describe America's mission and destiny. See, for example, Ernest Lee Tureson, *Redeemer Nation: The Idea of America's Millennial Role*, (Chicago: The University of Chicago Press, 1968); Walter

Micgorski and Ronald Weber, eds., *An Almost Chosen People: The Moral Aspirations of Americans*, (South Bend: The University of Notre Dame Press, 1976); Conrad Cherry, *God's New Israel: Religious Interpretations of American Destiny* (Englewood Cliffs, N.J.: Prentice-Hall, 1971); Sacvan Bencovitch, *The American Jeremiad*, (Madison, Wis.: The University of Wisconsin Press, 1978).

8. John W. Beardslee III, "The American Revolution," in James W. Van Hoeven, ed., *Piety and Patriotism: Bicentennial Studies of the Reformed Church in America, 1776-1976* (Grand Rapids: Wm. B. Eerdmans Publishing Co., 1976), pp. 17-18.

9. John A. Todd, "The Posture of Its Ministers and People During the Revolution," in *Centennial Discourses: A Series of Sermons Delivered in the Year 1876 by the Order of the General Synod of the Reformed (Dutch) Church in America* (New York: Board of Publication of the Reformed Church in America, 1877, pp. 113, 129-29).

10. *Ibid.*, p. 132.

11. A. C. Leiby, *The Revolutionary War in the Hackensack Valley* (New Brunswick: Rutgers University Press, 1962), p. 83. See also John W. Beardslee, "The American Revolution," in James W. Van Hoeven, ed., *Piety and Patriotism: Bicentennial Studies of the Reformed Church in America, 1776-1976* (Grand Rapids: Wm. B. Eerdmans Publishing Co., 1976), pp. 17-33.

12. See Beardslee, "The American Revolution," p. 21.

13. Earl William Kennedy: "From Providence to Civil Religion: Some 'Dutch' Reformed Interpretations of America in the Revolutionary Era," *Reformed Review* 29 (Winter, 1976), pp. 111-123.

14. William Linn, *The Blessings of America: A Sermon Preached in the Middle Dutch, on the Fourth of July, 1791* . . . (New York: Thomas Greenleaf, 1791), pp. 11-32. My source is Kennedy, *op. cit.*, pp. 118-120.

15. Kennedy, *op. cit.*, pp. 119-120.

16. *ibid.*, p. 121.

17. William Linn *A Funeral Eulogy Occasioned by the Death of General Washington, delivered February 22nd, 1800* . . . (New York: Isaac Collins, 1800), pp. 10-34. Again, my source is Kennedy, *op. cit.*, pp. 121-122.

18. Quoted in Beardslee, *op. cit.*, pp. 32-33.

19. Editorial, "The Birthday of Liberty," *The Christian Intelligencer* 60 (Wednesday, July 3, 1889), pp. 1-2.

20. Editorial, "Thoughts for the Hour," *The Christian Intelligencer* 47 (Thursday, June 29, 1876), p. 8.

21. Rufus Clark, *op. cit.*, p. 16.

22. *Ibid.*, p. 17.

23. See Winthrop S. Hudson, *Religion in America: An Historical Account of the Development of American Religious Life.* Third Edition (New York: Charles Scribner's Sons, 1981), pp. 149-58; and Sydney E. Ahlstrom, *A Religious History of the American People.* Volume I (Garden City, New York: Image Books, 1975), pp. 512-520.

24. Anson Dubois, "America for Christ," *The Christian Intelligencer* 32 (Feb. 14, 1861), p. 2.

25. *Minutes*, General Synod, 1876, pp. 456-457. I have quoted from John De Jong, "Social Concerns," in James W. Van Hoeven, ed., *Piety and Patriotism: Bicentennial Studies of the Reformed Church in America, 1776-1976* (Grand Rapids: Wm. B. Eerdmans Publishing Co., 1976), p. 111.

26. DeJong, *op. cit.*, pp. 116-117.

27. *Ibid.*, pp. 118-119.

28. See De Jong., *op. cit.*, pp. 118-119. For more on Muste's Reformed Background see A. J. Muste, "Sketches for an Autobiography" in *The Essays of A. J. Muste* edited by Nat Henthoff (New York: Simon and Schuster, 1967), pp. 1-32. For some biographical information on Taylor, see Peter N. Vanden Berge, *Historical Directory of the Reformed Church in America* (Grand Rapids: Wm. B. Eerdmans Publishing Co., 1978), p. 173.

29. *Minutes,* General Synod, 1931, pp. 986, 1124-1125; *Minutes,* General Synod, 1932, pp. 148-161; and De Jong, *op. cit.*, pp. 120-111.

30. Sidney Mead, *The Lively Experiment* (New York: Harper & Row, 1963), p. 12, quoted in Robert N. Bellah, "Civil Religion in America," *op. cit.*, p. 30.

31. Bellah, *op. cit.*, p. 31.

32. See De Jong, *op. cit.*, pp. 116-117.

33. Editorial, "A Patriotic Duty," *The Christian Intelligencer* 32 (Feb. 28, 1964), p. 4.

34. Editorial, "The Nation's Work," *The Christian Intelligencer* 33 (Aug. 4, 1862), p. 2.

35. Editorial, *The Christian Intelligencer* 35 (Feb. 4, 1864), p. 2.

36. Editorial, "The Price of Liberty," *The Christian Intelligencer* 35 (May 26, 1864), p. 2.

37. Editorial, "It is Finished," *The Christian Intelligencer* 36 (April 13, 1865), p. 2.

38. Editorial, "The Nation's Anguish," *The Christian Intelligencer* 36 (April 20, 1865), p. 2.

39. *Minutes,* General Synod, 1865, p. 648, quoted from Edward Tanjore Corwin, ed. *A Digest of Constitutional and Synodical Legislation of the Reformed Church in America* (New York: The Board of Publication of the Reformed Church in America, 1906), pp. 546-47.

40. See Wynand Wichers, "The Dutch Churches in Michigan During the Civil War," published by the Michigan Civil War Centennial Observance Commission, Lewis Beeson, editor (Lansing, Michigan, 1965), pp. 1-16.

41. Evert J. Blekkink, "Editorial," *The Leader,* 1 (Oct. 31, 1906), p. 1, and John H. Kleinheksel, "Editorial," *The Leader* (Trial Run) 1 (Sept. 13, 1906), p. 1.

42. Evert J. Blekkink, "America First," *The Leader* 11 (Jan. 10, 1917), p. 104.

43. For an excellent historical overview of this issue see Roland Bainton, *Christian Attitudes Toward War and Peace* (New York: Abingdon Press, 1960).

44. Editorial, "A Righteous War," *The Christian Intelligencer* 88 (April 11, 1917), p. 226.

45. Evert J. Blekkink, "The Love of Country," *The Leader* 11 (June 27, 1917), p. 578.

46. *Minutes,* General Synod, (June, 1917), pp. 260-62.

47. *Minutes,* General Synod, (June, 1918), p. 610.

48. See Ray H. Abrams, *Preachers Present Arms.* (New York: Round Table Press, 1933).

49. See De Jong, *op. cit.*, pp. 120-121.

50. "Editorial," *The Intelligencer-Leader* 6 (May 26, 1939), p. 3. Similar editorials include "God With Us." *The Leader* 17 (July 2, 1924), p. 2; "My Country," *The Leader* 20 (June 29, 1927), p. 2; and "Christian Patriotism," *The Leader* 25 (June 20, 1932), p. 2.

51. See De Jong, *op. cit.*, pp. 122-23. See also B. D. Dykstra, "From Christ to Constantine," *Intelligencer-Leader* 8 (July 25, 1941), pp. 3-4; and Luman Shafer, "Our Faith and a Durable Peace," *Intelligencer-Leader,* 10 (Jan. 29, 1943), pp. 16, 20; and (Feb. 26, 1943), p. 16. For a fascinating biography of B. D. Dykstra, see D. Ivan Dykstra, *B.D.* (Grand Rapids: Wm. B. Eerdmans Publishing Co., 1982).

52. *Minutes,* General Synod, (June 1940), p. 543.

53. *Minutes,* General Synod, (June 1941), p. 325.

54. See De Jong, *op. cit.*, pp. 124-125.

55. *Minutes,* General Synod (June 1969), p. 247; and *Minutes,* General Synod (June, 1971), pp. 228-30.
56. Third Reformed Church in Holland, Michigan, has so decorated its sanctuary on at least two occasions—the death of President Wm. McKinley in 1901, and during the Semi-Centennial celebration of 1917. See Elton J. Bruins, *The Americanization of a Congregation* (Grand Rapids: Wm. B. Eerdmans Publishing Co., 1970), pp. 52-53. More recently the North Park Reformed Church in Kalamazoo, Michigan, decorated its sanctuary with flags and bunting for the bicentennial celebration in 1976. See a photograph in *The Kalamazoo Gazette* (July 3, 1976), p. A-7. [See also Dennis N. Voskuil, *Mountains Into Goldmines: Robert Schuller and the Gospel of Success* (Grand Rapids: Wm. B. Eerdmans Publishing Co., 1983), pp. 156-57.—Ed.]
57. See H. Richard Niebuhr *Christ and Culture* (New York: Harper and Row, 1951).
58. Eugene P. Heideman, "Theocracy in the Reformation," *Reformed Review* 34 (Winter, 1981), pp. 81-88. For more on the Church/State relationship in Calvinist Thought see George L. Hunt, ed., *Calvinism and the Political Order.* (Philadelphia: The Westminster Press, 1965); John T. McNeill, *The History and Character of Calvinism.* (New York: Oxford University Press, 1967); and William A. Mueller, *Church and State in Luther and Calvin: A Comparative Study* (Nashville: Broadman Press, 1954).
59. Isaac C. Rottenberg, "The Kingdom and the State" *Reformed Review* 10 (April, 1957), p. 33. See also Rottenberg, "The Church and the State," *Reformed Review* 11 (January 1958), pp. 24-37; and John A. Vander Waal, "The Biblical Teachings on Church and State." *Western Seminary Bulletin* 11 (March, 1950), pp. 1-4.
60. For more on this issue see M. Eugene Osterhaven, *Our Confession of Faith: A Study Manual on The Belgic Confession* (Grand Rapids: Baker Book House, 1964), pp. 190-193; Albertus Pieters, *The Christian Attitude Towards War* (Grand Rapids: Wm. B. Eerdmans Publishing Co., 1932), esp. pp. 25-30.
61. Rottenberg, "The Kingdom and the State," *op. cit.,* p. 32.
62. *Ibid.,* p. 32.
63. Hans Kohn, *Nationalism: Its Meaning and History,* Revised Edition (Princeton: D. Van Nostrand Co., Inc., 1965), p. 9; and Carlton J. H. Hayes, *Nationalism: A Religion* (New York: The MacMillan Co., 1960), p. 10. See also, Winthrop Hudson, ed. *Nationalism and Religion in America: Concepts of American Identity and Mission* (New York: Harper and Row, 1970); James Edward Wood, *Nationhood and the Kingdom* (Nashville: Broadman Press, 1977); and Hans Kohn, *American Nationalism* (New York: MacMillan, Co., 1957).
64. Charles H. Kamp, "Law and the Christian Conscience," *The Church Herald* 20 (September 27, 1963), pp. 13, 21.
65. Winfield Burggraaff, "Don't Give Caesar Everything!" *The Church Herald* 22 (April 30, 1965), pp. 8, 31.
66. Isaac C. Rottenberg, "Proclaiming Liberty to the Cultural Captives," *The Church Herald,* 28 (December 17, 1971), pp, 14-15, 28.
67. "Christian Faith and the Nuclear Arms Race: A Reformed Perspective," in James I. Cook, ed., *The Church Speaks: Papers of the Commission on Theology, Reformed Church in America* (Grand Rapids: Wm. B. Eerdmans Publishing Co., 1985), pp. 165-182. The Cullmann quotation is from Oscar Cullmann, *The State in the New Testament* (New York: Charles Scribner's Sons, 1956), p. 75.
68. Gayle Boss-Koopman, Steven D. Hoogenwerf and Robert A. White, *Christ Is Our Peace: Biblical Foundations for Peacemaking* (New York: Reformed Church Press, 1982), p. 41.

INDEX